OPERA BIOGRAPHY SERIES, NO. 12

Series Editors
Andrew Farkas
William R. Moran

Dressed as Anatol for the world premiere of *Vanessa* at the Metropolitan, February 1958. (Photo by Louis Mélançon, New York)

Nicolai Gedda

MY LIFE & ART

by Nicolai Gedda
as told to Aino Sellermark Gedda

Translated from the Swedish by Tom Geddes

AMADEUS PRESS
Portland, Oregon

An earlier version of these memoirs was published in 1977 as *Gåvan är inte gratis* by Albert Bonniers Förlag, Stockholm

Translation by Tom Geddes, 1999

Where not otherwise indicated, the photographs in this book are from Nicolai Gedda's private collection. Some are photographs taken at rehearsals, commissioned by the relevant theater. Photographs of recording sessions were similarly commissioned. Other material from childhood and youth is from personal family sources.

ISBN 1-57467-048-4

Printed in Hong Kong

Published in 1999 by
Amadeus Press, an imprint of Timber Press, Inc.
The Haseltine Building
133 S.W. Second Avenue, Suite 450
Portland, Oregon 97204, U.S.A.

Library of Congress Cataloging-in-Publication Data

Gedda, Nicolai.
Nicolai Gedda : my life & art / by Nicolai Gedda, as told to Aino Sellermark Gedda; translated from the Swedish by Tom Geddes.
p.   cm. — (Opera biography series; no. 12)
"An earlier version of these memoirs was published in 1977 as Gåvan är inte gratis by Albert Boniers Förlag, Stockholm;"—T.p. verso.
Includes index.
ISBN 1-57467-048-4
1. Singers—Biography. I. Gedda, Aino Sellermark, 1927–   . II. Geddes, Tom.
III. Gedda, Nicolai. Gåvan är inte gratis. IV. Title. V. Series.
ML420.G32 A3   1999
782.1′092—dc21
[b]
98-42923
CIP
MN

Contents

Photographs follow page 32

Foreword

BY CHARLES OSBORNE

IN THE WORLD of opera, tenors have always caused the greatest excitement. Enrico Caruso, Beniamino Gigli, Richard Tauber, and John McCormack, household names in the first half of the twentieth century, are recalled even now, more frequently than their female equivalents. And it is those ubiquitous "Three Tenors" of today, not any three sopranos, who keep popping up all over the place. But the most versatile—and, incidentally, the most recorded—tenor in the world is Nicolai Gedda. Gedda made his debut at the Swedish Royal Opera House in his native Stockholm in 1952 while he was still a student, when no other singer could be found to cope with the title role of Adam's *Le Postillon de Longjumeau.* An instant success, within months he was singing leading roles in Milan, Paris, Rome, and Vienna, and recording operas and operettas with sopranos such as Victoria de los Angeles, Maria Callas, and Elisabeth Schwarzkopf.

When Gedda first appeared in Germany, *Die Welt* called him "the best lyric tenor singing today" and compared him with Caruso. His debut at the Metropolitan Opera led a New York-based critic to refer to him as "the poet among the lyric tenors." His command of nine languages and a huge variety of musical styles set Gedda clearly apart from his rivals. He was equally at home in the oratorios of Bach and Handel, French, Russian, and German opera, Italian opera from the bel canto period of the twentieth century, and even modern American opera. When he created the role of Anatol in Samuel Barber's *Vanessa* at the Met, several critics claimed that Gedda's English diction was much clearer than that of his American colleagues.

In his youth, Gedda's voice was one of great sweetness. The secret of his vocal longevity lies in the absolute security of his technique, while the secret of his stature as an artist lies in his extraordinary sense of style, something that is greatly admired by his fellow artists. A number of well-known singers, tenors especially, were to be seen in the audience at Covent Garden one night in 1996 when, accompanied by the Royal Opera Orchestra, Gedda sang eleven arias (plus encores) ranging from Tchaikovsky, through Donizetti and Bizet, to the operettas of Strauss and Lehár. His exquisitely and securely placed pianissimi in "Je crois entendre encore" from Bizet's *Les Pêcheurs de Perles* must have seemed "croce e delizia" to those younger tenors in the audience. In the final role of his operatic career, he scored a huge success at Covent Garden as the aged archbishop in Pfitzner's *Palestrina.*

Nicolai Gedda is the most amiable and amusing of companions—he does wickedly accurate imitations of several conductors he has worked with, Beecham, Klemperer, and Karajan among them—and is most generous in his praise of other singers. Gedda speaks of Jussi Björling, a fellow countryman-tenor, with reverence as "the true voice of the north." He is scathing, however, on the subject of trendy "concept" productions. "I'm shocked and disappointed," he once told me, "if the director deliberately destroys an atmosphere that the composer wished to communicate."

Geoffrey Parsons, who was Gedda's preferred recital accompanist for many years, described Gedda's voice as "very, very exciting and totally musical," adding that "apart from the sheen so characteristic of his sound, there is the subtle refinement of his legato line and his phrasing, plus a range of colors so wide that it seems as if he were using a whole collection of different vocal instruments." Luciano Pavarotti has said "there is no tenor alive with a greater ease in the upper register than Gedda."

Nicolai Gedda now enjoys teaching and passing on his knowledge to a younger generation of singers. But let us hope that he continues to give concerts and recitals to delight his admirers all over the world, among whom I consider myself one of the most fervent.

Preface

BY AINO SELLERMARK GEDDA

WHEN NICOLAI GEDDA and I got married in Stockholm one beautiful day in May 1997 we had known each other for nearly twenty-six years. For the last eleven happy years we had been living together in Switzerland.

The first time we met in person was on 6 December 1971 in Vienna. I was working as a freelance journalist for some of the leading newspapers in Scandinavia, and Nicolai was rehearsing the role of Alfredo in Verdi's *La Traviata* at the Staatsoper (Alfredo's Violetta was played by Ileana Cotrubas, the conductor was Josef Krips).

Nicolai had rented an apartment on Castellez Gasse next to Augarten Castle, and he received me there when the morning rehearsal at the theater was over. In a three-hour interview he answered my "searching" questions with honesty and thoroughness. When the article landed on the editorial desk I received a bouquet of roses—not from Nicolai Gedda, but from the editor, who believed that I had succeeded in opening up a clam. Our Swedish Court Singer had the reputation at that time of being a very shy celebrity.

Additionally encouraged by the praise I subsequently received from Nicolai himself, my enthusiasm was aroused for further interviews with him. As the years passed our friendship and mutual trust grew deeper, and Nicolai came to tell me more and more about his life and background.

In the mid-1980s he lost his elderly mother and his uncle at nearly the same time, which left him completely alone. At this point I was also able to offer him help of a practical nature in going through his mother's effects. There we found quite a number of interesting documents that cast a new light on his life with his parents.

9

This gave us both the idea of writing something more comprehensive, about Nicolai's personal life as well as his day-to-day work as a singer.

The present book comprises what Nicolai has told me in our many long conversations, which I recorded on tape to ensure that nothing was lost. The content of the book thus consists of his own words, his own subjective experiences of people and events in his life.

Nicolai Gedda has tried to give the reader a full account of all he knows about his own origins, since he has no male descendant to continue the line.

Youth

AS I GAZE at the yellowing photographs in the family album, recollections of childhood come flooding back.

My first really distinct memory is of a small apartment in the Södermalm district of Stockholm. This was my first home, where I lived with my father, Michail, and my mother, Olga.

I am sitting on the floor, playing. A big woman in a white apron and thick black stockings is standing in front of me. I am looking up at her inquisitively, pulling at her skirts, lifting them cautiously to see what there is underneath.

I found out later that the woman who seemed so large to me was quite a young girl. I do not know how that memory of a child playing by himself should be interpreted, but I refer to it here because it constantly comes to mind. The girl lived in the same building as we did on Brännerigatan and used to take care of me while my mother was out at work. My father was probably on tour with the Russian émigré choir, the Kuban Cossacks. They traveled throughout Italy and Germany; Russian singing was particularly popular in restaurants in Berlin in the early 1920s.

I was no more than two or three years old when my father first heard me humming. He taught me the Russian folk song "Vecherny Zvon" (Evening Bells) and then gradually went on to increase my repertoire of Russian folk tunes.

My mother and father have told me that as a three-year-old I was once lifted up onto the concert platform at the Amusement Park in Stockholm. The family had gone there to listen to a Russian balalaika orchestra called Kremlin. Dressed in a tiny Russian shirt that my mother had made for me, I started conducting the orchestra, to the delight of the audience. I have no memory of the event myself.

When I was four my father came home one day from a foreign trip with two offers of permanent employment. Times were extremely hard, and these offers came as gifts from heaven. The whole family went first to Berlin, where there was a job as a cantor in Tegel. I remember us traveling for hours by tram until we arrived in a district of ugly, dirty houses. My mother and father obviously did not like the church and its surroundings, because we resumed our journey.

Things were better in Leipzig. My father accepted the position of cantor and conductor of the choir at the Gedächtniskirche (Memorial Church), a Russian émigré church. His Russian title was "psalomchik," meaning reader of psalms.

The Memorial Church in Leipzig was built in honor of the soldiers who fell in the war against Napoleon in the battle that took place just outside the city in October 1813, known as the Battle of Leipzig or the Battle of the Nations. The church is beautiful, with gilded onion domes and two annexes. The priest lived in the annex on the left and the cantor in the one on the right. Our apartment consisted of two or three rooms and a kitchen. The area around the church was quiet and peaceful, and in front of it was a large park with splendid trees; I can remember their tops being clipped square. Not far from the church was the famous library, the Deutsche Bücherei.

Like all healthy children, I had a tremendous desire to play. I wanted to be out running around with the other Russian and German children in the neighborhood, but my father exercised an iron discipline over me. He wanted me to do useful things as well, so he started teaching me how to read music at this early stage of my life. He made time for it despite having a full workload in the church, and despite the fact that this and other matters often led to frequent unpleasant friction between him and the priest, who was a fanatically religious man. Thanks to my father's devoted teaching I could read music by the age of five and had almost perfect pitch, even though according to my father I had not been born with it.

My father taught me to play and sing as well as read music. We had a small harmonium, and although I cannot remember the day he first put me beside it to sing while he accompanied me, I do have a picture of it in the family album, and I look as if I must have been about five or six years old.

Many decades later, when I was giving a concert in the Gewandhaus in Leipzig in the late 1980s, Aino Sellermark, who is now my wife, and I took a walk in the city and returned to the district where I had lived as a child. We went to the church, of course, and I had the chance to show Aino the apartment where my parents and I had lived. Imagine my surprise when I saw the little harmonium still there. It felt as if time had stood still. It was here by this simple instrument that I had learned to sing my first notes and in this very room that my father had composed and arranged a collection of hymns that I still have in my possession. I recently telephoned the priest of the lovely old Memorial Church about donating my father's music collection, and I was pleased to hear from him that the harmonium is still in its original place.

My father's duties at the church included conducting the choir, which he had formed. It consisted of three girls—two sopranos and an alto—and myself, singing the tenor part. For festival occasions our little choir was augmented by adult singers, and we had a magnificent ensemble, particularly at Christmas and Easter.

He also found time to give me instruction in the Russian language, religion, and mathematics. I soon forgot the Swedish I had known when we left Sweden. Russian was spoken at home, and Russian or German outside among my friends.

In Russian, my father taught me both reading and writing, and there was no question of skipping over the grammar. I had a Russian arithmetic book that my mother would produce when she saw me with nothing to do. I can still remember today how much I hated that arithmetic book. She would shout at me and really have to drum into me anything that had to do with mathematics. Even a simple thing like 7 plus 8 was almost completely beyond my grasp.

Of all my Russian books, it was the wonderful fairy tales with their beautiful woodcuts that I loved best. I still have them and look at them from time to time. The worn pages bear the signs of my attempts to draw; there are houses and animals in profusion and my clumsy efforts to form numbers. My finest fairy-tale book is the one about the Fire-Bird, printed in Russia in 1909.

I do not remember actually enjoying learning anything as a child apart from singing. I cannot recall ever being unwilling to sing. From the start, singing was a means of expression as natural to me as speech. When I stood there in the choir and sang, I experienced a kind of liberation, mixed with a feeling of happiness and self-esteem, especially at the big festivals. It was wonderful to be able to take part in them and sing with the adults even though I was so small. At the same time, somewhere inside me was the knowledge that I was better than they were. A sensation, if not of arrogance, then at least of pride.

When there was a social gathering in the parish hall I was often put up on a chair to sing. Then old ladies and gentlemen would come up and kiss and hug me and say how sweet I was in my little Russian shirt and how beautifully I sang. It was an intoxicating feeling of happiness that surpassed the enjoyment of all the sweets I was given afterward.

To give me some company at home, my parents got me a little green canary that we called Canny. That bird was a fantastic songster. My mother was kindhearted enough to let him fly freely around the apartment so that he did not have to sit penned up in his cage. I was awoken one sunny summer morning by Canny sitting on the curtain rod singing nonstop. I lay there listening and wondering how he could sing like that. Didn't he breathe? Oh, if only I could learn to sing like my bird!

Then a remarkable thing happened: he flew down and sat on my chest. I lay absolutely still and he walked up on to my face and began kissing me. From that day on my canary was completely tame. He ate his food direct from my lips, and when I got dressed in the mornings he was always there to play with my socks and underclothes. He bit my toes and spread his wings to make himself look a real cock of the walk. And he never stopped singing.

My parents thought that Canny should have a wife, so they bought a yellow canary that we called Elsa. I stood and watched them when they celebrated their marriage up on the curtain rod. They soon had two little chicks. I christened the little boy bird Chirik and the sweet little girl Rosa. The two baby birds were also tame, but their mother Elsa never became so. Canny taught Chirik to sing, and we had a wonderful time at the dinner table when the birds sat on our shoulders and sang or walked around on the table eating bread crumbs. Sadly Canny's mate died when she was sitting on the floor one day and my father, not seeing her, crushed her under his big shoe. He went out and secretly bought another bird!

I have often thought of Canny later in life as I have become more and more convinced that there must be some form of reincarnation. Perhaps Canny was on his way to becoming something more than a little green canary.

My childhood years from then on consisted of music and singing and playing with my little birds. And my friends. I think I was a perfectly normal child. I was sometimes happy, often disobedient. Not infrequently I inclined to melancholy, which was perhaps my Slavic temperament. In adult life I have often been seized by a profound melancholy, and when it happens I usually put on a record of Russian Orthodox church music, preferably choral. It is a form of music I find exquisite to listen to. I would not describe my melancholy as an affliction; in fact I find that frame of mind very restful, and did so even as a child.

From the Leipzig period I remember my father as an exceptionally authoritarian person. He was very strict toward me, but that severity did not exclude tenderness. He always held my hand when we went for a walk together, and I often sat on his lap to be cuddled.

I looked up to my father as a god when I was a child and always believed he was right. When there was a quarrel with the priest it never occurred to me that my father might be in the wrong; it must be the priest who was stupid.

My father exuded calm and goodness. Perhaps that is why in later life I never reproached him for all the beatings he gave me. The slightest bad behavior or act of disobedience had to be punished. As soon as I did anything he thought wrong he would pick up a narrow Cossack belt that had once belonged to his uniform and I would be given a thorough thrashing. Born in the late 1880s, my father belonged to a generation that was convinced of the benefit of strict punishment. It was probably also the Cossack in him coming to the fore.

One episode from my childhood in Leipzig stands out. My family had quite a full social life with other émigré families, some of whom were fairly well off. On one occasion we were invited to the home of a family who had a son my own age. Just as we were about to leave, the boy opened the door of a large cupboard, in which every shelf was stuffed full of toys. Even to stand looking at such marvels was a delight, but then of course I also wanted him to take some of them out and let me touch them, just for one tiny, tiny moment. My parents were standing in the doorway, ready to go. When I realized the game was over even before it began, I was filled with rage and despair and began to howl. I refused to go home. To show who was in charge, my father said "You just wait, you're in for a proper hiding when we get home," and off I had to go. I can remember being frightened to death all the way home of what was to come. And as expected I was given a good thrashing with the Cossack belt.

That upbringing was completely misguided, since it instilled fear in me. I am totally opposed to corporal punishment myself, especially when combined with psychological punishment. I am convinced that such experiences are harmful to the development of a child's character. Why else would I have had such a shy temperament right into adulthood and found it so hard to open up to people, to dare to express what I really thought or felt? Why was my need to please everybody so great, and why did I brush all my personal problems under the carpet instead of coming to terms with them? I know now that much of the complex I suffered from stemmed from being frightened as a child. It was a long time before I found the courage to liberate myself entirely, but only after having been thoroughly duped and deceived in my own home. Nowadays I am not afraid as I once was, nor so childlike and credulous. I have developed a perspicacity over the years that makes it easier for me to live with others and for others to live with me.

My relationship with my mother was different from that with my father. She did not have such an equable temperament as my father. She would shout and scream at me when she thought I was being disobedient, and I responded by answering back for as long as I could. Our rows always ended with my mother smacking me. I never had the same respect for her as I had for my father. With my mother I always tried to see how far I could go.

My father Michail came from the small Russian town of Novocherkassk, northeast of Rostov, near where the River Don flows into the Azov Sea. His family were peasants from the village of Kachalino. As a young man he went to a training college that included music in its curriculum, and then he went on to become a teacher for a short while before joining the Czar's army.

When the Revolution broke out in Russia in 1917 my father fled from the Crimea to Constantinople across the Black Sea. He and another soldier succeeded in stowing away on board a cargo ship. The two young men hid themselves deep down in a recess in the hold. They were completely without food for the whole journey, which took several days, but the hold above them was full of sacks of flour. They managed to get some of the flour to run down in a steady trickle through a hole in the ceiling of their little recess. They collected it, moistened it, and kneaded it into small cakes, which they then dried on the hot pipes that ran the length of one side of the hold. By these ingenious means they kept themselves alive until they reached Constantinople.

As he was musical and had a powerful bass voice, my father joined a group of refugees who were organizing Russian choirs. It was in Constantinople that the famous Don Cossack choir started, and there too that a similar choir was formed, the Kuban Cossacks. My father belonged to the latter, and they sang on both secular and religious occasions. He came to Stockholm on tour, and after one of their concerts he met my mother, Olga, who had come to Sweden from Russia some time before.

Olga's father, Gustaf Gädda, came from the Helsingborg area of Skåne in southern Sweden, but the family also had offshoots in Denmark. As a young man Gustaf Gädda took up a position with the royal jewelers W. A. Bolin in Stockholm. He rose to become an engraver and was given a post in Bolin's branch in Riga, Latvia.

Over the course of the years he became a highly respected and sought-after artist. I often thought of him when I read Benvenuto Cellini's autobiography: there are many facets of the Italian Renaissance prince that could apply to Olga's father. By all accounts he was rather hotheaded. When I look at old photographs I am struck by how elegant he was, a tall man with a fine goatee beard and expressive eyes.

As a young man in Riga, Gustaf Gädda met a Russian girl named Anastasia, who came from a small town northwest of Moscow called Pskov. She was very pretty, with perfect regular features. The two young people married and had six children. At the turn of the century they owned a grand house with a garden in a residential district of Riga, big enough to allow them to keep animals.

My grandmother Anastasia had a large family that needed financial support, and when her own children went to school there was very little money available for their education. I have heard that there was also discord in the family over religion: my grandfather was born a Protestant and remained one, whereas my grandmother was Russian Orthodox and held to her own beliefs.

Of the six children, it was my mother, Olga, who got on best. She took a secretarial course and at the age of twenty obtained a post in the Moscow office of the German firm Siemens. She was probably one of the earliest typists. When the unrest began in Russia, Siemens was taken over by the Bolsheviks and Olga lost her job. She found temporary employment in the office of the Russian Navy.

My mother often told me about those dreadful years of 1917–1918, when there was neither food nor fuel to be had for money in Moscow.

Everyone lived in fear for their lives. One day when she went out to sell some jewelry to exchange for wood, she encountered an armed revolutionary. He subjected her to coarse abuse and turned his gun on her. Olga was very brave and shouted: "Go ahead and fire!" The man lowered his weapon and slunk away.

Olga and the whole Gädda family had Swedish passports, and she decided to try to leave Russia. Olga managed to get a seat on the last diplomatic train going through Finland to Stockholm. The family was reunited in Stockholm, but it was not long before the unity was disrupted.

Gustaf Gädda started a new life with a Swedish woman and moved with her to Malmskillnadsgatan, where he also opened his own engraving workshop. My grandmother Anastasia lived with three of her children in a small apartment at 41B Renstiernas gata in Stockholm. She was at the time a woman of about fifty, but judging by photographs she already looked quite elderly, with white hair. One daughter was married in Russia and had stayed behind. One son was dead, and another had married in Latvia and remained there, despite the unrest. In my grandmother's home on Renstiernas gata lived my mother and her brothers Harry and Nikolai, both teenagers who spoke Swedish very poorly, lacked any practical qualifications, and thus found it difficult to get jobs in their new country. Once again, my mother, Olga, managed best. She spoke perfect German and so was able to earn a passable living and even have her own little apartment after a while. Uncle Harry solved his problem by going to sea. Things were worse for Nikolai, the youngest: he went astray and got in with a gang of undesirable friends.

My recollections of my earliest years with my grandmother are of her being a profoundly unhappy woman. She was extremely taciturn and fervently religious. She went regularly to the Russian church on Birger Jarls gatan. I remember her praying in a whisper, always ardently, and constantly crossing herself and dropping to her knees. As a child I could not imagine what she was praying for. But the great unhappiness reflected in her face must have been caused by some tragedy, that much I could understand.

As I look back on my childhood, my lasting memory is of being dearly loved by my parents and the constant center of their attention. There can be no doubt that they devoted themselves to me entirely, as evidenced not least by my father's enormous ambition to instill knowledge in me, particularly in the musical sphere. I do not think I would have gotten where I am today if I had not had his solid tuition to build on. And despite the severe shortage of money, my mother always kept me well dressed, as I can see from the photographs of myself as a child. In retrospect, the good times in my childhood predominate.

We were better off financially during the Leipzig years than both before and after in my youth. My parents seemed happy and content. But as I got older terrible changes started taking place in society around us. I would be playing outside with my friends, and we would see to our horror groups of men suddenly engaging in bloody fights. The ones in brown uniforms were Nazis. The others, in black shirts, were Communists.

Our church began to fill up with people even when there was no service. The immigrants turned to the priest in their anguish. Would they no longer be able to retain their sanctuary in the new country? I must have been frightened to the core by this period of violence and hatred. I have been so adversely affected all my life by any quarreling; I have a constant longing for peace and harmony among people.

Strangely enough, we children were more afraid of the Communists than the Nazis. That was because we never saw any drunken Nazis, whereas the Communists would stagger around the streets in an inebriated state. But I remember the fear that gripped us when the Nazi storm troopers marched through the streets of Leipzig just before Adolf Hitler came to power: brown uniforms and brown boots, wide leather belts with shoulder straps, high caps with swastikas, and swastikas on their armbands.

Far too many of the Russian immigrants saw Hitler as a liberator. They had not read *Mein Kampf.* They knew nothing of his racial policies, which were based on the idea that the Germans should make themselves masters of all other races—the Slavic peoples were to become slaves. The uncomprehending immigrants formed a liberation army with markedly Nazi attributes. This army met in the cellars of our church, preparing itself for the day when Hitler would crush the Communist regime in the Soviet Union and the immigrants could return home to their beloved Russia and regain all the property they had lost.

In the autumn of 1933, after he was elected Chancellor of Germany, Hitler came to Leipzig. There was a large field between our church and the Deutsche Bücherei, and there he parked his truck and treated the citizens of Leipzig to a strident propaganda speech. My parents did not go out to listen to him, but they did not need to go out to hear the speech, because a good provision of loudspeakers meant that no one who had ears could fail to hear what Hitler bellowed out to the enthusiastic crowds, who responded with a resounding "Heil Hitler."

At that time I was in a German primary school. Every morning we were lined up in the school playground, where we would stand with our right arms outstretched to salute the Nazi flag and sing "Deutschland, Deutschland über Alles." One day as I was standing there in line I happened to giggle for some reason, whereupon the teacher immediately rushed over and grabbed me roughly by the short hair on the back of my neck and pulled sharply upward. It hurt so much that I never giggled again when we were saluting the flag.

My mother became increasingly uneasy during this period. Having experienced the horrors of the Russian Revolution, she could feel the reign of terror approaching again. She wanted to return home to the neutrality of Sweden. My father, the family provider, was not so willing to leave Germany. He had finally obtained permanent and reasonably well-paid employment, but what would await him in Sweden, since he spoke no Swedish and no other language except Russian? My mother followed the call of her strong intuition, however, and stuck to her decision. I can still remember my father's words to her: "Take Nicolai with you and go to Sweden, then. I'll stay for a little while longer and we'll see how things develop."

So my mother Olga and I set off, taking with us the few necessities we could carry. We had the canaries in their cage, which mother covered with a black cloth so that they would not be frightened.

I never did see any of my school friends from Leipzig again. I have not heard from a single one of them over the years. I know why. They long ago fell victim to the war.

TWO

Stockholm

IT WAS MAY 1934 when my mother Olga and I left Leipzig. Our journey began with a lengthy train ride through northern Germany, then the ferry from Sassnitz to Trelleborg, followed by another interminable train journey through Sweden. When we finally pulled into Stockholm it was in bright morning sunshine. I stood at the window and looked out over the city where I had been born nine years earlier, on 11 July 1925. My mother told me that to the left of the railway bridge was Riddarholmen, where, in the church with the tall black openwork spire, many centuries of Swedish kings lay buried. The building a little further over, adorned with three gold crowns gleaming against the blue sky, was the City Hall. There were white steamships everywhere, some puffing out black smoke as they glided over the water. My mother pointed out the huge House of Parliament and the Royal Palace. She told me about the Old Town behind the Cathedral, with its sixteenth-century houses and alleyways.

Everything looked so beautiful, seemingly floating on sparkling water. There was nothing to be afraid of here, no black or brown uniforms, no people shouting or fighting. I knew I would like living in Stockholm.

I do not remember whether anyone met us at the station, but we moved in with my grandmother Anastasia, who lived on Renstiernas gata near Sofia Church, which stood on the hill just above the apartment block. I stayed with her while my mother searched the area for an apartment that we could afford. My grandmother's place was not modernized, with its lavatory in a little red hut in the yard. But all around us spring was in full bloom with the sweet smell of lilac and cherry blossoms.

My mother quickly found a one-room apartment with a large kitchen and a sleeping alcove. It was on Gruvgatan below Åsöberget in Söder-malm, not far from my grandmother. In the early 1930s it was as quiet and peaceful there as out in the country, and the houses around us had big gardens with flowers and a profusion of greenery.

My father Michail came to join us in Sweden only a few months later. The situation in Germany had become even more militant. He was a stateless refugee traveling on a Nansen passport (a passport issued by the League of Nations to individuals without a home government), and things did not go so speedily. It would be a long time before he obtained Swedish citizenship and was able to get permanent employment. We had arrived in a Sweden suffering widespread unemployment in the midst of the Depression, and the country had not yet recovered after the big stock market crash. Unemployment was a hard burden for my father, but eventually he found a job as choirmaster in the Russian Church on Birger Jarls gatan. Now that he could devote himself to music again he quickly organized a choir in which I too could take part, just as in Leipzig.

The nominal salary that my father received for his services in the church was not enough for the family to live on, however, even though there were only three of us. My mother had to take on the responsibility of provider. I remember her mostly sitting bent over her sewing machine making up sheets commissioned by a shop. Later she told me that she seldom had even the few coins for the tram when she had to deliver the heavy parcels of sheets. She had to carry two packages, one in each hand, and the strings cut deep into her fingers.

I was too young then to understand how hard it was for us financially. I liked our little home. My bed was in the sleeping alcove, and I was to live there for twenty-two years. I recall my mother's kitchen with special delight, so cozy and snug. She had brought some of our china from Leipzig and some old Russian silver. Otherwise there were no ornaments in my childhood home, but always a clean and beautifully embroidered tablecloth on the table.

In the autumn of 1934 I was put in the third year of Sofia Elementary School, because I had completed almost two years in a school in Germany. I had totally forgotten the Swedish that I had learned in my early childhood, and I now spoke only Russian and German. Fortunately my first schoolmistress, Agnes Gustafsson, knew German and helped me along.

My schoolmates, however, were not so helpful. They tormented me mercilessly. They thought it was strange and frightening that I spoke a different language from them, particularly German at a time when all things German were regarded with deep suspicion among the working-class population of Södermalm. They christened me "the German." Sometimes a kind of frenzy came over them, and they would gang up together and decide to beat up "the German" and chase me around the school playground. I was so fast that I generally escaped them, and only once did an adult have to intervene and disperse my tormentors.

I suffered terribly from being persecuted. The name Nicolai sounded odd to their ears, and it was soon transformed into the ridiculous-sounding Nicodemus. Well into the 1940s there was a boy who would sit in the window of one of the houses on Åsögatan shouting after me so loud that it echoed over the whole of Åsöberget: "Nicodemus! Nicodemus! Nicodemus!" He had been shouting that ever since I arrived in Sweden. I remember thinking: "Will he never get tired of teasing me? Has he nothing else to think about?"

Since the atmosphere at school was hostile to me, I became introverted; I bottled up my suffering and was too ashamed to tell my parents that I was not popular. I remember one occasion in particular when I got a cut on my face trying to defend myself in a fight. When my mother asked me what had happened, I swiftly made up a story of having dropped a book on the classroom floor and hitting my face on the desk lid when I bent down to pick it up.

I foolishly lied because of my fear that I would also get a beating at home. My childhood was full of white lies instead of the uncomfortable truth. I once got a C in a subject at school, and I was scared stiff of coming home and showing my parents an inadequate mark. I felt I had to alter the grade to an A. When I took my report card with its alteration to my father he was very pleased and satisfied, but I suffered hell all summer. My torment increased as time went on and autumn term approached. What would my teacher say? By some miracle he noticed nothing and I was able to breathe freely again.

Lies and fear of various kinds characterized my early years. One day when I was playing with a little girl my own age, I had a sudden impulse to ask her to pull down her knickers. She did not do so, but she did tell on me to her mother. The next day her mother opened the window when she caught sight of me and shouted out "Shame on you!" I remember agonizing in fear that her mother would tell my parents and that I would get a beating.

I often felt dreadfully alone and lost as a child. It was a suffering that I was never able to identify properly. It may perhaps have been caused by my parents' overprotectiveness. My mother would suddenly come down and make me go home when I was right in the middle of playing. "That's enough now. It's time to eat." I used to get terribly angry with her. Nor did I like her Russian food that I had loved during our time in Leipzig; it was not the same as the food eaten in my friends' homes.

I was not dressed like the other boys either, which is always rather distressing at that age. In retrospect I realize that my mother could not afford to buy clothes for me. She made them herself and dressed me according to her own taste. I was particularly upset by a winter hat that I looked very girlish in, and I always took it off as soon as I got out of sight. My dearest wish was to look just like all the other boys, but my mother could not understand that.

All these little things together made me look unhappy as a child, or so I have been told by my teachers when we met in later life.

To be fair, I must admit that there were also good times. On Gruvgatan I remember we had nice, kind neighbors. As I became more fluent in Swedish, my persecution lessened and I began playing with the other children. We lads who lived around Åsöberget went about in little gangs. There was the Gruvbacken gang, which I belonged to, and the Åsö gang, consisting of working-class boys. A certain amount of tension existed between the two, but we rarely fought; it was mostly just snowball fights.

The local populace was quite a social mixture. There were workers' apartments in a big corner building on Åsögatan and also down the hill and along Danviksgatan. I think most of the workers in the neighborhood were employed at the Liljeholmen candle factory. Åsöberget had beautiful but unbelievably dilapidated houses that had once been red. In the 1960s the whole area was renovated and the almost crumbling buildings were transformed into housing for Stockholm's "artistic workers": writers, actors, and painters.

Number 4 Gruvgatan, where my parents and I lived, was a yellow brick building. Our home was on the first floor of the four-story house. There was a beautiful big studio apartment at the top, occupied by a well-known Swedish artist from the province of Dalarna. He actually painted a portrait of my father Misha.

I remember us children having fun in summer and winter alike. It was not usual then to have a summer cottage, nor could my parents afford to rent one, and they did not want to send me to a summer camp with other city children. After school finished at the beginning of June I would play for days on end up on the grass of the rocky hillside. Just below Sofia School was a large overgrown garden where we could do as we pleased. Nearby were some old semi-derelict houses where gypsies lived.

The gypsy children did not go to school, so we had no contact with them, though I did see them in the Russian Church when I sang in my father's choir. The gypsies came from Russia and were Greek Orthodox. I saw them every Sunday morning on the number 6 tram, which went right to the junction of Roslagsgatan and Birger Jarls gatan where the church is situated. Huge numbers of gypsies came to mass, and I recall in particular one ancient woman who always came without fail, despite her frailty.

The Russian Church on Birger Jarls gatan in Stockholm is the world's oldest Russian émigré church. It celebrated its 350th anniversary in 1967. It was originally located up near Slussen in the center of the city, on the block where the City Museum is today. A colony of Russian merchants had lived in the area during the Middle Ages, engaged in trade with Sweden.

In 1908 the Swedish Prince Wilhelm Bernadotte, a son of King Oscar II, married the Russian Grand Duchess Maria Pavlovna Romanova. She donated many beautiful icons to the Russian Church, which regrettably fell victim to a burglary in the early 1970s.

The unfortunate thing about the Russian Church in my childhood was that the priest at the time, Father Stefan, did not believe in cooperation between different nationalities. There was, and still is today, an Estonian and a Greek Orthodox congregation in Stockholm. Since then the streams of refugees from southern countries have brought in several other denominations. Each attended its own church. If they had all been allowed to come together in a single church, that church would have had a fantastic choir, among other benefits; but such was not to be.

Life for me personally improved when I entered Katarina Secondary School. I could talk completely naturally with the boys I met there. I felt as if I had moved to a different and better world.

In one of our first singing lessons at the school, the music teacher, Einar Ralf, divided us into groups. Each group had to learn to sing a tune, and we then had to sing in different harmonies. When he came to my group I sang the song without his having to teach me. I remember his being incredibly surprised and asking if I had studied music, and if so with whom. I replied that my father had taught me, and I could feel that he did not really approve. He probably wanted to be my sole instructor.

In any case Ralf was impressed by my ability, and he let me sing solo from time to time in the class. He was also cantor in the beautiful baroque Katarina Church, and one Christmas he asked me to sing a well-known carol. My mother and father listened with tremendous pride to this, my first solo public performance. I received 5 crowns from Einar Ralf afterward, and I gave the coin to my mother as a welcome contribution to the housekeeping money.

End of term at Katarina Secondary School was wonderful from a musical point of view: I always had a lot to sing. On one occasion we learned *Estudiantina*, a waltz by Waldteufel. Einar Ralf arranged it for a boys' choir, and the performance was rated a great success by teachers, pupils, and parents alike.

This success with my singing voice faced an abrupt, but fortunately temporary, setback when I hit puberty. One day I woke up and suddenly could not hit a single pure note—all that came out was a croaking sound. The period during which my voice was breaking took two years or so, and I could not sing at all. But as suddenly as it had disappeared, it came back when I was seventeen. My father and I were in church when all at once my voice returned as a tenor. That is what is so strange: many children have beautiful singing voices and enjoy singing, but extremely few get back their high, clear voice after it breaks. That applies to both boys and girls, and it is even rarer for boys. Thousands of boys have sung in the prestigious Wiener Sängerknaben choir, but I can only think of one who went on to become a famous singer: the superb Austrian baritone Walter Berry.

The transition from child to teenager was an extremely painful and oppressive time for me. I felt clumsy and constantly in the way, with no control over my body and growing limbs. I suffered a great deal of emotional anxiety too, perhaps partly because I was now able to understand my parents' severe financial problems. My father was very volatile and had trouble controlling his Cossack temperament. He became involved in various conflicts with members of the congregation of the Russian Church and with Father Stefan. His views probably were often justified, and all he wanted was for his choir to sound as good as possible. But he had no authority, so all arguments simply damaged his position. On one occasion it ended with him losing his post, so he did not even have that little income. He was later taken back, because he was so good at his job.

Like so many other young people, as a teenager I was constantly in search of my own identity. As soon as I had any money I would rush off to the cinema, and I would try to imitate my heroes' walk and gestures. I had seen Alan Ladd in one film dressed in a stylish pullover shirt with a high roll-neck. Somehow I managed to get hold of a similar yellow garment, and I put it on and went into the kitchen to show my mother. She looked at me angrily, asked what I was meant to be, and ordered: "Take off that ridiculous jumper!"

A particularly wonderful event for me was the summer that a Swedish film company was filming a comedy in one of the tumbledown houses up on Åsöberget (the ones that are now houses for artists and writers). I spent whole days watching what was eventually going to appear on the screen. Just seeing in the flesh these god-like creatures called actors filled me with delight. Once as I turned to go home I could not tear my eyes away from these "children of paradise," and I walked straight into a bicycle, which fell over with a crash. I heard one of my great film idols yell after me: "You might at least pick the bike up again!"

I was very unsure of myself and lacking in confidence as a teenager, and my awkwardness made me terribly shy and reserved, especially with girls. Yet I had the usual overheated sexual feelings that were so disturbing and unsettling and of which I was so frightfully ashamed. I thought that I was absolutely alone in the world with my misery. Much later in life I happened to be reading Leo Tolstoy's biography, by Paul Birukoff, and had to smile when I read that in puberty the great Russian writer felt exactly the same way I had. But when it was at its worst I had no one to turn to. I would go red in the face when I stood singing in the church choir and saw the women in the congregation fixing their eyes on me. It was a terribly painful experience for me, and once I actually fainted. But that was after the lengthy Good Friday Requiem.

My friends at school made wild boasts about their conquests of girls; some of them had already had sexual experiences, or at least they claimed as much. I felt that such things were not for me. My parents did not even let me take part in the school dances when the boys invited the girls' school and vice versa. They were born in the 1890s, and they simply did not talk to their children about sex. So I went around with false notions that sex was sinful and dirty, something to be done on the sly. It would never have occurred to me to ask my parents for advice on any sexual matter. That subject was taboo.

Women were a mystery that I could never stop thinking about. One rainy morning on the way to school I met an elegant woman dressed in light-colored clothes. I was gazing at her as we passed one another, my foot slipped off the pavement into a puddle, and I splashed her fine spring coat. She glowered at me angrily and shouted: "Watch where you're going, you oaf!" That was hardly a good encounter, and it affected me badly.

But wounds heal quickly when we are young. I started noticing a very attractive girl on my way to school, who I thought looked really sweet and pretty. One day I plucked up the courage to say "hello" to her. She responded with a delightful smile, and after this happened a few times I felt brave enough to stop her and chat. I ventured to ask if she would mind my inviting her to the cinema. She thanked me and promised to turn up at the appointed time.

I went off in a state of blissful intoxication. That girl was so wonderful in my eyes that I wanted nothing more than to be with her for a couple of hours in the darkness of a cinema. Just to sit beside her. But then came the sickly pallor of reflection. I had no money, and I also knew that my parents had none to give me. There was no alternative for me but to take a different route to school. I dared not meet the object of my love again, so agonizing was the situation.

Nevertheless women continued to occupy my thoughts. In summertime, on the grassy bank outside the building we lived in, there would be women sitting on blankets, talking and drinking coffee. When it was very hot they would take off their stockings. I would stand behind the curtains in our window and watch them gently unfastening their silk stockings and carefully pulling up their skirts. My erotic fantasies would be aroused, but with no other outlet than in my imagination.

Like the young Tolstoy (though I did not know it then) I tried to control my ardor through physical exercise. I was particularly interested in athletics such as handball. My sports club was called Hellas, and I was quite good at handball. Otherwise my best sport was running, and I felt incredibly proud when I ran 60 meters in 7.5 seconds. My running shoes were worn out every second or third day. My father was completely flabbergasted: my running knocked great holes in the domestic budget. My parents could not understand what enjoyment there could be in running fast. They did not understand how important it was for me: being the fastest made me the hero of the school.

Singing and sports and language lessons meant most to me at school.

I think I was something of a favorite with the language teachers, because I found their subjects so easy. I could speak several languages as a small child—Swedish, German, and Russian—and so I had no fear to hinder me when it came to others. I got As in all my examinations, which made me extremely pleased. When French entered our curriculum, that too went well. I loved French from the very first moment, which might have been because our young French teacher taught it so interestingly. And then I adored the wonderful French films that were shown in the local cinemas. I saw all the films that we nowadays regard as classics.

I had difficulties with Latin in school at first, but then I discovered the logic of the language, or rather of its grammar. As I learned more and more Latin, I noticed that French also became easier. Latin classes included much Roman history, which made the classes fascinating.

I did not particularly enjoy the rest of the subjects on the schedule. I had trouble with mathematics more than anything else: I could not understand a single thing. My marks were inconsistent, too. I had a weak period in the second year and had to repeat the year. This was probably because my sexual fantasies were taking over and drawing me into reading romantic literature. Luckily, when I repeated the year my interest in my studies revived. I was never a shining light at school, however.

I had classmates who were extremely clever, but only one of them achieved fame beyond the borders of Sweden. He was a disabled boy named Olle Hellbom. At school he was already a genius, and I thought he would be a prominent professor or scholar. He became a world-famous director of children's films through his cooperation with Astrid Lindgren, the author who created that idol of many a child, Pippi Longstocking. The only other boy from Katarina Secondary School to achieve fame outside of Sweden was myself, but that was something I could never have even dreamed of at the time. I simply hoped to get reasonable enough examination results to enable me to find a job and contribute to my parents' income.

My parents, by this time in their fifties, were having a great struggle financially. I was growing out of my clothes very quickly and constantly needed new ones, and my appetite was enormous and I was always hungry no matter how much I stuffed myself. I obviously had to work during the summer holidays; my mother needed the money I earned to pay for my clothes. One summer I was a delivery boy for a hardware shop on Sibyllegatan in Stockholm (the firm closed down long ago). My first task was to carry a hundredweight bag of cement on a trade bicycle. The bicycle had its rack above the front wheel, and it took me half an hour to figure out how to get the bag of cement onto the rack without the back wheel flying up in the air! When I finally got it in position and pedaled off, it turned out that the delivery address was five floors up in a building with no elevator. When at last, dripping with sweat, I stood outside the door with my bag of cement, I decided that if the next job was as bad, I would give in my notice.

Fortunately the next assignment was considerably easier. The owner of the hardware shop had a summer cottage out in the Stockholm archipelago, and on Saturdays he would send me to the steamer with things for the family. The archipelago ferries had such a wonderful smell of fried herring and bloaters. If only I could have a bloater, I thought. Even today I start to feel hungry when I am home in Stockholm and go past the white skerry steamers.

Another summer I worked for Nils Leander, first husband of the great Swedish-born singer and actress Zarah Leander. He owned a publishing house on Regeringsgatan in Stockholm, and while I was working for him he published a directory of everyone in the Swedish film industry, not just actors and directors but even cashiers, projectionists, and ushers. I think his business must have been quite profitable, because I spent many busy days packing books for the post to be sent out cash-on-delivery all over Sweden.

The summer of 1943, in the middle of the Second World War, was a hard time for our family. My father took work as a tree feller with a farmer in Märsta, about thirty miles northeast of Stockholm. My mother's younger brother, Nikolai, and I also worked with him in the forest. I remember that summer out in the country being exceptionally beautiful. We got up at three o'clock in the morning, when the day was at its best, not too hot and no mosquitoes. We went on working until three in the afternoon and then rested for the remainder of the day and evening. We were put up at the farm for these summer months and ate with the farmer's family. I remember the food tasting divine after all our hard physical labor. (Much later on, memories of that summer in Märsta made me realize what a pleasant life the great Finnish singer Martti Talvela must have had. He worked his own organic farm near Savonlinna in Finland, and he invited me several times to go out to his place for a week in the summer. I had promised to go but never got around to it. When I eventually did have the time, he unfortunately had already passed away.)

In 1944–1945 I took a nice clean job in the big NK department store in

Stockholm. The Swedish Count Folke Bernadotte was heading a relief action for the starving children of Germany, and NK had willingly placed at his disposal premises on a back street, where one person packed the parcels and I attached the requisite dispatch notes. When I recall that period it is not thoughts of the war in Europe that stay with me. The only thing in my mind then was the girl standing next to me. She was a few years older than I was, and she already had a brief marriage behind her. She knew a lot about men. She said yes to my shy suggestions and we started going out together. It went on like that for a month, until another co-worker, a drama student, asked whether we would like to borrow his apartment while he was away for the weekend.

I was nineteen that summer when I lost my virginity, and since the girl was experienced it was all reasonably successful.

Unfortunately my school-leaving examinations in the spring of 1945 were not so satisfactory. The Swedish paper in particular that year seemed appallingly difficult to me, and the only thing I could think of to write about was the Swedish poet Gustaf Fröding's poem "A Poor Monk from Skara." I had no idea what the poem was really about, so I made things as simple as possible for myself by just paraphrasing the words of the poem, for which platitude I got a C and never went through to the oral examination.

It felt terribly ignominious and upsetting to see one's schoolmates get their white matriculation caps, especially since I had already repeated a year. But somehow I managed not to lose heart and decided to do the last year's course again during the autumn term. I was good at history, and for the Christmas oral examination I had to give a talk on the United States, which I was interested in and knew a lot about. And when the Latin examination was over I remember my old teacher Per Venström coming up and poking me in the stomach and saying in his squeaky voice: "He knows his Latin!" I was very proud of that remark. French also went quite well and I got a Ba (equivalent to a B+ in the U.S.), but in everything else I was a B pupil.

My more gifted friends went on to university. I myself had no interest in continuing my studies, nor did my parents try to influence me in that direction. They were probably pleased that I was at last leaving school and could take up employment, provide for myself, and perhaps also help them out financially. At that time my father had the worst job imaginable. He was washing dishes in the basement of a big Stockholm restaurant. In winter, cold air mixed with exhaust gases came in through the window, and this, combined with the steam from the hot water, contributed to the deterioration of his health.

After finishing school my first position was with a small provincial bank, Sörmlandsbanken. The manager to whom I applied for the job discovered that I had an A in singing. He made special mention of it to me, and I was aware that he was well-disposed toward me during my time in the check accounts section; he was probably interested in singing himself.

Although I continued to sing a lot in my spare time, always with great enjoyment, neither I nor my parents at this point had the faintest notion that I would turn to singing professionally.

Here I am, one-and-a-half years old, wearing a fur coat made by my mother Olga.

With my mother Olga on the stairs of my uncle Harry's villa in Enskede, a suburb of Stockholm. I still have in a drawer the sweater that I am wearing in this photo.

With my father at the
little harmonium in our
apartment at the Russian
Gedächtniskirche
(Memorial Church)
in Leipzig.

Dressed up for my father
Misha's children's choir at
the Gedächtniskirche in
Leipzig, 1931.

Leipzig   20.VII.31

Back in Stockholm and now
nine years old, standing above
Åsöberget.

More than ten years later,
resting on the rocks where
I played as a child. At last
I can wear the white
graduation cap, having
passed my examinations.

On the hills of Södermalm in 1953. I have found a quiet place to practice my arias with only the birds as an audience. Behind me is Stockholm harbor.

An early publicity photo, circa 1953.

In costume as Chapelou for my debut, in Adam's *Le Postillon de Longjumeau* at the Stockholm Opera, April 1952. (Photo by Enar Merkel Rydberg, Stockholm)

With Kurt Bendix at an early recording session. (Photo by Harald Borgström, Stockholm)

Packing for my first trip outside Sweden, to Milan for my La Scala audition, July 1952. (Photo by Pressens Bild, Stockholm)

Dressed for my first role at La Scala, Don Ottavio in Mozart's *Don Giovanni,* January 1953. (Photo by Foto Piccagliani)

A scene from *Don Giovanni* at La Scala, with (*far left*) Elisabeth Schwarzkopf as Donna Elvira and (*center*) Carla Martinis as Donna Anna. (Photo by Oscar Savio, Rome)

Posing with Constantina
Arauyo for my Paris
Opéra debut, as Huon de
Bordeaux in *Oberon* by
Carl Maria von Weber,
1954. (Photo-Lipnitzki,
Paris)

With my *Oberon* co-stars. (Photo-Lipnitzki, Paris)

Dressed as the Duke from *Rigoletto* for my debut at Covent Garden in London, April 1954. (Photo by Helga Sharland)

As Tamino in Mozart's *The Magic Flute* for a guest appearance at the Stockholm Opera, November 1956. (Photo by Enar Merkel Rydberg, Stockholm)

Strolling through Times Square shortly after my arrival in New York in 1957. (Photo by Pressens Bild, Stockholm)

Standing outside the Metropolitan Opera House before my debut in *Faust*, November 1957. (Photo by Pressens Bild, Stockholm)

Getting ready in the dressing room at the old Met, November 1957.

Onstage with Hilde Gueden during a dress rehearsal for *Faust*, November 1957. (Photo by Pressens Bild, Stockholm)

With my teacher Paola Novikova and her husband, Werner Singer, my accompanist in 1958. (Photo by V. Sladon, New York)

At a recording session with Elisabeth Schwarzkopf in Paris. (Photo by Sabine Weiss, Paris)

With Gian Carlo
Menotti at the old
Met during rehearsals
for Samuel Barber's
Vanessa. (Photo by
Louis Mélançon,
New York)

Dressed as Anatol for
the world premiere
of *Vanessa* at the
Metropolitan,
February 1958.
(Photo by Louis
Mélançon, New York)

Scene from *Vanessa* with Rosalind Elias. (Photo by Mark Hagmann, Philadelphia)

The recording session for *Vanessa*, 1958. Seated to my right is Regina Resnik, and to my left are Rosalind Elias, Eleanor Steber, and conductor Dimitri Mitropoulos; standing behind Mitropoulos is the composer, Samuel Barber.

Rehearsing with Boris Christoff and conductor André Cluytens at the 1958 recording of *Faust.* (Photo by Jean Marie Marcel, Paris)

With Victoria de los Angeles and Sir Thomas Beecham during the 1959 recording session for *Carmen.* (Photo by Esselte Foto, Stockholm)

As Des Grieux in Massenet's *Manon* at the Met in the autumn of 1959.
(Photo by Louis Mélançon, New York)

My debut at the Holland Festival in Amsterdam, playing the title role in *Benvenuto Cellini* by Hector Berlioz, July 1961. (Photo by Maria Austria and Henk Jonker, Amsterdam)

Dressed as Alfredo in *La Traviata* at the Metropolitan Opera House, 1963.
(Photo by Louis Mélançon, New York)

With Mirella Freni at the July 1963 recording of *La Bohème* in Rome.

A scene with Mirella Freni in Donizetti's *L'Elisir d'Amore* at the Metropolitan, 1965.

Playing Nemorino in a production of *L'Elisir d'Amore* at the Vienna Festival in the summer of 1973. (Photo by Palffy, Vienna)

At a recording
session with
conductor Otto
Klemperer in
1964. (Photo by
G. Macdomnic,
London)

The 1964 recording of *Carmen* in Paris. To my right is Maria Callas, and
conductor Georges Prêtre is seated in front of us. (Photo by Sabine Weiss,
Paris)

With pianist
Gerald Moore.
(Photo by Rudolf
Betz, Munich)

Joking around with George London and Jean-Christophe Benoît during
the recording sessions for the complete *Tales of Hoffmann* for EMI in Paris,
September 1964. (Photo by Sabine Weiss, Paris)

In *Fra Diavolo* at the San Francisco Opera, 1970. (Photo by Carolyn Mason Jones, San Francisco)

The recording session for Rossini's *William Tell* at EMI studios in London, July 1972. With me are conductor Lamberto Gardelli, playfully placing an apple on my head, and baritone Gabriel Bacquier. (Photo by Macdomnic)

Preparing with conductor Sir Colin Davis at the recording session for Berlioz's *The Damnation of Faust* in London, 1973. (Photo by Mark Evans)

As Herman in Tchaikovsky's *Pikovaya Dama* (The Queen of Spades) at the Met, 1972. (Photo by Louis Mélançon, New York)

With Kurt Bendix for a rehearsal (above) and concert with the Stockholm Opera in 1984. (Photos by Enar Merkel Rydberg, Stockholm)

My final opera role, as Archbishop Abdisu of Assyria in Pfitzner's *Palestrina* at Covent Garden, 1997. (Photo by Clivebarda)

My Parents

ONE DAY soon after my final school examinations an event occurred that was to have a decisive significance for the whole future development of my life. I presumably must have done something to make my mother very angry with me, and in her rage she blurted out that I was not her and Misha's child. She had adopted me, and she regarded herself as having saved me from a children's home and thus from a fate worse than death.

Without my asking, the story came pouring out in a torrent. My natural father was actually her younger brother Nikolai, the youth who had been out chopping wood with us in the summer of 1943, the lanky fellow who occasionally threw me a coin and whom I had thought was my uncle. She told me that my natural mother was a woman named Clary Linnéa Lindberg, who gave birth to me in the Södermalm Maternity Clinic when she was only seventeen years old. The young couple was totally without means. Nikolai was an odd-job man but mostly unemployed. My natural mother was working as a waitress in a coffee house in Stockholm on extremely low wages when she became pregnant with me. There were already children of all ages in her parents' home, and Clary's mother had just had another baby herself, born the same year as I.

There was no place for me anywhere, and in their hour of need my natural parents decided the best thing was to give me to a children's home, and they had already talked to the matron. At that point Olga, who was actually my aunt, and my grandmother Anastasia came to visit Clary, as I was to be christened before leaving the maternity clinic. When Olga heard what fate was planned for me she performed a heroic act: she decided she would take care of me herself. And when the decision was made I was christened Harry Gustaf Nikolai, the first name after my uncle, the second after my grandfather, and the third after my true father, who spelled his name with a "k" in the Russian manner.

My mother Olga told me that I was six days old when I came home to her little apartment on Renstiernas gata, in the same building as my grandmother. Uncle Harry and my father Nikolai also lived with my grandmother, as did Clary Lindberg, to whom Nikolai was engaged. Once I started talking I called my natural mother, who also breast-fed me, "aunt."

When I was between one and two years old my mother Olga moved with me to Brännerigatan, and a year or so later she met Michail Ustinoff and they married. But I remember nothing of all that. I felt that my father Misha had always been there in my life and I grew up in the absolute certainty that they were my actual parents. When I enrolled at the German school in Leipzig in 1932 I had the name Nikolai Ustinoff, and I carried on using that name in the Swedish school that I entered two years later.

Having made this revelation to me, my mother warned me not to make contact with my real parents, and indeed I did not feel I had the strength to undertake such an initiative. I think I tried to suppress what I had learned, since I regarded Olga and Misha as my parents anyway—the only ones that I knew.

Before she died, my mother Olga told me that once, in the 1950s, when I was giving an outdoor concert in Stockholm after my international breakthrough, she recognized my natural mother in the audience. She was among the women who had come backstage, but she asked no questions, just put out her hand and touched my clothes. I was completely unaware of it myself, since I was probably fully occupied in signing autographs.

My father Nikolai, on the other hand, did not behave so discreetly. When I became a world-famous singer he sat down and wrote me a letter, explaining the situation at the time of my birth and expressing deep regret for what had happened. He wanted to declare himself as my father, and he even signed the letter "Your Father."

The letter landed in our house like a bombshell. He even had the bad taste to make disparaging remarks about my mother Olga, which hurt me so much that I wanted nothing to do with him.

When I responded with silence Nikolai went around the shops in Södermalm boasting of being my father. He even went to an evening newspaper and told them, a fact I learned indirectly from a journalist, who was kind enough not to publish this revelation. Not that it would have harmed me, but it would have saddened my mother Olga and father Misha after they had struggled for so many years to raise me.

I would not have minded having contact with my natural father had it not been only after I became famous that he wanted to know me. Before that he had pretended not to be aware of my existence.

The truth about my real parents was of course known to a small number of people. A few of them would point out the situation to Olga, but she would always stubbornly and obstinately deny it. One Russian woman was roundly harangued and told that it was none of her business: "You were there, then, were you, standing over me with a lamp and watching while I produced him?" was Olga's caustic reply. She would maintain and elaborate on her lie, and anyone who dared to assert anything else was in her eyes evil and malevolent.

I often questioned her attitude myself, but I also understood her perfectly. For reasons I cannot fully understand, she had taken me on as a newborn baby and then worked and struggled to make ends meet all the time I was growing up to ensure that I received the best care and education possible. She did everything a mother does for her children, but for me who was not really her child.

I wonder whether she should have waited so long to tell me the truth, and then in such an agitated state of mind. If I had been told as a child in a calm and sensible way that my real parents were her brother Nikolai and his fiancée Clary Linnéa Lindberg, then I probably would have come to accept that explanation. And I might have been spared all the emotional complications that being an adopted child eventually caused. I had many tormented moments when I convinced myself that my natural parents were so irresponsible that they did not want to know me, that they valued me so little they were willing to cast me off to a children's home. These thoughts always came to the fore when life was going badly for me. I imagined I was fit only for unhappiness.

When my mother Olga died in January 1985, at the age of ninety-two, I was the only one left to sort out her estate, no great task in itself since she owned nothing of any significant value. But what she had amassed on the other hand was paper, among which was a thick brown handwritten book—my father Misha's notes about me and my progress, and also their disappointments and frustrated hopes for me. There were two applications to the Swedish child-care authorities to adopt me as a baby. Both applications were rejected because of my parents' poverty; I remember the tone of the authorities being cold and impersonal. I assume therefore that I lived with Olga and Misha illegally.

In view of this I can understand how afraid my mother Olga must have been the whole time that I would be discovered and taken away from them. She must of course also have been worried all her life that I would disgrace myself or in some way fall foul of the law.

In character, mother Olga was a true original. She lacked psychological insight, was obdurate and even impolite when the mood took her, and many people found her difficult to deal with. Others simply accepted her as she was and saw her as straightforward and honest.

One of her closest friends was a frail little lady from Berlin, who came to be called Aunt Eva. The friendship between Aunt Eva and mother Olga was a long-standing one that they kept up into the autumn of their lives, talking for hours on the telephone in German. The following anecdote told to me by Aunt Eva will serve to illustrate how Olga could be.

It was 1956, four years after my breakthrough at the Stockholm Opera, and I was singing on the world stage. I was married and living in Paris, under engagement at the Opéra. One day my mother had a telephone call from the head of the Stockholm Opera, Set Svanholm, inviting her and her friend to a performance by Jussi Björling. He thought it would be fun for her to listen to a voice other than her son's.

Mother Olga accepted Svanholm's invitation, gracefully I hope, and she and Aunt Eva sat with him in his splendid box. She listened to the music and singing for a while, and then Jussi Björling came on and launched into a wonderful long aria. Mother Olga suddenly stood up and headed for the door of the box, declaiming loudly "Huh, he can't sing!" before marching out.

Aunt Eva said she felt like sinking through the floor, so ashamed was she. Svanholm took it quite calmly, however. He even offered me a longer season as guest singer.

Aunt Eva often said that she could write a novel about Olga's indiscretions. In the early 1970s I was singing a guest performance in Rossini's *William Tell* in Florence. Mother Olga and Aunt Eva were invited, I put myself out to make them feel comfortable, and everything went well. But then, on the flight home from Milan to Stockholm, mother Olga could contain her temper no longer. The two ladies were sitting right at the front of the cabin, and when the meal was served the cabin crew started from the back. Mother Olga was furious and screamed out, "Don't you know who I am? I'm Nicolai Gedda's mother." The stewardess gave her a faint smile and replied, "Sorry, there's nothing we can do about it." And they continued serving as if nothing was amiss while my mother went on gesticulating and moaning, "We won't get any food before we get to Stockholm at this rate."

Mother Olga suffered from an indefatigable desire for conflict. In the late 1960s after I took up residence in Switzerland I invited her down so that she could enjoy the flowers in the garden. But the bees were buzzing about industriously, and since mother Olga had no concept of the fact that if you get in their way and annoy them you are likely to come off badly, she started running around waving her arms in the air. She was soon so badly stung that I had no alternative but to put her back on the plane to Stockholm.

After my last season at the Metropolitan Opera in 1983–1984 I returned from the United States and spent a lot of time with my elderly mother during my recuperation in Stockholm. She had her ninety-first birthday in January 1984, and I tried to make things pleasant for her. She was suffering from hardening of the arteries and now living less in the present than in the past. She could narrate events that had occurred in her youth, even in her childhood, with crystal clarity. She often told me that she was firmly convinced there were ghosts, she had seen them herself. She recounted an incident from the period when the Gädda family lived on the outskirts of Riga, Latvia, in a large house with outbuildings for the animals. There was also a barn in the yard where the winter fodder was stored. Olga had woken up late one evening and looked out of the window and seen a man she did not know moving the hay by the barn. Her father, Gustaf, the goldsmith, was frequently away traveling and was not at home just then. I listened to her story but thought no more of it until one summer's day when I was visiting her brother Harry in his house outside Stockholm. We ate lunch in his little arbor and were sitting chatting about the Gädda family. I asked him to tell me something about the way things were before my time. He revealed that his father Gustaf thought that his youngest boy Nikolai (my biological father) could not be his own son. He did not want to know the child and when Nikolai misbehaved Gustaf would lock him out. I remembered then that my mother Olga had often defended Nikolai because she felt sorry for him, a feeling shared by her sister. I thought too of my grandmother Anastasia, who throughout my childhood had gone to church every Sunday and entrusted herself to the mercy of the Lord with so much praying and kneeling. Could there be a connection between Gustaf's dislike of his youngest son Nikolai and his divorce from his wife Anastasia when they arrived in Stockholm? And did my mother Olga's ghost from the family home in Riga have anything to do with it? If Anastasia had been raped, or had a secret admirer who turned up when her husband was away on his travels, who then was my biological grandfather? My uncle Harry could not provide any answer, and those who knew the truth had taken it with them to the grave.

Readers will wonder, of course, whether I ever sought out my natural mother later in life, as might be expected. I did eventually meet Clary Linnéa in person when I spent an afternoon with her in the late 1970s, listening to her version of the story of my birth and adoption, an account that confirmed much of what I had been told by Olga.

In 1977 Aino had published a detailed article about me in one of Sweden's largest newspapers, and some time afterward she received a letter from a friend of my natural mother Clary Linnéa. Aino had previously tried to find out about my mother through the registry office, but without results. I was convinced that she had been dead for many years. The friend explained that Clary Linnéa was too shy and frightened to make contact with her famous son herself; she asked Aino to let me know that my mother had but one desire in life—to be able to give her only child a hug.

I really felt like the prodigal son when with some trepidation I telephoned my birth mother to tell her I would like to come and see her. This was the autumn of 1977.

She lived in a very pleasant suburb of Stockholm. When she came to the door I presented her with a large bouquet of yellow roses. Our initial embarrassment was overcome by my mother immediately starting to arrange her flowers. It gave me time to look at this woman who had given me life. She was in her seventies, of average height, and slender, with dark brown hair curled prettily around her well-shaped head. She moved around easily in her simply but tastefully furnished home, which was exceptionally clean and well ordered with potted plants in every window. On a bookshelf directly opposite the sofa where I was sitting there was a large framed portrait of me. The photograph, which was from the time soon after my breakthrough as a singer, must have been bought from a photograph agency.

She put a ready-prepared coffee tray on the table between us, and there we sat together for the first time in fifty-two years.

To get the conversation going I asked her to tell me her version of what her and my father's life was like at the time I came into the world. In many respects it coincided with Olga's account.

Clary Linnéa Lindberg was only seventeen and working as a waitress in Södermalm. My father just had casual work and was mostly unemployed. These were the worst years of the Depression in Sweden. She told me of their simple pleasures when they were young. In their free time they would take a tram to a dance at one of Stockholm's numerous places of entertainment. According to my mother, Nikolai was an accomplished dancer, and all the girls were eager to dance with him. He was extremely good-looking and she was constantly jealous.

"I gave myself to him in order to keep him," my mother said. And that was how she came to be with child, the child that was to become me.

She went on to tell how my father's sister Olga was pregnant at the same time by a rich landowner's son, but she managed to get the money for an abortion. She, Clary Linnéa, was absolutely exhausted after my birth. Her own mother had come to the maternity clinic and told her that she could not bring her baby home, since she herself, the mother, also had a newborn child in the already over-large family. There was neither space nor money to feed another mouth. They solved the problem by deciding that I should be sent to a children's home. The nurse in my mother's maternity ward had already made all the arrangements.

My mother explained that for the sake of convenience I had been baptized in the little chapel attached to the maternity clinic. My grandmother Anastasia and Olga were present at the baptism, and they suggested the name Harry Gustaf Nikolai.

"I liked the names," my mother said. "Harry was your uncle's name and he had always been so nice. Gustaf was old man Gädda, and Nikolai, of course, was your father."

She fell silent, and it seemed to be the end of her story, but then she went on slightly more cautiously: "But what I have never understood is why Olga decided to take you herself. She had just as little money as we had. Maybe she had such overwhelming feelings of remorse for having had an abortion herself?" My mother could not get any explanation and had nobody to ask. Olga put up an iron curtain between herself and me and my natural mother.

A few years later Clary Linnéa married a good and kindly man who worked for a Stockholm newspaper. Since the new couple was reasonably well off, the husband proposed that they should take me themselves. But it was not to be. Olga apparently chased them off so abusively that they did not dare repeat the attempt.

My poor mother could not have any more children because my father Nikolai had given her gonorrhea, resulting in sterility. The break-up with Nikolai was caused by his perpetual infidelity. Old Gustaf called on Clary Linnéa for a serious talk, and she had to promise him that she would not throw her life away on a wastrel like Nikolai.

That was the essence of what my birth mother had to tell me on that autumn day in 1977. I embraced her and took my leave. She did not ask for my address or telephone number, and did not suggest further visits. Nor did I make any promises.

I must admit that the occasion had quite an impact on me. I was filled with contempt for the behavior of my biological father toward this wretched and impoverished girl who was my mother. I was suffering further internal turmoil from having met my biological mother and listened to her story behind the back of mother Olga, which felt to me to be an act of disloyalty. I decided not to have any more contact with Clary Linnéa, at least not while Olga was still alive.

Olga died in January 1985. On Mothers' Day (in Sweden the last Sunday in May) Aino thought we should call on Clary Linnéa; it was eight years since I had seen her. I rang, and when she answered I asked if she minded my calling her mother and wishing her a happy Mother's Day. Not at all; but when I went on to ask whether we could come and visit, she said that she was suffering from so many aches and pains (she was then eighty-one) that she was about to move into an old people's home. She added rather brusquely, "If you want to know more about all that ancient history, I've got nothing to say. Olga is dead; we should let her rest in peace."

That was the end of my contact with my natural mother. By now she must be dead. All I can do is send her my grateful thoughts and thank her for giving me life. And good genes in respect of certain aptitudes.

May she too rest in peace.

Pieces of the puzzle of my background continued to emerge late in my life. One evening in the early 1990s I was giving a concert at Riddarhuset in Stockholm. I had arrived in good time to go through the program with the pianist, and as we were rehearsing, an attendant came in and handed me a thick brown envelope. As luck would have it, I did not open it then and there. Not until Aino and I got home later did we unseal the mysterious envelope and read its contents.

It was from a woman I had gone out with for a few months during my youth. This letter was apparently an attempt to renew contact with me all these many years later. She must have heard that I had left the United States and my second wife, information she possibly gathered through a friend who was the wife of one of my former colleagues. Obviously in order to arouse my curiosity she revealed that she knew the truth about my life, about my background.

When we were going out those many years earlier, I had tired of her and she in her turn had sought out my biological father Nikolai and turned to him for solace. She learned from Nikolai that my mother Olga had been engaged to a rich Swedish landowner's son. The boy's mother did not approve of his fiancée but wanted her son to make a match more in keeping with his social position. Olga was apparently diverted by being sent off to train as a cook in southern Sweden. There she discovered that she was pregnant, but she managed to get the money for an abortion.

At the same time the young Clary Linnéa Lindberg was also pregnant, but without the means to procure an abortion. The months went by, and when Clary Linnéa gave birth to me, Olga was there and expressed her willingness to take me. According to what Nikolai had disclosed to my correspondent, Olga's would-be fiancé had by that time already married a girl that his mother had selected for him. Olga, a woman of wild temperament all her life, was furious at his perfidy and wrote to tell him that she had not had an abortion and demanded support payments for their child. According to Nikolai, Olga actually then received money from her former fiancé.

The letter went on to say that much later on Nikolai and Olga had a great quarrel. In his anger at Olga, he and his wife (Nikolai had eventually married a different woman from my birth mother) apparently visited the wretched landowner's son who had been frightened into providing financial support for me in the belief that I was his son. Nikolai showed him a copy of my baptismal certificate, which gave the names of the real parents. (In this case the information was absolutely correct, but in many cases the wrong man is named as the father in the church register and in the register of births—meaning that the woman has duped her husband.) The former fiancé, by then come of age and well-to-do, took it with a sad smile, folded up the certificate without a word and put it in a secret drawer in his writing desk.

The contents of this letter that I received disturbed and affected me greatly, and after reading it carefully I destroyed it. It is not a good idea to keep such reminders, and I did not have the slightest desire to make further contact with the writer of the letter, despite the fact that she clearly wanted me to.

Putting together now the fragments I have gleaned from all the secretiveness surrounding my origins, I think my correspondent who told me my father's story was telling the truth.

Sweden in the 1920s was an undeveloped country. Historians still talk of "Fattig-Sverige," Sweden's impoverished majority, in contrast to the welfare state that was yet to come. Unemployment was widespread and those without means starved or half-starved.

It is quite possible that mother Olga simply grabbed at a chance of getting money to survive. She was also of course livid at her fiancé's desertion, and by her own code of honor thought it no more than right that he should pay. The abortion rendered her sterile too, and I thus became her compensation for the lack of a child of her own.

Even if mother Olga acted unjustly toward her former fiancé, I nevertheless remain extremely grateful to her for looking after me so well. A poor and wretched girl gave me life, another equally poor and forsaken woman ensured my survival. By dint of incredible efforts I was given a happy childhood and a proper schooling.

What contact did I have with my natural father? None at all. I mentioned earlier that he tried to make money out of being my father after I became a well-known name. I remember that I despised him for the fact that only then did he want to recognize me.

One summer evening in 1977 I got into a taxi that I had ordered in my name, and the driver looked at me and said, "Funny, my last customer was called Nikolai Gedda too, but he was an old man and I picked him up from Kungsholmen. He was having heart trouble and I drove him to the emergency room." The name and the address left me in no doubt that it was my natural father. I heard from mother Olga some time later that he had died. My uncle Harry had attended the funeral.

My father Nikolai had eventually settled down after many years and married a respected woman who had borne a number of children who were for me half-brothers and sisters I knew nothing of. One summer's day in the early '90s Aino and I were walking through Södermalm in Stockholm, through an area I used to know well where old blocks had been demolished and new ones were being built. Suddenly a man of about forty clambered up from the building site, came over to me and asked, "Aren't you Nicolai Gedda?" When I replied in the affirmative, he said, "In that case, we're brothers."

FOUR

The Beginnings of a Musical Education

MY INTEREST in vocal music, and my joy in singing, has been with me all my life. I think I could sing even before I could talk properly. In my youth it was the radio that awoke and fulfilled this passion, listening to Gigli during the war years—and later also to Jussi Björling, the German singer Richard Tauber, and the Dane Helge Roswaenge. I remember admiring Roswaenge's tenor voice; he made a great career for himself in Germany during the war. But my most passionate feelings were aroused by Gigli, whose repertoire also enchanted me. He sang French and Italian operas. I spent most of my evenings doing nothing but listen to the radio. German broadcasts gave generous time to operas and operettas, with now and then an interruption for the victory fanfare, which I subsequently discovered was a motif from *Les Préludes* by Franz Liszt.

What was going on in the world outside, however, impinged on me very little. It was a long time before we could afford a radio in our house, newspapers were an unnecessary luxury, and my parents heard of world events through their visits to the Russian Church. I myself lived in total ignorance of the situation in Europe. I recall only one disturbing occurrence. My father received a letter from Germany in which the writer described how a mutual friend in the Don Cossacks had attempted to run across a road during a bombardment. He stuck fast in molten asphalt and was burnt to death. My mother and father were very upset and talked about the dreadful accident for a long time.

Just after the war ended, in the spring of 1946, I was called up for military service with the Army Service Corps in Linköping, and the transport role of my company meant that I had to learn to drive trucks. Because I had gotten a job at a bank immediately after completing my final school examinations, I was saved from being called up to the army as a potential officer, which would have committed me to the one and a half years' military service that was virtually compulsory in student companies. I was able to prove that my mother and father were dependent on my financial support to keep the household going.

The beginning of my military service was like a nightmare, but it was ameliorated somewhat by our having a decent lieutenant in our company. He looked like a film star, tall and blond, but with one eye blown out by a grenade. The first thing he told us was that we would have to shed our girlish looks. When he came into the barracks dormitory in the mornings, he always yelled: "Don't lie there like dames in a harem—get up!"

When we were ordered to call "To arms!" I used to sing it instead. There are always good acoustics in barrack yards, because there are usually buildings on all four sides, and when I sang "To aaaarms!" my mates would start laughing and even the lieutenant could not help smiling. So whenever we had a training exercise all the windows in the barracks would go up: people were curious to see this madman who sang instead of shouting.

Winter maneuvers began in February 1947 way up in the north, on the border with Finland. The temperature was around $-40°F$ when we set off one night in a convoy of trucks full of infantrymen. We drove in an enormous column with a gap of about twenty yards between vehicles. We could not use our lights; the only directional guide we had was the rear lights of the truck in front. We were on the road for several days and forbidden to sleep: we were playing at war.

The infantrymen were primarily from the northern provinces of Sweden. We southern lads had heard many shocking tales of their violent tempers and readiness to reach for a knife, so we were rather afraid of them.

As a driver I was warm and comfortable in the cab, and I also had a mate to change places with, so it was possible to catch some sleep from time to time. But while my mate slept I got so terribly drowsy myself that I fell forward over the steering wheel. When I woke I realized to my dismay that I could no longer see the rear lights of the truck in front. I had driven off down a side road and lost the convoy. Since I was in the middle of the convoy, I had taken another twenty trucks with me. My mind seized up and I had no idea what to do other than go on. Suddenly we were entirely surrounded by lofty fir trees: the road had come to an end.

My mate woke up when the column came to a halt. He stared at me in disbelief and yelled: "You bloody fool, what the hell have you done?" In the back of the truck the northern boys from Lapland were dressed only in short sheepskin jackets and ordinary uniform trousers in that tremendous cold. We were well aware that they must be freezing. When they discovered that I had taken a wrong turn, they would probably beat us senseless. We tottered hesitantly down from the cab.

The moon was peeking out between ragged clouds and we were surrounded by snow-laden fir trees. An indistinct murmuring could be heard from the back of the truck. Now the knives will be out, I thought. After a long pause one of the lads spoke up in his singsong northern Swedish accent: "You might just as well keep going and drive us straight to the cemetery."

As luck would have it there was a motorcycle orderly to keep tabs on the convoy. He discovered that I had turned off and managed to locate us. I falteringly explained that I had dropped off to sleep at the wheel. Eventually we were reunited with the rest of the convoy, but it took me a long time to get over the fear I felt when I drove all those men into the wilderness. And after that adventure my relationship with motor vehicles was totally destroyed—I hate them all.

We were stationed in Boden, where you might end up with any job, even washing dishes—and the pots to be cleaned were not little ones, either! When we had pea soup it was cooked in gigantic cauldrons. I remember a mate and myself dragging the pot down to a lake, where we first had to saw a hole in the ice and then scour the pot by hand in the freezing water. That job was the hardest I have ever had. It took hours before our fingers came back to life. I have suffered from gout in my fingers for the last ten years or so, and it seems to be worsening year by year; I wonder whether it stems from what my hands had to undergo washing those pots in Boden.

The worst thing psychologically was that we never got any sleep during maneuvers. In the end we were so exhausted we could barely stand upright and our nerves were totally shattered. But instead of resting for a few hours the whole company would be ordered out on a hundred mile ski-march. I always came last. As a child I had begged and pleaded with my parents to give me a pair of skis like the ones the other boys had, but they could not afford it. It was thus pure luck that I survived when we were ordered to go skijoring behind horses. My guardian angel must have been watching over me.

Perhaps military service was good for me, since I had been so cosseted and overprotected at home. In the military I discovered how incredibly tough life could be and how vindictive people sometimes were. When we were at last able to put up our tents after twenty-four-hour maneuvers and were about to crawl into bed, the order would come to take the tents down again. We would stand there mute with anger. Why the hell couldn't we lie down now that we'd finally got the damned things up? No, we had to be toughened.

Luckily I managed to avoid the really brutal officers. Our captain was a pompous little ass. When it was approaching Lucia, the Swedish festival of light on 13 December, we asked permission to celebrate it. The captain responded with a grimace: "Lucia? What nonsense! If we celebrate anything here, it'll be Charles XII," referring to the Swedish warrior king who wanted to conquer Russia in the eighteenth century.

It felt good to leave Norrland when winter maneuvers were over, and I have never returned there of my own volition. I did hold a master class in the town of Arjeplog, just south of the Arctic Circle, in the summer of 1986, and while all the rest of Sweden had a heat wave, the temperature there hovered around 55°F and the weather was stormy. Never again Lappland for me.

Because my military service came the year after the end of the war, the whole thing seemed totally pointless to me, as indeed it did to most of my fellow recruits. But of course there were careerists who took it seriously and would go on to become officers. I could not understand them. I was a bad soldier; I just wanted to sleep, I was so utterly exhausted all the time.

When I went on leave it was to Stockholm to stay with my parents. I used to go to the cinema with a girl I had met before I was called up. She would accompany me to the last train after the Sunday evening film show. I would get three hours' sleep in the warm compartment before Monday morning's reveille.

After my military service was over it was not my cinema companion who came to play the primary role in my life, but rather a priest. One summer day in 1946, my school friend Ola Woxström had suggested that I go on an excursion to the old fortified town of Vaxholm in the Stockholm archipelago with the local Högalid Youth Club. When we arrived at the church my friend introduced me to Johan Movinger, the curate of the parish of Högalid. He mentioned to the priest that I enjoyed singing. Movinger was immediately interested and asked me to sing something, since we had the organist at our disposal. I chose Handel's *Largo*, which I used to sing to myself at home.

Johan Movinger was delighted and asked me to sing in his church, which I did, sometimes in Högalid church itself and sometimes in the parish hall. Our friendship grew closer every time we met, and I even went with him when he held services in hospitals and old people's homes. Then I also began singing at weddings and funerals at which he officiated.

Movinger was a fine and upright man whom I could treat as a pal and talk with about anything and everything. I could not help but make comparisons between Movinger as a spiritual guide and Father Stefan at the Russian Church on Birger Jarls gatan. The latter had embarrassed me on numerous occasions. At one confession during puberty when my sex urge was at its most troublesome he exhorted me to tell him what was "tormenting" me; I did not do so. He also hinted several times that he knew that my father Misha was not my real father. Instead of calling me Nicolai Michailovich he would say Nicolai Nikolaivich. Of course, this was correct, but I felt humiliated to be put in my place like that.

Movinger was totally different. He was a human being who had the ability to impart trust and confidence. He was a simple and true Christian. It was uplifting to listen to his sermons or to hear him talking to young people at a youth service. He always found the right words, too, at weddings and funerals. Movinger was the son of a fisherman from the west coast of Sweden. For him, as a man of the people, religion meant primarily common humanity. Everyone loved Johan Movinger, and as a result he took on more work than he could manage.

He was also always ready for a laugh. I remember once when I was to sing Bizet's "Agnus Dei," I happened to see the program before Movinger. I noticed right away that the "g" was missing in Agnus. I wondered whether I dare point it out to him—after all, he was a priest. But I plucked up the courage and told him there was a misprint in the program. He laughed: "So it says God's bottom—that's not bad, either."

It was comforting for me to have Movinger around in those years of my youth, as I began to develop as a singer despite not having any formal singing lessons then nor even having decided to devote myself to singing. One high point for me was the Christmas play that Movinger inaugurated in his parish hall in 1948. I sang the part of Joseph, and the part of Mary was played by Margareta Hallin, a student at the Stockholm Opera House who lived with her mother in Högalid. The play was very successful, and it included Christmas carols. Margareta sang "The Cradle" and I sang "Silent Night." Margareta Hallin has a beautiful coloratura soprano voice and went on to a splendid future with the Royal Opera House in Stockholm. She could have had an international career, but she preferred for some reason to stay at home in Sweden.

Even after I had become an established singer I often sang in Movinger's church on my visits back to Sweden. Sadly, on one occasion that I was to sing a program in his church, I arrived home to discover that he had suddenly died and I had to sing at his funeral instead. His death was a great loss for the whole of his congregation, and not least for me personally. I still miss him today.

My early voice training extended beyond the Högalid district of Stockholm, however. In the platoon that I had belonged to there was a chap, known as "Big Dick," who had a magnificent bass voice. (I only discovered his real name in the 1980s, and I knew him only by his nickname while in the army. We all had nicknames there, like "Pixie," "Snow White," or "Jesus." My own actual name was bad enough, but sometimes I was just called "Fish," since Gedda is the Swedish word for pike.) Big Dick was active in the drama section of the St. Matthew's Boys' Sports Club, and he asked me whether I would like to play the first lover in the operetta *Blue Beaver Inn*. The piece was written and composed especially for them by their pianist Curt Henricson. Henricson was a jeweler by profession, and I found out later that he had learned his trade from Gustaf Gädda, my grandfather.

Our opening night was in the spring of 1949 at the Scala Theater on Norra Bantorget in Stockholm. Wearing rented white evening dress, I sang a series of charming operetta airs. The operetta also had a comical pair of lovers, as there should be. We young people had enormous fun with our operetta, but it did not run for long, playing only four times. The following year I made a fiasco of a serious drama and brought my career as an amateur actor to an end.

After my military service had ended I took a post with Skandinaviska Banken in their branch in central Stockholm. I was perfectly content with my duties, and it was only at Christmas and New Year that I felt a slight despair. In those days we had to work every evening until nearly midnight; everything had to be checked on adding machines (that was long before the age of computers). Thousands of account calculations had to agree. If there was a mistake somewhere, we had to carry on searching until we found the error, which could take an inordinate length of time. When I walked home on Friday nights and met happy, sometimes inebriated, revelers, I hoped I would not have this job for the rest of my life!

The idea came to me then of trying to find someone who could help me train my voice. This subconscious notion had been activated by conversations with a school friend, Sven G. Hansson. Sven's mother was very interested in singing and often urged me to get a teacher. I sometimes sang for my former singing teacher, Gustaf Wiebe, at Södra Latin Grammar School. He was choirmaster at the little red Methodist church on Majorsgatan in Östermalm. I told him that I wanted to try to get into the Royal Academy of Music, and he wrote a very good letter of recommendation to the principal, Einar Ralf. I was given the opportunity to sing for Einar Ralf and the head of singing at the Academy, Joseph Hislop. They both agreed that physically I was not up to an adequate standard for the Academy and gave me a written notification to that effect.

Perhaps they were right. Perhaps not. My parents' reaction was an angry one and they thought I had been treated unjustly, not least because Einar Ralf had previously been my music master at secondary school. I found it rather strange myself that they did not recommend that I go to a suitable teacher if my vocal instrument was so clearly not yet fit for more serious studies.

I used to talk to some of the bank customers about music, and the one who had the most significant impact on me was Bertil Strange, who was the French-horn player in the Royal Opera House Orchestra. When I told him that I hoped to find a singing teacher, he recommended Martin Öhman: "I think Öhman would suit you."

Bertil Strange arranged a meeting and I went for an audition at Öhman's house to sing a few arias. One of the arias was from *L'Elisir d'Amore*. Öhman accompanied me admirably and I felt that I had come to an expert musician.

When I finished singing my numbers, Öhman remarked that he had not heard anyone sing those arias so beautifully before—except for Gigli and Björling, of course. I was very pleased and decided I wanted to work with him. I explained that I was a bank clerk and that the salary I earned was needed to help support my family. The money for lessons was not an immediate problem, declared Öhman, and he offered to work with me without payment for the time being.

It was the autumn of 1949 when I began studying with Martin Öhman.

A few months later he arranged an audition for the Kristina Nilsson Award, which was then 3000 crowns—or about $2000, a sum nearly equivalent to the average annual salary in those days. Öhman was one of the judges, along with the director of the Royal Opera, Joel Berglund, and the singer Marianne Mörner. Öhman told me afterward that Mörner had been especially enthusiastic but that Berglund was not. Nevertheless, I received the whole award, the highest amount, and was able to pay Öhman for my tuition.

Öhman telephoned one of the directors of Skandinaviska Banken and requested that I be given a half-time post so that I could pursue my singing studies properly. I was moved to the head office on Gustav Adolfs torg. He also organized a second audition for me at the Royal Academy of Music, and they took me on as a visiting student, which meant partly that I was there on a trial basis and partly that I was excused from certain lessons because of my half-time job at the bank.

I continued my classes with Öhman and worked solidly every single day in the years 1949–1951. Those were the most delightful years of my life to that point. The wonderful world of music was beginning to open up to me.

FIVE

The Royal Academy of Music and the Opera School

MY PARENTS were very pleased when I started making serious progress with my singing, although I remember that whenever I was called and asked to perform, my mother never really understood why I was "going to sing for practically nothing again." She was convinced that people were exploiting my voice, a view I did not share. Being allowed to sing publicly was very important for me at that stage, and in any case everyone who offered me a job had a budget to stick to and did not have the means to pay more than a modest sum. Besides, I was a totally unknown young singer. My mother could not accept that.

What I did not fully come to terms with, not until later in life when I had become an established singer, was that I had to learn to say no when people did try to exploit my singing. I thus found myself singing without payment or for practically nothing for thousands of societies and similar venues. Why did I not refuse when I was reluctant? Because I was a coward and did not dare—I so much wanted to be liked. In fact I was probably regarded as stupid. One of my old Stockholm schoolmates always used to joke "Gedda will sing for nothing over coffee."

At the beginning of my career I was pleased to get every little commission, however, and I really felt that I had found my vocation. Thinking back on that time now, I cannot value highly enough the fact that Eric Ericson, who later was to become world-renowned as a conductor, let me sing in his choirs so frequently. I was at St. Jakob's Church opposite the Royal Opera House every Sunday, and I always received a fee. Then I sang for Ericson in the Chamber Choir on Swedish Radio, all types of music, modern as well as classical. I also sang with Fylkingen ("Phalanx"), a choir that specialized in medieval music on original instruments, which was good for my development since it required so many different styles. I was accustomed from childhood to singing a cappella and had a well-tuned musical ear, so it was easy for me to change from one musical style to another.

I also had no difficulty learning things quickly, which was a necessary prerequisite since I often had to come in on short notice. The Chamber Choir consisted of professional singers who really were musical. They included Erik Saedén, the music director from the Academy, and singers like Elisabeth Söderström and Kerstin Meyer. We all read directly from the page and needed no special rehearsals. In two or at most three days we could turn up and perform extremely intricate works. In my case it was my father Misha's early instruction that made even the most complicated music easy for me.

The most difficult thing in medieval music is pitch and polyphony. I sang many works by medieval French and Belgian composers, particularly Guillaume de Machaut and Guillaume Dufay. They were songs for small ensembles and also for solos with instrumental ensembles that specialized in medieval instruments. The accompaniment was entirely polyphonic, so there was not a single melody to help. That meant it was very hard to hit the right pitch, despite all the instruments playing in harmony. Of course it was not twelve-tone music, though medieval music has a lot in common with it.

The feeling of happiness that permeated my life at this time arose from the fact that my days were filled with doing what I liked best—I was young and carefree. I did find alternating between bank work in the mornings and music lessons in the afternoons difficult at times, however, a difficulty that only other musicians can fully appreciate.

In the evenings after classes at the Academy or the Opera I had rehearsals or perhaps a performance; I often sang at weddings and funerals. I gave all the money I earned to my mother, apart from a modest sum that I kept for myself to go to a film or occasionally a café. I had no thoughts of moving away from home but was content with the little sleeping alcove in the kitchen where I had slept since 1934 when we moved to Gruvgatan.

I have since wondered occasionally whether it was the best thing for me to live in my parents' house for so long. Many of my friends had their own apartments or rented rooms in order to have their freedom. But the thought of leaving my parents never occurred to me, and it would proba-

bly have been financially impossible anyway, since we had to help one
another out. Everything was suddenly moving so fast for me during this
period, and I needed the comfort and care my mother could give. It felt
good to live in a home where I was not only looked after but where I could
also discuss with my father my new musical experiences.

I cannot claim to have had any social life at all while I was studying. I
was so totally committed to learning more and more new musical works.
Of course I might take a girl to the cinema from time to time, but I was not
going steady with anyone during those years. It was not exactly the life of
a monk—that would have been against my nature. At one of the banks
where I worked after leaving school I would flirt a little with a female colleague a few years older than myself. We went to films together or out for
walks and to cafés, all very innocent. One Saturday evening she invited me
to her home, and her charming mother, with whom she still lived, provided an exquisite meal. After supper she decided to entertain me with
songs, sung to her own guitar accompaniment. Picking up her instrument,
she began to sing a Spanish love song in a hoarse, seductive voice. I listened politely, but it gave me goose bumps. My sensitive musical ear
reacted so violently that I had to bid a swift farewell, not only for the evening but to the relationship forever.

I can honestly say that I preferred to remain faithful to my own Lady
Musica.

The additional earnings from my singing meant that I did not need to
borrow money for my studies, apart from 1000 crowns that I needed for
the purchase of a second-hand piano. Some members of the Oddfellows
signed my loan application to the Bank of Sweden, which issued loans to
young Swedes who wished to pursue studies in various professions. The
money meant a lot to me indeed at that point. The loan was soon paid off,
and I even repaid the Oddfellows' signatures many times over by "singing
for nothing over coffee."

I started at the Royal Academy of Music and then the Opera School in
1950. The first piece I had to do at the Academy was a short scene from *The
Magic Flute*, together with a young man who had already been accepted at
the Opera School. Our first performance at the school was a scene from
Wagner's *Mastersingers*. Erik Saedén played Hans Sachs and I sang the part
of Walter. Kerstin Meyer sang at the same performance and was praised
for her interpretation of Orpheus in Gluck's *Orpheus and Euridice*. Both she
and Elisabeth Söderström became famous throughout the world, and I had

the pleasure of singing *Faust* with Elisabeth at the Metropolitan during the 1959–60 season.

I continued my private singing lessons with Martin Öhman all the while. He was extremely strict and demanding, but his rigor was alleviated by an inspired sense of humor. He was tall and strong, though not fat as he was said to have been in his younger days. I soon discovered that the rumor about his enormous appetite for young women did not entirely lack foundation. We were walking once in Kungsträdgården Park in Stockholm and I of course was busily talking about music. Suddenly he was no longer by my side. I turned around and saw him standing like a statue, staring intently at a young woman. One may perhaps cast a glance if a beautiful woman passes by, but to break off a conversation as Öhman did, forgetting everything and just staring, that I could not understand.

He had an extremely fine collection of pornography at home, much of it artistically beautiful. The collection was not exactly on view to all: he kept his treasures on a high shelf in his wardrobe. He once took them out after a lesson and showed them to me. I had a feeling he was thinking of selling them—financially things were sometimes quite difficult for him. He earned his big money in his heyday in Germany before the Second World War, but he lost everything in the "Kreuger Crash" in Sweden. Kreuger owned the company now called Swedish Match. Many a Swede put money into the "Match King's" stock. Kreuger shot himself in Paris in 1932, and the shares came to be worth absolutely nothing. Öhman told me that he had bought lots of so-called Mussolini shares too; these also turned out to be completely worthless. Poor Öhman certainly had no flair for finance.

What he did have, however, was a knowledge of singing technique, which, together with his wide musical experience, was of the greatest benefit to his pupils. During his years in Germany he had worked with the foremost conductors and directors of the time, and he had constant contact with Bruno Walter, Wilhelm Furtwängler, Otto Klemperer, and many other big names.

When I started with Öhman I had little understanding of correct breathing technique and what we singers call "covering." When the voice comes to a certain position where you cannot sing completely open, you have to make a bridge in order to reach the highest notes. If you were to sing these notes open, you would have to sing them with your throat and you would "crack," as we say. "Covering" is a method of saving the voice, of reaching the highest notes without damaging the vocal cords.

From a technical standpoint covering is quite complicated. Let's say you are singing an open vowel, an open *a*. You get to the high notes that the Italians call *passaggio*, F, F-sharp, and G, which are so high that they cannot be sung on a completely open *a* but tend instead toward an *o*. This involves darkening, or rounding, together with work from the diaphragm and rib cage and the repositioning of certain muscles. You do this "covering the voice" not just by rounding toward *o* but also by using the yawning position of the throat and adding some support. A singer breathes as people generally do, not in the throat but deep down in the lungs. The correct breathing technique is like filling a carafe with water from the bottom. You fill your lungs to the deepest point so that there is enough air to sing a long phrase. The problem then is to be economical with it so that you do not run out before reaching the end of the phrase, when you have the opportunity to fill up again. Martin Öhman was very good at teaching all that because he himself was a tenor and knew the difficulties.

I studied with Öhman for almost five years, and in that time I assimilated everything he had to teach. Many singing teachers are renowned for their lust for power and their desire to interfere in young singers' private lives. I never experienced that with Martin Öhman.

One thing Öhman could not ameliorate was my shyness. He often told me the posture I should adopt when I walked on stage: "Out with the chest. Here I come." You can sometimes see this kind of attitude in the types we call prima donnas. "I am the one who is speaking. Who are you?" They may indeed be uniquely talented singers, but you nevertheless feel a sense of discomfort at their lack of awareness that there is actually a world outside of opera. There are plenty of famous and successful people in a variety of fields who behave modestly and discreetly in their personal lives. All my life I have upheld the principle of remaining true to my original self in all situations, and of not regarding myself as anything out of the ordinary just because I have the God-given ability to sing.

Kurt Bendix, Master of the King's Music, was our rehearsal teacher at the Opera School. He was my musical father, an extremely kind and friendly person. He died in May 1992 at the age of eighty-four. He made even difficult things pleasurable. In one class he picked up a sheet of music with a complex melody and said: "I'll give 10 crowns to anyone who can sing this piece faultlessly." We tried as hard as we could, but not one of us could manage it, and Maestro Bendix was able to keep his 10 crowns!

Ragnar Hyltén-Cavallius, the Royal Opera's first director and our instructor in acting, was a completely different sort of person from Bendix. He was severe and often carping, but that was balanced by his expert knowledge of music, theater, film, and languages, and he was a talented teacher. The whole group of students had to rehearse, both musically and dramatically, pieces from Mozart's operas *The Magic Flute*, *The Marriage of Figaro*, and *The Abduction from the Seraglio*. Then came Wagner operas such as *The Mastersingers* and Gounod's *Faust* and *Romeo and Juliet*. During my time at the Opera School Hyltén-Cavallius celebrated his sixty-fifth birthday, and we paid our respects by singing the quintet from *Romeo and Juliet* in class; I remember how much he appreciated the gesture.

In addition to these main tutors we had various coaches. Arne Sunnergårdh helped us practice many works, both musically and in singing technique, and some of my fellow students also took private lessons with him. I had quite a lot to do with him, but not for singing technique—for that I stuck with Martin Öhman. All the teachers at the school were very good, and I acquired a solid foundation for my further training. Thanks to my musical background I was able to skip the solo singing class completely, which otherwise takes two or three years before the rest of the two-year course.

While at the Opera School I had a few miscellaneous assignments at the Opera. The first was in Verdi's *Aïda*, as one of the many soldiers. Then I was in the chorus for Mascagni's *Cavalleria Rusticana*. I was also in a quartet in Sutermeister's modern opera *Der Rote Stiefel*, which Herbert Sandberg conducted and which we sang a cappella in the orchestra pit.

In the middle of a rehearsal one morning in the autumn of 1951, Kurt Bendix suddenly asked me: "Listen, Mr. Gedda, can you reach this note?" He struck a very high note on the piano. I sang it successfully. "Yes, that was excellent." Nothing more was said, and we carried on with what we had been doing. I wondered throughout the course of the lesson what he had in mind.

Some weeks later we had a private conversation, which Bendix prefaced by asking for a promise of secrecy on my part. Then he continued: "Hyltén-Cavallius and I have a little surprise for you. We are doing a new production of Adolphe Adam's *Le Postillon de Longjumeau* and we would like you to sing the lead."

Needless to say, I was overjoyed.

SIX

From the Stockholm Opera to the World Stage

KURT BENDIX and Ragnar Hyltén-Cavallius took a great risk when they gave me the lead role in *Le Postillon de Longjumeau*. Hjördis Schymberg, the comedian Arne Wirén, and the bass Sven-Erik Jacobsson were all experienced celebrities at the Stockholm Royal Opera at that time, and I was the only new member of the cast.

Le Postillon has a rather boring story, but if its typical comic-opera arias are sung the right way they can be little pearls. The last time it had played at the Royal Opera in Stockholm was in 1928, with David Stockman in the principal role. He had been a neighbor of mine on Gruvbacken in Södermalm, but he died a few days before I was given the role. I worked hard on *Le Postillon*, and in a few weeks I knew my part inside-out. It is a lengthy part for a very high tenor voice, so I really needed the exceptional help that both my teachers were able to give.

In retrospect I am not so sure that the new 1952 production was much to boast about. The set was garish and made a rather sickly impression. The previous production may have been better, but that was far from my thoughts at the premiere on 8 April 1952. I felt right from the beginning that it would go well. The famous "Postilion Song" comes in the first act, and as soon as I had finished that there was wild applause in the auditorium. I continued singing with an intense elation that carried me through the entire evening.

Martin Öhman was pleased on my behalf and told me it was a dream of a debut, that I had been given a fantastic opportunity, but he also said that I put myself at great risk by starting with a major role. Many renowned

58

singers started with smaller roles; Jussi Björling, for instance, began as the Lamplighter in Puccini's *Manon Lescaut.*

On the night of that successful premiere Martin Öhman invited me to supper with his wife and daughter. My parents had been at the performance of course and were extremely saddened not to have been invited. It was pure thoughtlessness on Öhman's part not to include them. Or he may have assumed that as a grown man I had the freedom to leave my parents for a few hours in the evening. He was wrong there. My parents always wanted to have me entirely to themselves; they showed their love by their exaggerated solicitude.

They went home alone after my big night at the Royal Opera House, and I can understand their feeling upset. My mother had a further grudge against my tutor. In her opinion Martin Öhman was only interested in getting money out of me. My father was my singing teacher, my only singing teacher. She could not understand that my father could not teach me everything, that he had given me a good grounding but that I had to build further on it. My father, on the other hand, was in full agreement that I had to continue my studies with Öhman.

I spent the day after the premiere at home with my parents. Newspapers from all over the country kept calling to ask for interviews. I received them one after another, and our home on Gruvbacken was filled with flowers from friends and the public. I was delighted with the excellent reviews that appeared in all the Swedish newspapers that featured opera. *Le Postillon* was a lucky charm for me, although the production as a whole was not successful and had to be taken off after a few nights.

The music critics' columns suggested at least a dozen different roles they thought I should try. I think the Opera management had quite a headache, since I had a useful voice and had also displayed a tiny bit of acting talent. When it was time for a new production of Offenbach's *Tales of Hoffmann* many people thought that I would get the principal role of Hoffmann, but instead I was given the subsidiary part of Nicklaus, which is really a woman's part for a mezzo-soprano.

I sang Nicklaus in the autumn of 1952, and the only major role left on my schedule was the Singer in Richard Strauss's *Der Rosenkavalier.* The conductor Nils Grevillius did not want me to sing at the premiere, however, which was to be attended by King Gustav VI and his consort Queen Louise. The part of the Singer is short but extremely difficult. If you lose your way, or "die," as we say in musician's slang, there is no chance to remedy matters. Einar Andersson played the part for the premiere and a few subsequent shows after that; then I took over and carried it off successfully at every performance.

I was next given a completely insignificant part in *The Beggar Student*, and that was all I had after my successful debut. Nor did the director of the Royal Opera, Joel Berglund, make any promises for the future. I do not remember whether I was directly upset by that lack of recognition, however, because other exciting things were happening in my life.

A month after *Le Postillon de Longjumeau*, a good friend of mine, the conductor Gunnar Staern, told me that Walter Legge was in Stockholm. Legge was the head of EMI, at that time called HMV-Columbia. He was married to the soprano Elisabeth Schwarzkopf, who was giving a guest performance at the Royal Opera in *The Marriage of Figaro*, a production conducted by Issay Dobrowen. Gunnar Staern revealed to me that Walter Legge had plans to make the first complete recording of Mussorgsky's opera *Boris Godunov*. Dobrowen would conduct, and the singers would include the Bulgarian bass Boris Christoff, who had just had a big breakthrough and obtained an exclusive contract with HMV. The recording would be done in Russian, and Walter Legge was frantically searching for singers who could sing in more or less presentable Russian. Staern suggested to Legge that he listen to me, as well as the Finnish bass-baritone Kim Borg and others.

I auditioned for Legge with Tamino's aria from *The Magic Flute*, an aria from Donizetti's *L'Elisir d'Amore*, and Lenski's aria from Tchaikovsky's *Eugene Onegin*. I sang Lenski's aria in Russian, a language I knew faultlessly. Legge was full of praise. We signed a contract immediately after the audition for the recording of *Boris Godunov* with me as Dimitri, the false pretender son of the Czar, a tenor part.

Before Walter Legge left Stockholm he said to me: "In a few years' time the whole music world will be talking about you." I was extremely pleased by these laudatory words from such an authority on music, but I did not dare believe them—after all, I was still no more than a pupil at the Stockholm Royal Opera.

Legge told the famous conductors in the world outside Sweden that he had met a young man in Stockholm with a promising tenor voice. The first foreign letter that dropped through the mail box at our home in Gruvgatan after *Le Postillon* was an invitation from La Scala in Milan: Herbert von Karajan, the conductors' conductor, had heard of me. La Scala's general secretary, Luigi Oldani, wanted me to come down for an audition; the theater would pay for the flight plus board and lodging.

It was in June 1952 that I flew to Italy. Since it was the first flight of my life, I was convinced the whole time that the plane would crash. The flight passed without mishap, however, and I was not even nauseous. Upon arriving at the airport in Milan I felt terribly alone and lost. I took a bus from the airport to the center of Milan and there found my way to the hotel. In my hotel room I was even more lonely. There was no overprotective but well-meaning mother to fuss around me, no father to give me good advice. I had to look after myself.

I can still remember today how much I was trembling as I set off for the venerable La Scala. I asked for Dr. Oldani, and luckily he received me in a very friendly manner and asked me to sing right away. I had chosen something from *Faust* and a few other pieces that fit my voice. Those listening to the audition immediately recognized the suitability of my voice, and to my amazement they offered me the chance of returning that winter to sing the part of Don Ottavio in Mozart's *Don Giovanni* and Lo Sposo in Carl Orff's opera *Trionfo di Afrodite*.

With the La Scala contract in my pocket I took a flight to Paris. The little plane bumped and shook so much over the Alps that I was just as frightened as I had been on the flight down to Milan. But Paris itself was sheer delight. I was met at the airport by Peter de Jongh, a representative of HMV, who had arranged dinner for me in a wonderful restaurant up in Montmartre. In the glimmer of candlelight, the delicious French food melted in my mouth as the alluring voice of Madame Patachou, dressed in white blouse and black skirt, enveloped me. I was fetched the next day for a tour of Paris, a city that until then I had only marveled at on the screen. I could feel my confidence returning.

The following day work began on the recording of *Boris Godunov* at the Théâtre des Champs-Elysées, and I thought it went very well. Legge himself produced the recording, with Issay Dobrowen conducting. Paris had been chosen as the site because at the time there was a large choir of Russian immigrants, and the best voices could be selected from the various churches. I was very critical myself and did not think the choir was particularly successful, but I was probably listening to the singers through my father's sensitive ears.

After the recording Walter Legge signed me to an exclusive contract with HMV for two years.

In Paris I did not have cause for loneliness as I had in Milan. Since I spoke fluent Russian I immediately made many friends among these "choral Russians," and we would go to a bistro for a glass or two after a day's work. The French cafés were exactly as I had seen in the films that I had imbibed during my schooldays when I rewarded myself with a cinema visit after finishing my homework. The Russians were also keen to show me their churches, and older Russians in the choir who were supporting themselves in their new country as taxi drivers took me around not just to churches but to every atmospheric corner of Paris.

I was young and romantic and enjoyed being surrounded by the Russian girls in the choir, who said they were thrilled that I also sang in a church choir. I started going out with two of the girls; they were both quite attractive, though not exactly beautiful. I used to joke and flirt with them the way young people do. One day a member of the choir came and whispered in my ear that I should not bother with one of the girls. He advised me instead to consider the other one more carefully. I was so incredibly romantic and inexperienced myself, I was in love with Paris and with my youthful life, and I was greatly enjoying my ever-growing successes. I took the whispering man's advice without suspecting that he was a "matchmaker," a not unusual phenomenon in Russian circles at one time.

That was how I came to start courting the young daughter of a Russian émigré family. What I did not ask myself was whether or not I actually loved the girl. Everything was so wonderfully exciting and it felt liberating to be free at last of my parents' supervision.

When the recording sessions in Paris were over, I promised I would write to the girl, and I kept to my undertaking. When I got back home and told my parents I had met a Russian girl, I remember my father at least being pleased. My mother had more of a wait-and-see attitude. That same autumn my father flew with me to Paris and I celebrated my engagement.

While I was in Paris recording *Boris Godunov* I also auditioned at the Opéra. Its director, Maurice Lehmann, engaged me for the principal role, Huon, in a new production of Weber's *Oberon*. It was scheduled to open in the late autumn of 1953.

But the Royal Opera in Stockholm was my base, even though I had no permanent post there. I had a scholarship contract of 500 crowns a month, an agreement that involved a number of interesting obligations on my part but almost no benefits for me. My first foreign engagement was rapidly approaching, and in December I wanted to take a few days off to do a recording of Stravinsky's *Oedipus Rex* oratorio, a very difficult piece, with Herbert von Karajan, to be broadcast by Radio Italia on 20 December 1952.

I was called into the office of Artur Hilton, the Royal Opera's financial manager. "It's too early for you to sing abroad," he said, sucking on his fat cigar. "Everything you say about offers from outside sounds fine enough, but it's far too soon. You've got to do your apprenticeship here first."

Joel Berglund's idea was that my apprenticeship should begin with the role of Pinkerton in Puccini's *Madama Butterfly*. When I told Martin Öhman and Issay Dobrowen, they both were appalled and advised me against it. They thought my voice was still too "narrow" to sing the wide range of Puccini. By narrow they meant it was too young and undeveloped. My volume had increased during my years of study with Öhman, and I had evolved a proper technique, but the instrument itself was still that of a twenty-seven-year-old. I had not yet fully broken myself in, so to speak—far from it. Puccini is dangerous for young singers; he has long-drawn-out phrases for both sopranos and tenors, and because the whole orchestra plays the melody, you really have to force your voice to be heard above it. For a young singer to strain his voice even for a single evening can have damaging consequences for years to come.

So I went to the director and explained that I would like to be excused from singing Pinkerton, that I was much too young and would not be able to manage it. Berglund asked me to sing it nevertheless. He called in Sixten Ehrling, Master of the King's Music, who was to conduct *Butterfly*, and the three of us went off together to the Queen's Foyer, a little room in the Royal Opera House decorated in rococo gold and green. Ehrling went over to the piano and Berglund sat in a chair to listen to me. Since I did not want to sing the part, I forced my voice as much as I could, and soon became quite hoarse. I broke off and said: "You can hear that I can't do it. I'm completely hoarse." Berglund then embarked on a lesson, starting to sing himself and forcing his own voice. He as a bass was going to show me, the tenor, how to reach the high notes! It was not very intelligent of him, I remember thinking. But the result anyway was that I got out of taking on the role.

With great difficulty I managed to get a few days off to go down to Rome to see Herbert von Karajan. I arrived more or less unprepared, since I had not been able to find a single person in Stockholm with enough musical ability to help me with *Oedipus Rex*. So my first rehearsal with Karajan was a complete disaster, and he was very distressed. "You have put me in a difficult position, Mr. Gedda. I have engaged you for this recording of Stravinsky, but it's absolutely obvious that you don't know the piece." I told him the situation. Karajan took the great risk of giving me a couple of days to study the part. I was to be assisted by a pianist from Italian radio. I do not recall how many hours a day we worked, but by the time we came to the dress rehearsal I knew both the Latin text and the music. The concert went extremely well and Karajan was really impressed. He thought I was born with perfect pitch, but as I said earlier, I was not.

To cope with my offers of work abroad I applied for a leave of absence from the Royal Opera in Stockholm. I received a flat refusal from the administrator. Apart from my engagements in Milan and Paris, I had also been asked to do Orff's *Trionfo di Afrodite* as a concert in Munich, and HMV was planning a recording of Gounod's *Faust* with Victoria de los Angeles as Marguerite. And I had an inquiry from Denmark about singing Bach's *St. Matthew Passion* for radio.

I could only write to Walter Legge and explain my embarrassment. I expressed my gratitude for the splendid recording contract, but unfortunately I was unable to fulfill it because the Royal Opera in Stockholm refused to give me the time off for recording. Very quickly I had a response from Legge, asking how much I was paid at the Royal Opera. I told him of my contract, a serfdom of 500 crowns a month. Legge was furious and wrote to Joel Berglund to say that if the Royal Opera did not give me two years' leave of absence he would make sure that I was never heard again at the Theater of the Royal Opera on Gustav Adolfs torg.

After receiving Legge's sharply worded letter, Berglund asked me to come to his office for a talk. He laughed slightly sneeringly, looked up and said: "I have an exceedingly strange letter here from Walter Legge. I don't know why he has written like this." He continued to hem and haw in the same manner until it finally ended with his giving me a leave of absence to perform my roles at La Scala. But I only got away at the last minute.

So on the second occasion that I met Herbert von Karajan I was equally ill prepared. At the same time that I was hurriedly cramming in Don Ottavio, I was also having to work on my next part, Lo Sposo in *Trionfo di Afrodite*.

For *Don Giovanni* I rehearsed opposite Elisabeth Schwarzkopf, who was playing Donna Elvira. The rest of the cast was also a rather elite group. Karajan could not find fault with my voice, but as far as the acting was concerned, I was a total disaster. I had no experience at all in roles that demanded graceful, elegant movements and gestures. The postilion Chapelou was a simple country lad, but this was Mozart in gracious rococo style.

As was his typical manner, Karajan made sure to point out my weaknesses in full public view. When he saw my miserable acting on the stage he was there as quick as a flash with his bullying tactics. He did it in as hurtful a way as possible: I first was made to pass across the stage and then had to join the rest of the cast and watch as he demonstrated how clumsily I had moved my legs, how absurdly I had flailed my arms.

It upset me to be ridiculed like that in front of my friends and colleagues. Naturally not one of them commented on Karajan's demonstration, they were all loyal and kind, but it was nevertheless a horrible feeling for me.

I was often deeply depressed in my isolation during those months at La Scala. I had no one to talk to, it was too expensive to telephone my parents at home, and there was nobody else to confide in. Hotel rooms in the early 1950s had no radio or television to relax with. I tried to persuade myself to stick it out and fight on despite the humiliation. After all, I had nothing to lose. If things went badly, I could always return to the Royal Opera in Stockholm.

Fortunately, luck was with me, and my debut at La Scala on 28 January 1953 went fantastically well. The following month I had equally great success with *Trionfo di Afrodite*.

I offered up many prayers of thanks before my little icon that I had pasted on a piece of cardboard. The picture had been given to me as a child by my father, Misha, who bought it in Bari, Italy, and had it blessed in the Orthodox Cathedral there. Saint Nicholas was my patron saint, and he has accompanied me on all my journeys throughout the world. I always ask him for help before every performance and always thank him afterward when it is successfully completed.

My collision course with Herbert von Karajan was only just beginning at my 1953 La Scala debut. The following summer I was in Aix-en-Provence, where I had been engaged to sing two operas, Mozart's *The Abduction from the Seraglio* and Gounod's *Mireille*. I heard from Walter Legge of HMV that Karajan wanted me to go over to London immediately after the Aix Festival to record Mozart's *Così fan tutte* and Strauss's *Ariadne auf*

Naxos. Both parts were completely new to me. *Così fan tutte* suited my voice and I would very much have liked to sing it if only I had had time to study it properly. I knew from experience that one had to come to Karajan completely prepared and ready to record. *Ariadne,* however, did not suit my type of voice. It has too many high-pitched phrases for the tenor, and it would have been dangerous for me to take part. And there would have been no time to practice, since I was already contracted to do a recording of *Mireille* for EMI immediately after Provence. I also had no contract with Karajan. I therefore turned down his two offers. He showed no understanding at all, however, and just flew into a rage and let me know that he was not a conductor one could refuse with impunity.

It could not be helped: I had a responsibility to my own voice. I thought then that I would probably hear no more from him, but it turned out that he had need of me. In 1955 I did Johann Strauss's *Fledermaus* for him, with Elisabeth Schwarzkopf as soprano. In 1958 he wanted me for a recording of Beethoven's *Missa Solemnis* in Vienna, and in 1961 we did a series of concerts in several locations, including Salzburg where I sang Don Ottavio in Mozart's *Don Giovanni.*

I sang for Karajan over a period of ten years at longer or shorter intervals. My decision in 1962 to accept no more offers from him stemmed from a specific occasion working with him in Vienna. I was in the middle of rehearsing a new production of Mozart's *Magic Flute* at the Theater an der Wien, with Karajan conducting and Rudolf Hartmann directing, and Karajan asked me to take on at the same time the big tenor role in Bruckner's *Te Deum* for a concert at the Vienna Musikverein.

The concert was a great success for him, and also for us singers, four well-known soloists. When the thunderous applause died down, Karajan thanked the two ladies, but he totally ignored us two men. I was very annoyed, as this was an affront far worse than all the minor acts of persecution he constantly indulged in. I remember going back and taking one curtain call, but then I went off. I decided never again to work with this great fiend of a conductor after *The Magic Flute,* a production that in itself was a joy to do, particularly since it was the first production following the major restoration of the theater, which had been damaged in the war. I knew that Karajan wanted me for his productions and recordings, because he loved my voice. I, on the other hand, felt that our personal chemistry was utterly incompatible. If I did not go along with everything he suggested, he became intensely angry.

Karajan was never an easy person to deal with. He was extraordinarily egocentric. He always saw himself as the great star, beside whom there were no others. With Karajan you were there because you contributed to making his concerts and operas better—and I could understand that as a professional ambition. What I could not understand, however, was that Karajan never saw the singers as living individuals but only as cogs in the machinery of his own music-making. He never passed up an opportunity to humiliate a singer or a member of the orchestra. Later in life I came to the conclusion that Karajan was not in fact a good conductor. What I learned from him was musical flow and style, but it was so tiresome to have to live with the stringency that he demanded at all times.

I used to advise all young singers who were offered a role by him to tread very cautiously. They should first check that the part was actually suited to their voices. If it was not, how important would it be for their careers to sing specifically for him? It is certainly true that Karajan was considered the foremost orchestral conductor in the world for several decades, but his ability as a director was another matter entirely. In my opinion he was a bad director, and for young singers who still had things to learn he was worse than useless. He gave nothing of himself.

One reason for this was that Karajan did not attempt to understand a voice and its limitations. If he heard a particular voice and thought it sounded beautiful, he was immediately seized by an overwhelming desire to use it. He would expect the singer to sing parts that not only did not suit the voice but actually damaged it, perhaps forever. There were many who dared not refuse, singing as long as they could. Then when things started to go wrong, Karajan simply did not care; there were others waiting in the wings, so he took them instead. As far as I know he never lost out himself through that approach, but one has to feel sorry for the young singers whose careers were curtailed.

I found Karajan difficult on many levels. Not least, I disliked his impersonal manner. He would come to rehearsals, give a curt greeting, carry out the task in hand, and then disappear to one of his many beloved hobbies outside music, such as driving race cars, skiing, sailing, flying, and mountaineering. If you met him at a party he would give a nod of acknowledgment, but his gaze immediately wandered off in search of a new object.

As time went by and I had more and more experience with Karajan, my dislike of him increased. He was cold, impersonal, power hungry, and unpleasant. But that is my subjective impression; others may have loved him. The music-going public all over the world certainly loved his opera productions and concerts, anyway. He was a respected conductor and had the kind of personality that many people admire.

The reason I was able to progress despite Karajan was my innate ability not to let problems get me down. When things were at their worst and I felt depressed, I would remind myself that I did not have a lifetime contract with him. As soon as the project I was working on ended, there would be a new conductor, one who would be quite different. Thinking and saying such things to myself certainly saved me, even if I continued to fluctuate between joy and despondency.

I expect it would amuse a psychologist to hear of my early unconscious attempts to make contact with Karajan. Once in the early 1950s we were giving a concert in East Germany, and Karajan and I were on the night train together from Vienna. When I entered my compartment I was inquisitive and wanted to explore every inch of it; I had never been in such a fine-looking compartment before. I opened every cupboard and every door, but there was one door that would not budge. I pushed and pulled with all my might, refusing to accept defeat. Finally I gave a tremendous heave and it flew open. I leapt back just as fast and slammed the door closed again. I had broken through to the next compartment, and there was Karajan trying to get to sleep! As I went crashing in I could hear his irritated voice: "Was ist es? Was ist es?" I spent a sleepless night feeling the most terrible shame and anxiety: I was convinced that he must have seen and recognized me. The next day he gave no hint at all of the nocturnal interlude.

SEVEN

Paris and an Unhappy Marriage

FOLLOWING MY FIRST ROLES at La Scala in *Don Giovanni* and *Trionfo di Afrodite* in early 1953, I went to Munich and performed the latter in concert. From there I went on to Copenhagen and Bach's *St. Matthew Passion* with the genial Danish conductor Mogens Wøldike.

Then came Paris and the recording of Gounod's *Faust*. Walter Legge had engaged the best-known singers available: Victoria de los Angeles was Marguerite, Boris Christoff was Mephistopheles, and the baritone Jean Borthayre was Valentin. André Cluytens was brought on as conductor.

Young, green, and shy as I was at that time, I thought Boris Christoff a difficult and pretentious man. He was at the height of his career, and he made sure to let that be known. If we ever needed to go over a passage again, the cry would always come from him: "No, I can't do that, I'm tired and I have to get away."

Victoria de los Angeles was the complete opposite: a gentle, quiet angel, happy and kindhearted, never resorting to such outbursts. The Spanish soprano, then in her thirties, was also at the zenith of her world career, having made her breakthrough as a singer when she was only twenty.

This was the spring of 1953, and I was engaged to the Russian émigré girl in Paris. Her parents lived on the outskirts of the city, though I never stayed with them. We had set our wedding day for 5 July, and I was to give a concert in Paris a few days earlier.

Before we could marry or have the wedding ceremony in Paris, I had to obtain certificates of my personal details from the Swedish authorities. I remember a certain amount of resistance from my mother, Olga, who had already fallen out with my fiancée's parents. Tired of these incomprehensible obstacles, I wrote to my mother to say that I would call off the wedding. Then she did a complete about-face, wanting me to get married, and she obtained the necessary papers.

I took the certificates and went with my fiancée to the appropriate office in Paris. I felt extremely uneasy. The Swedish church birth registration certificate said that my parents were Clary Linnéa Lindberg, trainee, and her fiancé Nikolai Gädda. As we sat in the office of the French authorities, I tried to keep my hand over the two names that would be unfamiliar to my fiancée. She was not so easily distracted, however, and I had to explain that Misha was not my father and that Olga was my aunt. To judge from the documents, they had not even adopted me.

This revelation gave rise to endless discussions, and I was regarded with suspicion by my fiancée's family as they wondered who I really was and to whom they were actually entrusting their daughter. Even so, they did not wish to prevent her from marrying an up-and-coming young man.

Over the years I must have suppressed the memory of how apprehensive I felt in that July of 1953, but it all came back to me in May 1995, when my old schoolmates and I celebrated the fiftieth anniversary of our graduation from Södra Latin in Stockholm. One of my friends, Sven G. Hansson, who had traveled to Paris for the wedding in the summer of 1953, reminded me: "I was sharing a room with you the night before the wedding. You suddenly sat up, wide awake, and cried out from your bed in a voice laden with fear, 'Sven, Sven, let's pack and go home to Stockholm. I don't want to get married.'" He told me that he spent the rest of the night persuading me to go through with the ceremony.

After the wedding my wife and I had to think about finding somewhere to live. Since I had an exclusive contract with HMV, Walter Legge arranged for an advance of future royalties, and with this cash in hand I was able to make a down-payment on a little house for us. My parents-in-law insisted that it should be registered in my wife's name and not in my own. By way of explanation they quoted something about a foreigner not being allowed to own property in France—which turned out later to be completely untrue.

The reason they wanted the house registered in their daughter's name was that they were trying to ensure that she would be able to live comfortably. What they had learned about me from my birth certificate meant that they had a hold over me.

The marriage was unhappy right from the start. We traveled to Sweden after the wedding, because I was giving a concert in Göteborg followed by one in Stockholm, where my dear old teacher from the Royal Opera, Kurt Bendix, was my accompanist.

We also visited an old friend of mine from school who lived out in Saltsjöbaden, a Stockholm suburb. One evening we walked to a nearby outdoor dance. It was a perfect summer evening: the air was balmy and a gentle breeze wafted over us like velvet, the trees and bushes giving off a sweet scent—it was unbelievably beautiful back home in Sweden. The dance tunes were the old favorites, and the young men and women glided past two by two. I looked at the long-legged blonde Swedish girls in their thin summer dresses and thought: "Shall I never again be able to ask a pretty Swedish girl to dance?" I felt tied and oppressed, imprisoned far too early in the heavy shackles of marriage. It was not made any easier by the fact that my Russo-French wife was angry at not being able to understand any of our conversations. It was a natural reaction, of course, but she was still discontented when we were with my parents in the house on Gruvbacken, even though they were speaking her own language, Russian.

Back in Paris, work was awaiting me at the Opéra, where the recently appointed administrator, Maurice Lehmann, was staging a new version of Weber's *Oberon*, in which I was to sing Huon de Bordeaux. Huon is a very static role, a handsome war hero in exotic surroundings, and I was dressed up as a fairy-tale prince in vivid colors. My opposite was Constantina Arauyo, a Brazilian soprano very well known at the time. She wore a dress covered in pearls and with feathered plumes. She had a strong but unfortunately rather harsh voice. One of the more soubrette-like roles was played by a Frenchwoman, who interrupted Arauyo in the middle of a rehearsal to say: "If Miss Arauyo intends to carry on making that dreadful noise I don't want to be part of this." Arauyo affected a sheepish grin and said: "But my dear friend, I sing with the voice I have." Then she added: "You French singers are just shit, anyway." The Frenchwoman stood there speechless. After a few minutes' silence the rehearsal continued as if nothing had happened. It was the first time I had witnessed the bitter rivalry among opera stars.

The Paris Opéra was big, dusty, and muddled. There were always swarms of people on stage during rehearsals running around in a state of chaos. It was hard to grasp what they were all doing, ballet troupe, choir, extras, officials, and assistants with their assistants. There was no order to anything and the opening night kept being postponed.

Oberon was not ready until 12 February 1954. My parents came over from Sweden, and it felt marvelous to have them sitting there in the auditorium. They had a large and splendid program to leaf through and were very impressed. It was the first time they had been to a performance of mine abroad. I remember how happy my father was. He wept a lot and was deeply moved. Perhaps he was thinking about how the early training he gave me in singing was finally bearing fruit.

My Paris debut in *Oberon* was a great personal success. The premiere was attended by President René Coty and his entourage. After the performance we singers had to line up on stage and the President shook our hands. There was a Swedish photographer there who missed my handshake with the President and insisted on taking it again. I felt terribly embarrassed and foolish, but the President understood and we ended up with a very good photograph. For me the moment remains a painful memory, however, and since then I have always endeavored to avoid the photographers' flashbulbs.

Oberon had a long run. I sang it about forty times at the Paris Opéra. Immediately after the premiere Maurice Lehmann asked me to sign a contract for 1955 as well, and I did.

As far as my marriage was concerned, it was not long before more problems arose. I was convinced that my wife and her parents felt that they had power over me since I had been exposed as being illegitimate. The marriage was hardly made any better by the fact that both my wife's parents and my own tried to interfere and tell us how we should run our lives. Before too long we were quarreling over every tiny thing; for example, I had a dog that I loved which hated my father-in-law's cat. It sounds laughable, but it was enough to sour the atmosphere.

My parents wrote from Stockholm to say that they felt as if they had totally lost touch with me and that they were horrified to see how my wife's family increasingly dominated me. They also were afraid that I would no longer be able to afford to assist them financially, though they had no need to worry on that score: I made sure that they lacked for nothing for the rest of their lives.

I myself felt miserable and discordant, as if I were being torn apart by the stronger wills of others. My wife would take the side of her parents and I would side with mine, which finally led to a complete break in the relationship between our two sets of parents.

Despite this personal disharmony, my career progressed. In April

1954 I traveled to London on my own to sing the Duke in Verdi's *Rigoletto* at Covent Garden. The role was particularly difficult because I had to learn the English text. The prevailing opinion in Britain at that time was that all operas should be sung in the language of the audience, a view that luckily has since fallen out of favor. My conscientious study of the part led to my receiving special praise for my clear English diction—perhaps not undeserved after having worked hard on it every day for three weeks.

The arguments with my home base at the Stockholm Opera were still going on at the time of my English debut. The administrator, Joel Berglund, did not want to relinquish his slave-contract over me. I explained that I had contracts with the big opera houses abroad for a whole year ahead and that I quite simply could not return to Stockholm.

After the guest performance in London I returned to Paris that autumn to rehearse the role of Tamino in Mozart's *Magic Flute*. The production was directed by Maurice Lehmann, but I cannot, even with the best will in the world, describe it as a masterpiece. Instead of approaching it in a simple and natural way (as Ingmar Bergman did in his world-renowned television version in 1974), Lehmann had turned the opera into a play in the style of Louis XIV, with plumes and feathers and fussy costumes. It gave the impression that the director had not understood a thing about either the text or the music, or that he had been spoiled professionally by his previous post at Le Châtelet, with its flashy and spectacular operettas so beloved in postwar Paris. *The Magic Flute* was not such a success as *Oberon* had been, but it was my experience that the role of Tamino is theatrically extremely difficult for any tenor, a feeling confirmed later in life when I came to the part again.

My marriage rubbed along somehow. In the summer of 1956 I was engaged for the festival at Aix-en-Provence for the third year running. Without consulting me, my wife decided to spend the summer with her parents in another part of France. Since I was the sole income earner I thought she had acted rather highhandedly. When my contract ended in August, I gathered up my belongings and left our house in Viroflay. My wife was still "on holiday."

I found myself a Russian lawyer and advised the relevant authorities of my intention to seek a divorce. All I took from our home were my clothes, my music, and my first gramophone records, and I went to stay in a hotel.

I soon heard through the lawyer that my wife would not agree to a divorce. I arranged for her to receive an allowance, and I also proposed that she keep the house and other belongings. Despite that, a long-drawn-out legal process began, increasingly indicative of her acrimonious attitude. She did everything she could to blacken my name among the Russian émigré community, where I had previously been so liked and respected.

I let my lawyer handle the divorce proceedings, and both he and my wife's lawyers prolonged the negotiations; all they seemed to do was send me bills from both sides, and the amounts were not small. The years passed and the proceedings continued, since my wife was not prepared to allow a divorce under any conditions. I was by this time very definitely up-and-coming in the music world, and if she could not keep me she would at least make sure that I paid.

It was an extremely oppressive situation. Whenever I returned home to Stockholm my parents' question was always: "How is the divorce going?" That was how it went on year after year.

As it turned out, it would be another ten years before I was able to finalize my marital separation, and only after turning to the Swedish Embassy in Paris. They suggested a lawyer to me who finally succeeded in arranging a divorce.

I mostly blame myself for my failed French marriage. I should have followed my own intuition when I felt that something was wrong even before the wedding and had wanted to call it off. I had many new commissions awaiting me, and I felt the need to be free to move on in life.

EIGHT

The Metropolitan Opera

IT WAS 1956 and I had other things to think about rather than immersing myself in bitterness over a failed marriage. The Metropolitan Opera made me an offer, the whole music world was starting to open up to me, and I was not yet thirty years old.

Back home in Stockholm, Set Svanholm had taken over as administrator of the Royal Opera after Joel Berglund. The first thing Svanholm did was get in touch with me, and we agreed on a two-month guest run for the autumn of 1956. I accepted this offer from my home theater despite the fact that it meant refusing a long series of European engagements.

I was delighted to be facing a Swedish audience again. I was given a warm welcome by Set Svanholm when I returned to Stockholm in November. He wanted me to sing in a new production of Mozart's *Idomeneo* that was to have its premiere at the beginning of the new year. Until then I did a series of guest performances in the ordinary repertoire, the first of which was on 9 November in Mozart's *Don Giovanni*, singing the part of Don Ottavio. The title role was sung by Sigurd Björling (no relation to Jussi), with the Norwegian Aase Nordmo-Løvberg as Donna Anna. In Verdi's *La Traviata* I played Alfredo opposite Hjördis Schymberg's Violetta on 19 November. I continued with Mozart's *The Abduction from the Seraglio*, where again I sang with Schymberg. With her beautiful coloratura she gave as superb a performance as she had in my debut opera *Le Postillon de Longjumeau* in the spring of 1952. I sang Belmonte and thoroughly enjoyed the two magnificent arias in the role. On 27 November I was Prince Tamino and Elisabeth Söderström the most wonderful Pamina in Mozart's *Magic Flute*.

The Stockholm audience really showed their appreciation and the critics were overwhelmingly positive, which also pleased me. On 13 December, the Lucia festival in Sweden, I took part in the Royal Opera's annual performance of Handel's *Messiah* in the Cathedral, next to the Royal Palace in the Old Town. Arne Sunnergårdh, then choirmaster at the Royal Opera, was responsible for the arrangement. On the day after Christmas I played the Duke in Verdi's *Rigoletto*, opposite Margareta Hallin's Gilda. Hugo Hasslo played her father, the court jester Rigoletto. Kerstin Meyer was Sparafucile's sister, Maddalena. It was a superb production with many curtain calls and deafening applause.

Nearly every one of my guest performances was sold out, which was splendid because our staging of the Swedish premiere of Mozart's *Idomeneo* was approaching. Mozart had composed this operatic tale of the end of the Trojan War for the carnival in Munich on 29 January 1781. He was then just twenty-five years old, and he wrote in a letter to his family: "As far as so-called popular appeal is concerned, you need not worry, because there is music in my opera for all types of listener, except for asses."

We too had a varied audience for our successful opening night on 10 January 1957. There was King Gustav VI and Queen Louise in the Royal Box with Princess Sibylla, mother of our present king, and in the stalls and circle were both regulars and newcomers, Stockholmers and tourists.

The production was directed by Herbert Sandberg. Set Svanholm played King Idomeneo of Crete, and Hjördis Schymberg was a passionate Elektra. Elisabeth Söderström gave a superb rendering of the shifting moods of the young Ilia. The High Priest was sung by my fellow student from opera school, Erik Saedén, and I took the role of Idamante.

All the January performances of *Idomeneo* were equally successful, and my farewell performance came far too quickly. I will remember that evening for the rest of my life, and in fact I have an auditory memento of the performance as well, since one of my mother's friends recorded it for me.

As the audience applauded us, Set Svanholm came on stage with a laurel wreath that he put around my neck. He gave a beautiful speech thanking me for my guest performance. My colleagues gave me flowers, presented by my beloved Ilia, Elisabeth Söderström. She also gave a charming speech and said how much all my friends had appreciated having me back home. Although my heart was overflowing with joy and gratitude, I was too shy to dare say anything but a simple thanks. I could not forgive myself afterward. I had behaved like an idiot in my own eyes, just standing there receiving the adulation.

Immediately after the final performance I went home with my parents to pack for my departure from Sweden. My mother and father had moved to a large apartment in the Stockholm suburb of Hässelby, in beautiful natural surroundings on the shores of Lake Mälaren, which they absolutely loved. I, on the other hand, never having spent any significant length of time there, always felt my roots to be in Södermalm in central Stockholm, where I had lived for more than two decades of my life. Nevertheless, I was very sad as I prepared to leave. My time in Stockholm had been so wonderful. I had been able to work and enjoy success in the theater where I had started out, I had been with my closest colleagues, had met old schoolmates and many other friends.

After the break-up of my marriage I no longer had a base in Paris, since I had let my wife keep the house that we purchased in her name. Paris seemed like a closed chapter, yet at the same time I felt a deep sense of gratitude for my three years at the Paris Opéra. I had learned a lot there, not least by experiencing French tastes and styles and by learning the language, which is more beautiful than any other.

Ahead of me now was a concert tour in Canada. From there I would be going on to the United States to do several concerts and finally an audition at the Metropolitan Opera in New York.

My singing debut on the continent of North America took place in Quebec in February 1957 during a dreadfully cold winter with masses of snow. The streets of the city were slippery with ice, so it was by no means easy to tempt the public out. I remember the concert was attended primarily by the French-speaking population, who gave me a warm reception. The recital included French, Russian, and Scandinavian songs as well as some classical pieces by Schubert and Mozart. The little town of Chicoutimi, 100 miles north of Quebec, was also included in my tour program. This former American-Indian settlement had a sizable music society that had invited me, and they were a fine group of friendly people who really appreciated my singing.

My first appearance in the U.S. was in Pittsburgh at the end of March 1957. I sang the title role in *Faust*, with George London as Mephistopheles. Following that performance, the *Pittsburgh Sun-Telegraph* published the banner headline: "Swedish Tenor Sings Like Devil." Another article in the same newspaper acclaimed: "The young Swedish tenor Nicolai Gedda

. . . can boast of a voice of extreme purity, excellent range, secure technique and unusually intelligent conception of the role."

My journey next took me to Chicago, where I had a sizable Swedish audience since many Swedish immigrants lived in the area. I then continued on to California to give concerts in San Francisco and Santa Barbara.

After my American tour I was due in France for another concert, and I had arranged to travel via New York so that I could have an audition with the administrator of the Metropolitan Opera, Rudolf Bing.

Perhaps I should say a word here about why it was so important to sing at the Metropolitan Opera. In Europe we aspire to reach La Scala, and the next step is the Met. At that time the Met represented the ultimate stage in a singer's career: if one sung there successfully, one had in fact conquered the world. Nowadays it is not so essential for a singer to prove successful at the Met, because the Met no longer manages to maintain the high artistic level it once did. Nevertheless it is still physically the largest opera house and one of the three or four greatest in the world.

As I walked onto the Met stage for my audition on 2 February 1957 I was conscious that it was the largest theater in the world, with its 3800 seats. The old Met was located on the corner of Broadway and 39th Street, in the most chaotic of surroundings. It was in the so-called Garment District, with gigantic skyscrapers and the clothing trade all around. I felt extremely small and lost in this concrete jungle. But then I thought of Caruso and Gigli singing here and I took heart again; I did not want to be less courageous than my own favorite singers.

I stepped onto the stage and stared out into the immense auditorium, wondering how I would ever be able to make myself heard. Once I started singing, however, I discovered to my surprise that my voice in some strange way expanded into the space. It was easy for me to sing, because I was in good form; I went through the Faust aria with its high C, and then a Mozart aria. As I sang I could hear my voice carrying, and I completely forgot that I was standing in such a gigantic auditorium. The people listening to me were spread out through the stalls, and I was told afterward that they sat in the places known to have the worst acoustics. In addition to Rudolf Bing and his producers, there were some conductors among the listeners, including the Met's chief conductor, Dimitri Mitropoulos, who had heard me sing in Paris previously and declared that he loved my voice.

Bing arranged a meeting with me directly after the audition. The other assessors were also present, as was my agent Ronald Wilford, who had introduced me to the management of the Met. It was a rule that one had to have an agent, insisted on by the opera soloists' union, known then as AGMA (American Guild of Musical Artists).

In the course of that meeting I got my first insight into the hard-nosed world of the opera business. I remember Rudolf Bing commencing the discussion by saying something like "We are very interested. . . . Mr. Gedda absolutely must sing here at the Metropolitan. Our terms are $600 a week." They offered a weekly salary because you first had to prove your success at the Met before there could be any question of payment per performance. My career had been going for only four years, but I was not an unknown name in America, because Walter Legge had already produced a dozen recordings of me for HMV. Half of the recordings were operettas that sold incredibly well, as had my first three complete operas. On the other hand, I was totally unknown on the opera stage.

My agent considered the offer to be far too low. Bing laughed at him: "Even if I were to offer Mr. Gedda a thousand dollars, you would say it was too little." I understood the irony, since the agent would of course take his percentage on everything I received. My first fee was thus set at $600 per week, but that was a long way from the exploitation once intended by Joel Berglund at the Stockholm Opera. At the Met I was to sing once or at most twice a week; the rest of the time was my own and I could use it as I wished. The salary was guaranteed even if I got sick and was unable to appear on stage a single evening. The contract covered four roles in three months, so the salary was actually not too bad for the late 1950s. My first season at the Met was to extend from November 1957 to January 1958, and then I was free until April when I was to go on tour with the company.

After the audition, with the Metropolitan contract in my pocket, I returned to Europe for a series of concerts and performances there. As soon as I set foot on French soil I received a message from my lawyer: my ex-wife had instructed her lawyer to take me to court for failure to pay her alimony. For some reason I had not sent off the latest installment in time for it to reach her by the specified date. Her lawyer had sent a sharply worded letter threatening imprisonment, and my own lawyer advised me to pay up immediately and to avoid delays in the future, adding that French prisons were unpleasant institutions.

Despite such distractions, the excitement of my first night at the Metropolitan Opera arrived on 1 November 1957 in *Faust*. It was a great personal success. Of course, some critics wrote that it was impossible to judge

what my voice was capable of after only the one performance; they wanted
to hear another performance from my repertoire to be certain. After *Faust*
came *Don Giovanni*, and there too I received unequaled praise from the
critics. I was immensely pleased and felt spurred on to be even better. I
only wished it were not such a long way home to my singing teacher Martin Öhman.

Being at the Metropolitan Opera also allowed me the great pleasure of
renewing my acquaintance with that wonderful conductor Dimitri Mitropoulos. He was in his sixties when I first met him, and he gave the impression of being a deeply religious man and seemed to live like a monk.
Whenever he stayed at a hotel he would have all unnecessary furniture
cleared out of the room and then set up his altar; a large Bible would be set
open on the altar, and apart from that there would be just his bed and his
score. Mitropoulos died of a heart attack in the middle of a rehearsal at La
Scala in Milan, just a few years after my first season at the Met. It was in the
afternoon as he stood on the podium conducting, and when he collapsed
the sun suddenly streamed through the window and a broad golden shaft
of sunlight shone on him at the very moment of death—an ideal passing
for a great artist.

In January 1958 the Met was putting on the world premiere of Samuel
Barber's *Vanessa*, with the librettist Gian Carlo Menotti as producer and
Mitropoulos conducting. The music was a mixture of Puccini, Strauss,
and Stravinsky, the plot thoroughly confusing and sexually complicated,
and it was set, of all unlikely places, in a castle in Sweden. I took the part
of Anatol, a young man who arrives at the castle and seduces both his
father's former lover, Vanessa of the title, and her niece, Erika, a wretched
and poverty-stricken girl.

The part of Erika was played by the Lebanese-American mezzo-
soprano Rosalind Elias. In one scene in which Anatol is having dinner with
the poor girl, I was to light a candle. The atmosphere was very romantic.
At the dress rehearsal, after having just poured the wine into our glasses, I
approached the candelabra with a match, but there was no sign of a flame.
Menotti yelled at me: "Light the candle!" I replied calmly that I had, and
suddenly a giant flame leapt up before me. The whole auditorium burst
into laughter—the only time during the entire opera, in fact.

Despite this one mishap, the public and the critics were with me, and
I was praised for my musical interpretation of the unprincipled Anatol.
The critics also said that I was the only one who sang clearly enough for

them to hear the words and follow the plot. I was gratified by the praise: I had worked extremely hard, not least on the articulation, with an older actress and speech trainer. I realized from the start that if you are going to sing in the audience's own language, you have to sharpen the pronunciation to get the libretto over clearly. The other singers who were using their own American mother-tongue never fully understood that.

I did fall victim to one other little episode while working on *Vanessa*. Because the Met was in a good financial state at the time, it was able to take productions out to nearby cities during the season. Everyone was interested in *Vanessa*, since it was a new American opera that had been well received by the critics. We were sent to Baltimore and Philadelphia.

As a singer I had made it a rule on performance days not to eat anything between a late breakfast and the performance itself and to have a late supper afterward. When we were in Baltimore I went for a walk in the afternoon before the performance and kept passing one aromatic food stall after another. Ever since childhood I have had a passion for hot sausages, and I found myself getting hungrier and hungrier. Eventually I gave way to temptation and had a hot dog with relish and pickles.

That evening, just as I was about to go on stage, I felt terribly ill and was violently sick in the wings. It passed over and I went out on stage and started singing. But the nauseous feeling came creeping back, and as soon as I made my exit I was sick again. It went on like that for the whole performance. I had been poisoned by that damned sausage. The strangest thing was that despite feeling so ill I sang better than ever! The mucus from vomiting probably had a lubricating effect on my throat.

For the next three decades my colleagues never ceased to joke about skidding on my vomit whenever they went to Baltimore.

NINE

A New Teacher

WHEN I FIRST CAME to New York City I felt so small and oppressed among the skyscrapers. What got on my nerves most about the city were the police and ambulance sirens, an uncomfortable penetrating noise night and day that made me feel as if I was living at the center of a permanent combat zone.

I soon began to make friends in the city. To find some peace and quiet for my soul I made my way to the Russian Orthodox Cathedral, where I met with the conductor Nicolas Afonsky, whom I had known since my childhood when he came to Stockholm in the 1930s. My father had friends among his choristers, old friends from his time in Constantinople. Afonsky had been the choirmaster in the cathedral in Paris before he moved to New York in the '50s. He received me with open arms and let me sing as a soloist with his choir. I cemented many bonds of friendship with the choristers, friendships that lasted for as long as some of them lived.

My popularity among the Russian émigrés also had its disadvantages, however. Whenever a celebration or a charitable event was being arranged, my presence as singer was expected. These organizations were not all genuine charities; many raised funds simply for the benefit of themselves. I learned of that from the many angry letters I received from poor Russians who wanted to know what I was doing singing to raise funds for people already rolling in money.

So with this increased awareness, the next time I was asked to take part in one of these bazaars I said I would not be able to do it. My response of course was received with ill grace, and I was not allowed to escape so easily. A desperate Russian lady from the organizing committee made her way to my dressing room one evening at the Metropolitan (despite its being strictly prohibited) and tried to force me to take part. I really lost my temper and gave her a piece of my mind before getting a security guard to remove her from the dressing room. But this was not the last of it, and it did not mean that I was left in peace from then on.

My home during these first few years in America consisted of one hotel room after another. The first was an unpleasant place near Carnegie Hall. The guests at the Great Northern Hotel included a number of women who earned their living as prostitutes; since it was illegal to solicit customers on the street they frequented the hotel bar. One morning I was singing in the shower, as I always do, when I suddenly heard a woman screaming a string of obscenities at me. My bathroom was obviously adjacent to her bedroom. The fact that I then changed hotels had nothing to do with the whore who hated the sound of my singing, however: it was because of the Russian singing teacher Paola Novikova.

My situation at this time was such that I could no longer continue working with Martin Öhman, since he was in Stockholm and I was mostly in America. I felt encouraged by the excellent reviews I had received and wanted to learn more, and at the same time I felt that I might soon lose my way as far as my voice was concerned if I did not get assistance. When I was in Paris I had heard from the Russian conductor Igor Markevich about Paola Novikova's great abilities as a teacher, and in New York George London reiterated the commendation. London was studying with Novikova, and he had reached the pinnacle of his achievement as a bass-baritone. We also had become very good friends, and London had made some extremely generous remarks about me in a television interview: "On a visit to America right now is a very promising tenor from Sweden. His name is Nicolai Gedda, and I'm sure we're going to hear a lot more of him in the future."

During the 1957 production of *Don Giovanni* at the Met, in which George London had the title role and I was playing Don Ottavio, the elderly Russian lady came to my room to meet me. Paola Novikova was very short and thin and red-haired, a classic Russian woman. She invited me to visit her and her husband, Werner Singer.

I called on them and found her to be genial and charming, just the teacher I needed. To be closer to her I took a small suite in the Westover Hotel near her apartment on 72nd Street by the Hudson River.

Paola Novikova was about sixty years old at the time, and she told me that she had fled from Russia during the Revolution and taken up residence in Italy. She maintained that she had been the sole pupil of the great Italian baritone Mattia Battistini, who was as famous as Caruso in his day. Battistini was known not to take pupils, so it may be true that the young Paola Novikova was a unique exception.

Novikova had a very fine technique indeed, as was evident in a gramophone recording she played for me, which was recorded at the time she was a singer in Italy. Her voice was not particularly big, but it was extremely well controlled. Those of us who heard her thought she had the same technique as Tito Schipa. Schipa was an Italian tenor, a contemporary of Gigli, and although Gigli had a much more beautiful voice, the way Schipa handled his voice was astonishing. He also sang with exquisite taste and style, and later in life I came to think even more highly of Schipa than of Gigli. Gigli sang anything and everything, sometimes in a rather banal manner. On the other hand, his glottal stops and glissandos admirably suited many Italian works.

Unfortunately Paola Novikova's career ended prematurely because of a complicated inflammation of the lungs (it was before the advent of antibiotics). With the rise of Fascism and the outbreak of war in Europe she went to South America and established herself as a singing teacher in Rio de Janeiro. From there she moved to New York.

Novikova completed the work that Martin Öhman had begun with my voice. I devoted myself assiduously to my studies and went to her at least four times a week. She also helped me work on the operas that I was to sing at the Met. She was particularly skillful at getting the words to sound clear and distinct. Her phrasing was extremely fine.

The most sensible thing I did was to return to the basics with her, despite having studied for six years with Öhman. I must have subconsciously told myself that I had come to her to learn everything from the beginning. I did not question her knowledge or ability for a single instant. I never argued with her, I just accepted that she knew these things better than I did. And magically I was soon singing even more proficiently than before: my voice became more flexible and equalized.

With a correctly equalized tenor voice one should not be able to detect any differences between the various registers; the sound should be the same all the time. The voice should be well positioned in the "mask," the sinuses in the cheeks and nostrils. When these are opened and the note transmitted there, the sound will be more resonant. The real difficulty for a singer is that the quality, strength, and positioning has to be just as good on the high notes as on the low ones. If the voice is equalized, there are no muscles to block or harm it, and the note flows freely and unrestrainedly. An equalized voice moves unhindered in all positions, with no joins, from the lowest notes up to the highest. That takes a long time to learn; you have to get the brain to understand and the singing apparatus to put that knowledge into practice.

Under Paola Novikova's guidance my voice became not only equalized but also bigger and more powerful, and indeed more beautiful in timbre. After only a few months I had overcome the problems that I had when I first went to her. Her system of instruction was excellent, and she was able to help many singers in their careers. Unfortunately she also destroyed a good number of relationships by her manner. She was the most undiplomatic woman I have ever met, and she made many enemies. She was very domineering and keen to check on everything one did when not singing. She had that penchant for overprotectiveness that so many teachers have, wanting to act as a kind of parent. Then came the comments: "So, you were out with her again. You should stop that. It can't be good for you." And if one day I did not sound as good as I ought, she would remark: "You've had a rough night, then."

After I began studying with Paola Novikova I would say in interviews that I had two teachers. But when notes on my career were compiled for record sleeves I mentioned only Martin Öhman. Why I excluded Novikova I do not know—probably out of loyalty to my first teacher and the man who discovered me.

What is learned must also be put to use, and these improvements to my voice led to a major breakthrough for me. In 1958 I was invited to sing at Carnegie Hall in New York. It was regarded as a great honor to sing there, in a concert hall that, with 3000 seats, not only is among the largest in the world but also has the best acoustics. It was built with the help of a donation from Andrew Carnegie, the wealthy American steel baron, and the hall opened in 1891 with a Tchaikovsky concert conducted by the composer himself.

In March 1958 I had my debut concert at Carnegie Hall in Bach's *St. Matthew Passion* under the direction of the Austrian conductor Erich Leinsdorf. I had the role of the Narrator. The following year, on 12 March 1959, I took part in Debussy's opera *Pelléas and Mélisande*.

My first significant performance at Carnegie Hall was a solo concert with a wholly Russian program on 12 February 1960. I sang with a Russian men's choir led by Nicolas Afonsky. By my next solo concert I no longer thought it so remarkable to sing at Carnegie Hall. By then I had also achieved success at the Metropolitan Opera; I felt secure and confident and knew that the audience had come to listen to me. In that second concert, which took place in November 1962, I did scenes from French operas, including a duet from Giacomo Meyerbeer's *Les Huguenots*, which had been requested by a music society called Friends of French Opera. *Les Huguenots* includes bel canto in the true meaning of the term—that is, "beautiful song," with its long extended phrases and pianissimo phrases— and also a cadenza where the tenor goes up to a high D-flat, half a tone higher than high C.

That concert was my great breakthrough as a bel canto singer, and all the reviewers were in agreement—they had not heard such bel canto since Caruso's prime. The audience was completely ecstatic.

During my third season at the Met, at the end of October 1959, I had the pleasure of meeting Victoria de los Angeles again, one of my favorite sopranos. She was singing the title role in Massenet's opera *Manon*, and I was playing her unhappy lover Des Grieux. Nathaniel Merrill directed, Jean Morel was the conductor, and although it was not a new production, the stage set was very impressive. It was an enormous success. The critics wrote that I was born to play the part.

Jules Massenet's opera, based on Abbé Prévost's famous novel, is better than Puccini's version, which is entirely in the Italian style. One could say that *Manon* is the most French of all French operas. I have always been enthralled by the plot, which opens with the portrayal of a young man's tender love. After discovering that his beloved, Manon, is deceiving him he is gripped by the deepest sorrow and despair. He becomes a priest and seeks solace in religion. Manon eventually seeks him out in church and begs him to cast off his cleric's garb for her sake, which he does. But Manon leads an extravagant life, and Des Grieux takes to gambling in order to acquire the large sums of money that such a lifestyle requires. One of Manon's many lovers, jealous of Des Grieux, gets both him and Manon arrested for cheating. They are banished, and during their flight they perish.

The opera is very romantic, and we did it in the beautiful eighteenth-century costumes of the Met production. I never mind playing these romantic parts, but I am always careful to appear as virile as possible to counteract the soft, sweet, and sentimental deception of romanticism. At the beginning of my career I was a little too weak on stage and must have given an almost effeminate impression, but I soon matured and realized that I had to project manly strength in roles like Des Grieux and Don Ottavio in *Don Giovanni*—to name but two examples.

The 1959 production of *Manon* also allowed me the pleasure of participating in one of the most significant elements of my twenty-five years at the Met: the weekly radio broadcast. Every Saturday during the season an entire Met opera was transmitted. Obviously not all operas could be covered, but the most important and most popular ones were included. The program aired at two o'clock in the afternoon and was extremely well regarded. It reached from coast to coast and could even be heard in Canada and parts of South America. Surveys revealed that the Met had about thirty million listeners on those Saturdays, so it was very beneficial for singers to appear in operas that were scheduled for broadcasting. One's name became more widely known as a result of the broadcast, and that in turn had a favorable effect on both concerts and record sales.

My first experience traveling with a Met tour came in the spring of 1958. After the Met's season ended in April, they took three or four operas out on tour. We generally played the first week in Boston and then went on to Cleveland, Washington, Dallas, Atlanta, Memphis, St. Louis, Chicago, and Toronto, among other cities including Oklahoma City and Birmingham, Alabama. The performances were always held in the largest venues the cities had available, often enormous conference halls. The biggest place I sang in was an ice-hockey stadium in Cleveland.

It may sound from these extensive tours as if I have seen most of America, but that is far from being the case. I found the train journeys between cities slow and depressing, so I always flew and thus missed the American terrain.

The wonderful thing about touring was the opera fans, many of whom had been waiting for us for a whole year. Admittedly many of them did not understand much of what was sung, but they so much enjoyed the whole spectacle and were incredibly hospitable. Our arrival was a high point for them. A great many parties were arranged, and many of the events were very enjoyable, depending of course on the hosts' ability to create a good atmosphere. Sometimes after a long performance it was a little too much to stand for hours with a glass in your hand, when you were longing just to sit down and have something to eat. The conversation could also be a bit vacuous. George London told me that he was accosted on one occasion by a raucous, whisky-drinking old lady who asked him what he was going to sing next. London replied, "I am going to sing *Don Giovanni*." The woman shouted back, "Don Joe who?"

During one visit to Detroit, I and a few other artists from the Met were invited for drinks at the home of Henry Ford II, the car king, and his wife, Anne. Mrs. Ford was very interested in music and frequently held musical evenings at her house. They lived in a huge mansion outside of Detroit. It was like stepping into a film set depicting the nineteenth century. The rooms were enormous and packed full of art treasures from all over the world, thousands of small ornaments, Chinese porcelain, and delicate little statuettes. I believe that Mrs. Ford was the one responsible for the refined taste in the arrangement of their art treasures. I asked her how they protected their treasures from theft; it would have been quite easy to stuff a suitable object into one's pocket. She replied that they only invited small numbers of guests that they could easily keep an eye on. During our visit I stood for a long time admiring one particular painting, a detailed study of a sunflower by van Gogh. It had three-dimensional depth and the light was absolutely right. I just stared in total amazement that the sunflower could look so true to life.

Henry Ford and his wife also arranged a larger party, though not at their home, for the entire Met touring company. Those of us connected with the production sat at a long table and were interviewed as a panel by a reporter from the local radio and television station. The public sat at separate tables, eating lunch. There must have been several hundred people present. It was customary for various officials of the Met to be asked about the year's current operas from their professional viewpoint. On this occasion the interviewer wanted to discuss *Faust*, and he received a formal and uninspiring reply from the director's and conductor's representative, who was a real bore. After these expositions about money and production plans, one of the female singers stood up and said some very complimentary words about herself.

I sat squirming the whole time at all this depressing conventionality. When my turn came, the devil got into me. The reporter asked me what I thought of *Faust*. I replied that I had sung the part a great many times and had to admit that I still did not know what the opera was about. The audience interrupted with a roar of laughter, but the reporter struggled on and asked whether I had read Goethe's *Faust*. I had indeed, but I could find nothing of his *Faust* in the opera of the same name. "The music is extremely beautiful, but as for Faust himself, it seems to me his only purpose is to go around sighing for Marguerite."

Everyone suddenly came alive and started to laugh uproariously. The audience began to ask me lots of questions. They wanted to know what I thought of Maria Callas. An elderly lady shouted, "Is it true, Mr. Gedda, that when Maria Callas comes to rehearsal, the orchestra stands up and plays a flourish for her?" "It's quite likely," I replied, "but it's by no means certain that they'll do so after the rehearsal." The jests hit the mark and the guests had great fun.

Quite honestly, the reason for these big parties was not always an interest in music; the effort was more likely made because the hosts and their event would get a mention in the local newspaper. They would spend huge sums of money to get a few paltry lines, such as "Mrs. X gave a party last night for so-and-so-many hundred guests." I should also add that I did not attend many of these events. More often than not I took a plane home to New York after the performance and worked for a while on my voice until it was time for my next appearance in a new city.

After the Met tours I always returned to Europe, where I had concerts awaiting me, and when they were completed I would hasten back to Stockholm and my parents' house. I was forever eager to return to my beautiful homeland, whatever success I may have achieved around the globe.

TEN

Divas, Agents, and Producers

I MUST SAY a little more about the image I have of that legendary tigress, Maria Callas. She and I had some recording sessions together, the first being of Rossini's *The Turk in Italy* and later Puccini's *Madama Butterfly*, but we never appeared on stage together. When I was at the Metropolitan, Maria Callas was singing at La Scala in Milan, and when she did guest performances at the Met it was opposite other tenors.

Callas had her big breakthrough in May 1955 at La Scala in a new production of *La Traviata* directed by Luchino Visconti. She proved there as Violetta that she was as great an actress as she was a singer. She also showed what can be done with Verdi opera at its best. I still remember what Visconti told the press about Callas: she was always the first at rehearsals and the last to leave. She had an enthusiasm for work like nobody else, and this, together with her acting talent, intelligence, and complete realization and expression of character, was without equal. She was the incarnation of the great tragic figures of classical antiquity.

I witnessed one of Callas's two performances in *La Traviata* at the Met in February 1958. Since I am in the profession myself, it is hard for me to be moved by anything I see on the stage—too much awareness of technical detail tends to inhibit empathy. But when I saw Maria Callas I was so deeply affected by the intensity of her performance that I sobbed. I was especially moved during the second act, in which Violetta is visited by Alfredo's father, who forces her to renounce her love for Alfredo. He asks her to keep his visit secret from his son, and when Violetta agrees to that he offers her a large sum of money, which she proudly rejects. Instead she reverts to her former life as a demimondaine. Then, in the third act, comes

90

the cruel scene in which Alfredo, in a rage of jealousy and despair, insults her in front of all her guests and throws the money after her. Maria Callas played all this with enormous presence and depth of emotion, and all with very strong vocal qualities.

Unfortunately Callas's fantastic career was cut short, probably because she performed too many and too varied a sequence of roles at the height of her powers, which is a great temptation when one is in demand. Even if a soprano has the most technically well-equipped voice in the world, she cannot sing a coloratura part like Donizetti's Lucia di Lammermoor followed immediately by a dramatic Lady Macbeth. No voice can withstand such stress, and Maria Callas's was no exception. By the time she was forty her voice was almost gone.

It is said too that the decline of her voice began when she started losing weight. In a very short time she transformed herself from corpulence to extreme slenderness.

The Callas legend is based not only on her greatness as a singer but unfortunately also on the notoriety she attracted with her "scandalous" behavior. On many occasions, however, she terminated her performances for the purpose of pure self-preservation, in order not to put her voice at risk. Rudolf Bing, administrator of the Met, was furious when she refused to sing what she was contracted for; when she retaliated in kind, he finally broke with her altogether. Big black headlines appeared in newspapers all over the world in October 1958: the great Maria Callas had been dismissed by the Metropolitan Opera.

Earlier, in January 1958, she broke off a gala performance of Bellini's *Norma* at the Rome Opera, and the President and members of the government who were there as guests of honor had to go home disappointed. The next day the by-then customary headlines appeared.

Callas's tangled tax affairs also became fertile ground for the newspapers. In the United States Internal Revenue officials can turn up in the middle of a performance and demand the amount the artist owes. If they do not receive payment then and there, they impound the performance fee. One evening a tax collector came to Callas's dressing room. She immediately metamorphosed into a tigress and roared at the poor man to get the hell out. Unfortunately for him, he chose not to obey. She took a firm grip on the back of his trousers and threw him out into the corridor.

By the time Callas and I did a recording of *Carmen* together in 1964 she had almost no voice left. (It was also during the period of her life when she was with Aristotle Onassis, the Greek shipping magnate.) She sang as if she had a hot potato in her mouth. But I think the public loved her despite that; she was the greatest opera personality of our age. I was in the audience at a concert that she gave at Carnegie Hall in the mid-1970s with the Italian tenor Giuseppe di Stefano, and although her voice was no longer top ranking, she was nevertheless able to fill that great concert hall down to its last seat.

To judge from what the press later reported about Maria Callas, her life ended tragically. Onassis left her to marry Jackie Kennedy, a blow that Callas took hard. She died a few years later of a heart attack at the age of only fifty-four. Even in death she was the same intensely dramatic lady. She had specified in her will that her ashes be cast into the Aegean Sea. When the boat bearing the urn was out at sea and they prepared to scatter the ashes, the wind suddenly and unexpectedly changed direction and blew her ashes straight back into the faces of the priest and others present.

As I have already mentioned, Victoria de los Angeles was a different kind of personality. She was endowed with a divinely natural voice, and she very rarely allowed herself any temperamental outbursts even when something did not suit her. I know nothing of her life outside her work. She was married to an elegant and very pleasant Spaniard who was also her manager; she is a widow now. She must have led a healthy and sensible life, because she is still singing beautifully despite her advanced years, a couple of years older than I am. We did two concerts together in Barcelona and Madrid in 1992, the year of the Olympics. The audiences were enthusiastic and other theaters offered us concert contracts, including one at the Opera in Rome in January 1993 and three in May 1993 in London, Glasgow, and Brighton.

Over the course of my career I have noticed the increasingly objectionable attitudes of some of my fellow singers, who assume an air of superiority simply because of their professional success. Partly the result of my own shyness and partly the result of a strong belief in keeping true to one's self and one's origins, I have tried to make myself aware of the dangers of developing in the same way. It is easy to confuse your own self with the inflated praise that may appear in the press. If you are not careful, you can easily convince yourself that you are more remarkable than other people just because you can sing.

The attitude of trying to distinguish oneself from the crowd simply because one has had the good fortune to "get on" in society annoys me. For me the arts, and especially singing, have always been something holy. I have devoted the greater part of each day to work and tried to carry out everything I have done as conscientiously as possible. I have never arrived late for a rehearsal or a performance, nor have I ever been in a bad mood or behaved capriciously in the theater. If I have been unwell and felt that I could not give my absolute best, I have always canceled the performance rather than disappoint the public or degrade my art.

From the very first, my art has been the most important thing in my life. Even in my spare time I have involved myself in activities that directly or indirectly enriched my work. I have assigned all my resources and energies to it; my private life never took precedence. By that I do not mean to suggest that I am thus a greater artist than anyone else. I know many colleagues, not least women who have husbands and children, who handle both sides of their lives magnificently. They presumably immerse themselves totally in their art when they rehearse and perform, and then relax completely when they are together with their family. They probably thus avoid much of the anxiety and hysteria of life in the theater.

People like to speak of the egotism of the artist in general, but it may just be a purely temporary phase of the initial upward climb. You suddenly find yourself surrounded by so much that all you can think of is striving further in the direction you have embarked upon. Time is severely limited and so you behave selfishly and no longer have room in your life for former friends and acquaintances because they do not further your career. A singer's career comprises many different fragments that need to be fitted together like a jigsaw puzzle to make a complete and meaningful whole.

It is essential to acquire a sufficiently extensive repertoire, which must be both an appropriate one and comprehensive enough to allow for possible substitution for another singer. How many young singers have been launched because they rescued a fully booked production with an excellent performance of their own? I always advise my pupils today to build up a repertoire, even if they are not going to use particular material right away.

On top of that you also have to meet all the people who help pave the way toward your goal. And in the theater you have to fight against rivals, for there are always singers who think they have a monopoly on certain roles. If young singers then come along with equally good credentials, the established ones become jealous and try to spoil their chances, often by

intrigue and slander. Having to contend with all that requires both physical and psychological strength in young singers.

I have managed to get through all my years in various theaters without ever once being caught up in any intrigues. Nor have I ever allowed
myself to come into conflict with directors or conductors, though that
should not imply that I went around as meek as a lamb. Whenever anything felt wrong to me I asked for a private conversation with the director
or conductor. More often than not we arrived at a solution together that
seemed right for both of us, or at least an acceptable compromise. There
were, of course, occasions when I had to submit to a director's concept
that seemed wholly at odds with the music in an opera, and that was terribly hard. I would suffer inner turmoil and conflicting emotions. In my
opinion, there is a great difference between opera and a spoken play. In the
latter so much is unexpressed and the director can therefore interpret it in
various ways. For opera it is the other way around: the plot must surren-
der to the music, since the music always expresses what is concrete. If the
music is dramatic, the dramatic events on the stage have to be made to
correspond.

That may sound obvious, but unfortunately it often can be the reverse
in an opera production. As a singer I cannot influence it at all. Long before
I come into the picture the theater management has decided on the director and accepted his concept of the work. Large sums of money have
already been expended on costumes and scenery. It is hard to start protesting at that point. That was precisely the situation I found myself in
with my final opera, *Gustaf Wasa*, in 1991, the story of which I will describe
later in the narrative.

I have always been hesitant to make additional difficulties in such
cases, for I have thought it wrong to leave a theater in the lurch just because
my ideas differed from those of the director or choreographer. Throughout my career I strove for persuasion and compromise and tried to
approach each new production with an open mind, forgetting all previous
ones. I also would frequently ask myself whether my instincts were right.

The fact that I do not create conflicts does not mean that I am cold or
indifferent by nature. I do hate losing control over my emotions, however.
I am not like the Italians, Spaniards, or French, for whom it is natural to
vent their nervousness or anxiety by shouting and gesticulating. Instead I
withdraw into myself; that is my method of holding my worst reactions in
check.

I have thus acquired the reputation of being exceedingly calm and confident—which is far from being the case. I too am temperamental and am just as anxious and apprehensive as all other artists; the difference lies only in the way I keep it to myself. It is hardly likely that my method of dealing with anger and disappointment is the right one. It is probably much better to emulate those from southern countries by flaring up and giving expression to one's displeasure, and then everything is all right again. But I am the way I am, and there is little one can do about one's inherent disposition.

Another aspect of such a disposition is that I have never expected people to behave differently toward me because of my success. I was always embarrassed, for example, when I flew home to Sweden during my years in America and the airline staff would offer to look after my luggage to save me the trouble. I have never been used to being paid special attention, even in childhood. I had to take responsibility for my own life and my own finances at an early age. My teacher Martin Öhman hammered into me that I had to concentrate on singing and not bother myself with anything extraneous. I therefore never adopted attitudes or mannerisms to draw attention to myself. By feeling a responsibility to my singing vocation I was at the same time protected against the many disagreeable aspects of being famous.

Nor did I have a family pushing me and expecting me to become a great star. My parents were proud and pleased that things were going well for me, and grateful that I was able to relieve them of financial worries in their old age. As I stated earlier, I have had an interest in vocal music all my life. When I started listening to beautiful voices like Beniamino Gigli's and Jussi Björling's on the radio or occasionally at a concert, I was enthralled by the ability of such singers to inspire their audiences. I began to long to attain the same blissful heights myself, to be able to transport people into a state of ecstasy by means of my voice. But I do not remember any special day or particular occasion when I decided to become a professional singer. Many artists have such experiences; they may, for instance, have heard somebody singing with rare beauty and that was what determined their own professional career. I have met and continue to meet young people who say, in all seriousness, "Mr. Gedda, I want to sing like you." The young singer is already dreaming of forging the same career that I had the good fortune to find. I was myself by no means so firmly set on a singing career. I admired Beniamino Gigli and wished that I could sing like him;

when he came to Stockholm in my youth to give a concert I went and listened and enjoyed it, but I would never have dared go backstage and ask for his autograph. I never had any thoughts at all of following a Gigli career. Unless it was a dream deep in my subconscious.

I remember listening with astonishment as one of my female colleagues in the United States spoke of having even as a little girl set her heart on becoming an opera star—by that she meant an opera singer with the same glamour surrounding her name as the Hollywood stars of that time. And when she had achieved her goal, she demanded that her name be displayed in giant letters on posters and in advertisements. She also insisted that the names of her fellow performers be in smaller lettering and put below her own trumpet fanfare, even when they had roles at least as big and as difficult as hers in the same production. Since she had created star-status for herself, the other singers were there just to fill the space around her. And she got her own way.

I have never been able to understand such an outlook. That may be because I do not have the neurotic qualities that great stars are made of. It has always been enough for me to be a good artist and to be aware that you are never so good that you cannot be better. I was pleased if I thought people were coming to my operas and concerts not to see a star but to enjoy a fine performance.

The egotism of musical artists is largely due to the fact that we are involved with matters not based on solid reality, that we do not have a physical product we can handle. When I stood on stage I was always dreadfully nervous and so absorbed in my task that I could not really enjoy the music or the melodiousness of the singing. My reward was the effect I could have on the audience. The instant I got that beautiful warm response I knew I was alive and counted for something. The moment of recognition was always so disconcertingly short, however, that the worry and anxiety would soon prevail again, and I would be wondering how it would go the next time!

Some people now say that I misused my career by not going along with all the trappings of stardom, and that it is after all the big stars that the public wants to see. My American agents in particular disapproved of my modest self-presentation. When they saw me arriving at the theater on foot they tore their hair: a star must arrive in a limousine! But I have never fallen for status symbols such as cars, boats, and so on, and my wardrobe has never included unnecessary luxury garments. Even in my early years in Paris and then at the Met I was surprised that my colleagues, both male and female, took such delight in dressing themselves up and had such bourgeois outlooks. Art for them was a means of acquiring all the comforts they had dreamed of. Many American singers believe that their success depends on frequent appearances on television talk shows. I always stubbornly refused. The only programs I willingly took part in were those on which I could sing, and if the program was not entirely devoted to turning its subjects inside out.

I like to live in a way that I personally find enjoyable. In the summer I cycle, nowadays with Aino, in Switzerland and in Stockholm. We are fond of using public transportation, both buses and trains. And there are always taxis for journeys to the airport with luggage. To all external appearances I continued to look like the staid Stockholm bank clerk rather than the international and adventurous artist.

Being a star would not have given me any personal satisfaction. From the first moment I started singing I have only wanted the audience to experience beauty. That is why I like singing in churches, where I have the opportunity to sing fervent and melancholy songs that capture people's hearts. There is indeed a God in song, and one can thus bring joy on a more elevated plane by singing sacred music. I think that I have attained my highest achievements in churches. During the last ten years I have had more time to sing spiritual songs. In Stockholm I formed a male-voice quartet that sings Orthodox hymns. I also sing in a little Orthodox choir that was formed in my name in Salzburg at the end of the 1980s. Singing this kind of music brings no money, of course; it is something I do because it enriches the soul.

All the rest has gradually become rather banal over the years. Why should people hold me in such adulation? Yet after every concert large numbers come to thank me for what they have heard, to ask for my autograph, and perhaps to exchange a few words about the music. I am happy to listen to what they have to say and to answer to the best of my ability.

What I object to, however, is when the public's admiration becomes too intrusive, when I realize that the lauding and fawning is just a means of basking in the reflected glory of somebody famous. I have had to live with that over the years. It is not always easy to ask a too importunate female admirer to go away when she is determined for a more intimate acquaintanceship. Subtle requests to be left in peace are not always understood. I have suffered whenever I have arrived in a certain city and have been met by an admirer waiting with her car to drive me to the hotel, where she had even booked a room right next to mine. On several occasions I have had an attack of hysteria and told the person in question to get out of my sight forever. But that usually has had no effect. Several people like that are found in every country, and when you arrive alone, as I often do, it is easy to feel vulnerable. I know that I am not the only one to experience such difficulties. Our great Swedish soprano Birgit Nilsson wrote in a newspaper article that she had been pursued all over the world for twelve years by a tenacious female admirer. Such things are dreadful for us singers. When we arrive at an airport and no one from the theater is collecting us, we would rather get straight into a taxi and drive direct to our hotel. We are heartily glad to be left in peace to gather ourselves before the impending performance.

There are also many people who seek to profit personally by another's success and connections. I experienced that myself in my early years in Paris during my first concert at the Palais Royale in 1953. On the morning of the concert there was a dress rehearsal with the public present. I remember singing Rossini for the first time, among other things, and I was in good form and singing high and beautifully even at that early hour of the day. After the rehearsal a young man came up and introduced himself, handing me his visiting card as he complimented me on my singing. He was a great music lover and his parents had musical gatherings in their home; he wondered whether my wife and I would like to come to their next meeting.

We went to the reception at their house, which turned out to be exceedingly affluent. There were crowds of singers and instrumentalists, composers and music lovers of all ages. I recall we were first given a delicious meal and then went into the family music-room. Everyone sat around relaxed and comfortable on cushions listening to the musicians entertaining us in turn.

We attended many musical soirées at that house, and I had the opportunity to hear the French singer Hélène Bouvier, who sang ballads, and many others, including big-name pianists like Juri Boukov, Daniel Weienberg, and Aldo Ciccolini. I found contact with these people from the music world quite essential to me.

The young man began telephoning me, both at our home in Viroflay and at the Opéra. He insisted on coming to the Opéra every day to collect me after rehearsals and would then accompany me to the Gare Saint Lazare, where I caught the train home. I felt quite oppressed by this per-

sistent attention and began to wonder what he was actually up to. One day
he asked if he could come to my dressing room in the theater and help; he
had no employment yet and was just living at his parents' expense. A short
while later he entreated me to introduce him to one of the senior managers
at my record company, HMV. Since that involved no particular difficulties, I arranged it. Shortly thereafter the young man had a position with the
company, and as he was very capable and interested in his profession he
rose through the ranks and later became one of Herbert von Karajan's closest colleagues. It makes me smile to think that it was actually by hanging
on to me that he got into the realms where he so craved to be but which
he found so hard to break into without help. There is even opportunism in
the world outside the theater among people who want to advance their
careers!

Thankfully the majority of the public is not so persistent and pre-
sumptuous. Most people understand that we singers are just human beings
too and want to be able to choose our own circle of acquaintances.

My terror of obdurate females now confessed, the reader might infer
that I do not enjoy the company of women. But I certainly do, and after my
divorce from my first wife I met quite a number and had longer or shorter
relationships with several of them, though I never considered remarrying
over all those years. The memory of my Paris marriage, which took ten
years to dissolve, was just too much of a deterrent. I was always critical of
women and was often irritated by their bad habits. I was particularly put
off by women who talk in loud raucous voices. Whenever I saw such a
woman with her husband I would wonder how the man could live with it,
how he could stand hearing that voice every day of his life.

The trouble is that we do not discover each other's bad sides until we
are married, and then it is too late. When a man and a woman meet, they
are seldom their true selves: they both accentuate the best features of their
own characters. Then after marriage the real person emerges, in both part-
ners. That is my experience with marriage. I was foolish enough to enter
into a hasty marriage a second time, but I will come to that later in my
story.

As far as my international recording career is concerned, I owe a great
debt of gratitude to Walter Legge and his wife, the world-famous singer
Elisabeth Schwarzkopf. He helped me in every possible way, and I made

a long series of operetta recordings with Elisabeth Schwarzkopf throughout the 1950s, singing parts I had only dreamed of doing when I was a young music student. Legge had a significant and lasting influence on my recording career, yet I cannot be entirely uncritical of either him or his wife. I knew her only as a colleague, and despite the fact that she was always extremely kind and helpful if one felt poorly and needed a doctor, to me she seemed to radiate coldness. Of course she was really looking after their own interests; her husband after all was the big boss.

Walter Legge was the person who discovered me in Stockholm and then helped me in all aspects of my career, but it must be said that he also benefited greatly himself. As an artistic director he was the very devil. If a singer came to a recording session and wasn't in the condition he expected, he would be completely hard and turn them away without further ado. Many of my colleagues suffered from his ruthlessness.

Financially Legge was difficult and parsimonious. If someone was invited to record in London and asked if a spouse could come too, Legge, despite being the head of the worldwide company, would categorically reject such extra expense, even though it would have made life easier for the singer.

In London we would often rehearse in the various homes of Legge and Schwarzkopf (perhaps to save money). What struck me was the lack of any real homey feeling, as if the couple lived out of suitcases all the time, entirely intent on their careers.

As an aside, I will retell one regrettable incident from my career with HMV/EMI. It was the mid-1960s and the German EMI record company had arranged a big celebration for me. A magnificent castle near Hamburg had been hired for the occasion, and at the banquet I was presented with the record company's "Ring of Honor" made of thick gold. They had invited high-ranking executives from other countries, including Britain. Several speeches were given, and then I too had to say a few words. I expressed thanks for the sumptuous feast in my honor but then ended with a dreadful faux pas. Without even holding, let alone intending to express, such an opinion, I heard myself say: "Nothing so magnificent could ever have been arranged by the British." And there sat the head of the British firm, a good and kindly man! Despite this youthful solecism, I have always been treated well by my recording company.

Walter Legge remains to this day a mystery to me. What did he and Herbert von Karajan have in mind when they proposed that I make recordings of Mozart's *Così fan tutte* and Strauss's *Ariadne auf Naxos* in 1954? Were they so egotistical that they only thought of making use of my fresh young voice, without even considering the risk that my career as a singer might be finished forever after the ordeal of singing Bacchus in *Ariadne* with an undeveloped voice?

But the central question is, What truly constitutes a career in opera? A successful debut, first of all, followed by the right parts, and then of course a speedy rise in engagement fees. In this last respect one is dependent on the assistance of a good agent, and on that front I was not so lucky.

My first agent after my breakthrough in Sweden was Mia Adolfi, an Austrian lady living in Stockholm. She was a tough negotiator who recognized my worth even though I was still young, and I cannot fault her.

When I arrived in France for my recordings with HMV, Walter Legge suggested that I use Ibbs and Tillet, a well-known British agency. I never got as far as them, however, because I was surrounded by various agents during the recording of *Boris Godunov*, and the first to approach me was Lies Askonas, an Englishwoman. She arranged my first guest performance at Covent Garden in *Rigoletto*, and she remained my agent until she retired. The fees she negotiated were probably quite good by British standards— it is well known that one is paid poorly in England. Her agency was then taken over by younger talents, who never did much for me.

The French agent Leonidoff was also in Paris during the recording of *Boris Godunov*. He arranged an audition with the big American agency, Sol Hurok. I auditioned and was immediately offered a series of difficult roles at the Metropolitan. Fortunately I realized that I was far too young to take on those roles, and had I accepted the assignments I probably would have ruined my voice.

Another of the agents I met in Paris was Gabriel Dussurget, one of the triumvirate who organized the summer festivals in Aix-en-Provence. He sought me out in my rented room one day. At first I had been staying free of charge in the elegance of a stylish hotel in Paris where Walter Legge was also living, but a Russian émigré who was the leader of the choir in *Boris Godunov* persuaded me to move to the rue Alésia as a lodger with a Russian émigré couple, and I was naive and foolish enough to agree to anything.

Looking out of my window one day I saw a smartly dressed gentleman standing staring up at the dirty cement facade of the inner courtyard. I wondered what such a man of the world was doing in these slum surroundings. It turned out that it was Dussurget looking for me. We signed a contract for Aix-en-Provence for the following summer. He also took me to the Paris Opéra for an audition, and I was engaged immediately. Whether everything was done as it should have been, I don't know; I can only hope so. I certainly felt that the taxes deducted from my fees were unusually high.

I also had German and Austrian agents and they were quite good, although the fees were not particularly generous.

I went to America through a Canadian agency and there I met Ronald Wilford, a small-scale one-man agency based in New York. I liked Wilford, and even in my first year at the Met he arranged for me to participate in a television program. Unfortunately this experience came to have some negative consequences: as soon as the Russian émigrés in America heard that I had Russian connections, they immediately went on the make. A man named Misha Hoffmann, who introduced himself as a singing coach, suddenly turned up, praising me to the skies. He assured me that he could create a career in television for me, taking part in programs that included operatic elements. I soon had a call from my agent, Wilford, who wanted to know who the hell Hoffmann was. I told him what had happened. It turned out that this man had done nothing less than purloin Wilford's commission for the TV show I had already taken part in and that Wilford had organized for me. Hoffmann had usurped my agent's rightful due.

Wilford realized that I was young and inexperienced, and he forgave me and carried on working for me. I actually thought that he could have exerted himself a little more to obtain higher fees for me—in fact I had to negotiate with Rudolf Bing myself for a better contract.

I told my singing teacher, Paola Novikova, that I was unhappy with the situation, and she thought I should go to a big agency with better resources and a greater breadth of coverage. She suggested Columbia. The head of the agency was Frederick C. Schang, and he had been looking after the interests of Jussi Björling very well. We met over lunch. He was a solid, straightforward sort of man, and he brought his young son with him. Schang agreed to act as my agent. What he did not tell me was that he was not intending to look after me himself but was putting me in the care of his son. The son was totally incompetent and could not do a thing. My performance fees became worse and worse, and I had to do my own negotiating. I seldom appeared on television, which had become so enormously popular. With a good agent my career in America could have been completely different. What I also failed to realize was that to get anywhere at all in that jungle I should have had a publicity agent.

After leaving the younger Schang I found myself back with Wilford again. He had suddenly become one of the top bosses in the Columbia agency, but this brought no results either. I did my seasons at the Met and a few concerts here and there in America, but nothing else.

So I decided once more to change agencies, and again found myself having lunch, this time with Sol Hurok, well-known as having been at one time the agent of the great Russian singer, Feodor Chaliapin. Hurok expressed his pleasure at my joining his agency, but I had another bad experience. What I did not know was that Hurok had no intention of concerning himself with me: his interests lay in large ensembles and the ballet, and he was no longer personally committed to individual singers. He, too, passed me on to an underling. My old agent, Wilford, was extremely annoyed with me, and rightly so. I stayed with Hurok and did a few concerts until Hurok suddenly went bankrupt. He sustained a huge loss by taking on the whole Bolshoi Ballet, which cost more than it earned. The shock was so great that I believe Hurok died of it.

My last agency in New York was Herbert Shaw, which was reasonably good. In my final contract with the Met my performance fee for the autumn of 1983 was $6500 per night (for five performances of *La Traviata* between 24 October and 11 November). Although this was by no means a bad income, my domestic expenses in America were so high that my fees from the Met were never adequate and I had to keep transferring money from my account in Switzerland.

Because of my naiveté, credulity, and ignorance, I feel that my years in America were wasted years. I would probably have made greater progress if I had chosen to continue my career by singing more in Europe, with shorter seasons at the Met.

Despite (indeed perhaps because of) my own mistakes I find it hard to advise young singers on a choice of agents. Finding the right agent demands great acumen, and it is essential that one settles on an agreement that is satisfactory to one's own best interests. The situation is more difficult now than it was in my youth. I have heard that very few agents today will go to the trouble to promote their young singers properly or to arrange auditions with the right people.

ELEVEN

The Singer as Artist

BEYOND THE purely practical aspects of developing a significant operatic career—agents, recording contracts, and the like—is the sense of vocation, of making the most of one's vocal gift. For me this feeling was extremely strong, and it brought with it a sense of duty to serve art by becoming a true professional. That meant never tiring but constantly striving to learn more and more, trying to penetrate the mysteries of every work. I was particularly concerned with interpreting the composer in every individual piece as skillfully as I could, and to do that one has to have a voice that consistently responds. Every new role presents a new challenge, a new perspective on the operatic art. Indeed, there is something to discover with every subsequent performance of a role, no matter how many times you may have sung it before.

I am thankful that I was always aware of how assiduously I had to work on developing my voice. I am also happy to note, with a deep sense of gratitude, that success followed success and the critics eulogized my performances, so despite the lack of a supportive agent I soon became a big name. My public and critical reception at the Metropolitan Opera in turn put me much in demand with opera houses all over the world. Appearing at the Met at that time conferred prestige, especially if one was advertised as first tenor.

Everything has been extremely easy for me as far as singing is concerned. My difficulties have all been on the acting side. Reviews of my various opera roles in the 1950s and '60s always had very positive comments on my singing; for the dramatic aspects, there was often mention of my detachment. I was not born with natural acting ability, and my shyness as a person made me hold back as an artist. I am not an exhibitionist who enjoys revealing his own persona and seeing himself reflected in the admiration or fear displayed by others. My shyness was my great handicap at the start of my career, and I have had to struggle incredibly hard over the years to overcome that and go out on the stage at all. Despite such difficulties, however, I continued in the theater right up until the early 1990s, and I have more than sixty operas in my repertoire. I believe I succeeded in overcoming my shyness to some extent, but never entirely.

Apart from a Russian actress with whom I worked during my debut as Lenski in a production of Tchaikovsky's *Eugene Onegin* in 1958, I have never had guidance from anyone but opera directors, and that has often been inadequate. The Opera School in Stockholm offered a much more solid grounding in this area than is usual for singers, but since I took the opportunity to enter the world arena early on, I did not learn there as much as I could have and my dramatic training was never completed.

Since I did not have any innate acting ability, I gave rather awkward stage performances in the first few years of my career. There is little chance to think about body movements when one is fully occupied in remembering what to sing and in trying to sing as purely and correctly and beautifully as possible in time with the music. On stage one has at least half a dozen different factors to concentrate on, so it is easy not to notice that one's arm and leg movements are gauche. The difficulty for singers is that they must not make a single gesture or action that is inconsistent with the context. If that is an impossible demand, it is actually better just to stand still with your arms by your sides. Not all singers realize this, unfortunately; they adopt poses and their singing becomes tense as a result of their prancing about.

For me, rehearsals have always been worse than the performances themselves, because of my over-sensitivity and shyness. When I struggle to accomplish something in a rehearsal, the fact that others are watching only makes my movements worse. A real actor, on the other hand, does not mind making a fool of himself in front of any number of people. I have heard Laurence Olivier and others speak about their special rehearsal technique: they exaggerate everything, not afraid of looking unnatural or absurd. They then pare it down and take away everything superfluous, and it would be all right by the first night. A female colleague once said to me that she would rather make herself look ridiculous in front of her friends than in front of a public audience—a perfectly logical attitude.

I found all this preliminary work very laborious, however. On the whole, therefore, I hated the theater, because it made me so nervous. I knew that one should never overdo things and strain oneself in performance, but I had to strain myself to be able to get every little thing right. It was such a mistake. The right contact with the audience comes from being relaxed and playful.

Visual impact, of both singers and productions, is even more significant nowadays than it was during my early years in opera, when the principal necessity was for the singer to have a fine voice. Such emphasis on visual impact is one reason that I hesitated doing *La Traviata* opposite sopranos who looked all too substantial for the part, because almost everyone who goes to see *La Traviata* knows that the young woman at the center of the story is mortally ill with tuberculosis. If the audience sees a healthy and exuberant 250-pound lady coughing so that her chins quiver, the illusion of tragedy is shattered.

There are exceptions, however, and in October 1970 I sang *La Traviata* at the Civic Opera House in Chicago opposite the divinely talented Spanish soprano Montserrat Caballé. In the death scene of the final act, Alfredo enters Violetta's boudoir unexpectedly and there is a moving reunion. He sits down on the side of her bed and they sing the exquisite love duet. The bed that Montserrat Caballé was lying on was covered with a synthetic leopard-skin coverlet. She took up nearly all the space, leaving only a narrow edge for me. As I sat there singing and at the same time trying to embrace her, I could feel myself gradually sliding off the slippery bed. I almost panicked, convinced I would land on the floor at any moment, to general ridicule. Caballé noticed nothing, of course; she just sang and coughed, and then suddenly she threw herself on to me with all her might. I fought against her with every muscle in my body, desperately trying not to fall. The sweat was pouring off me and I became quite breathless under the strain. The duet lasted only three minutes, but it seemed an eternity as I struggled there on the edge of that bed.

Montserrat Caballé has without doubt one of the most beautiful voices in the world for both lyrical and dramatic effect. When we sang together it was as soft as velvet, from the lowest right up to the highest registers. She is also totally musical. She has specialized in Verdi and prefers playing Greek goddesses in the Norma mold. She thoroughly deserves her triumphs.

Some may believe that her fantastic voice is partly due to her bodily volume and that that is why she has kept her weight up. But her physical size is in many ways a hindrance to her, as I have seen myself. She and I did a performance of *The Sicilian Vespers* at the Met in January 1974, which was broadcast on the radio from coast to coast. In the finale of the second act Montserrat Caballé fainted and fell to the floor. We were all terribly anxious and wondered how we would get her out to the dressing room. Fortunately she came around. I was apprehensive about the third act, which begins with an extremely long duet that is demanding for both the soprano and the tenor. To everyone's great relief, Caballé emerged from her dressing room and we began to sing, and she managed the whole act without further mishap.

Genuine music-lovers today are still willing to disregard physical size in the case of singers of the prestige of Montserrat Caballé or Luciano Pavarotti. It was the same with Jussi Björling and Beniamino Gigli: at certain periods they too were very stout, but audiences forgave them for the sake of their delightful voices. An immense stomach appearing first did not matter if it was followed by Björling or Gigli.

I have tried not to let this happen to me. I know that however forgiving the music-loving public may be, a body in physically poor shape can have an irksome effect. So I always try to take care of my figure, although I willingly admit it is difficult, especially with evening performances and having to eat at midnight.

What can be done to keep trim? With the passing of the years and a slowing metabolism, I have disciplined myself to a fairly strict routine. I start the day with a large glass of spring water and follow it with a filling but simple breakfast of Norwegian crispbread, a boiled egg, coffee, and orange juice. After that, an hour's walk with Aino and our neighbor's cheerful and lively Gordon Setter Blackie. We eat a calorie-rich meal in the middle of the day and a lighter early dinner between six and seven in the evening. The experts seem to think that the stomach should have a chance to rest so that the body can renew itself during the night's sleep. Before going to bed I like to drink a glass of skim milk and eat a couple of biscuits. We are often asleep by ten o'clock in the evening, which means that we rise with the sun. In any case we never sleep beyond seven or eight in the morning.

When I am performing in concerts it is obviously not possible to get to bed so early, but I always try to be asleep before midnight on such occasions. I have for a long time refused late-night parties where one eats and drinks into the early hours. They make me feel so tired and listless afterward.

More than just maintaining a healthy daily routine, a singer must avoid anything that can unduly jeopardize the vocal apparatus. I was constantly given advice by my teachers that I nowadays pass on to my own pupils: a singer should never sing if he or she feels the slightest infection in the throat. But many of my colleagues regarded singing as a game. However tired and ill they were, they obstinately decided to carry out their engagements. That is reprehensible, pure madness. It can lead to a career being severely curtailed and cause serious damage to the vocal cords. My now-departed friend and colleague George London is a classic example of what can happen if one ignores a throat infection. He succumbed to various illnesses, including jaundice, but he started singing again before his health was fully restored. As a result one of his vocal cords became paralyzed. He consulted every throat specialist he could find, but no one could help him, and he just became increasingly hoarse. He finally had to admit the bitter truth: he was finished as a singer. George London's misfortunes continued, and for the last few years of his life he was confined to a wheelchair as the result of brain damage caused by heart failure. It was a tragic end.

I have never really been afraid of losing my voice, since I have always taken care of myself and am so aware of what can happen. If you look at the breathing apparatus in cross section, you can see that small tubes branch off from the trachea into the lungs. They get narrower and narrower the further into the lungs they go, and they can be infected without necessarily provoking the symptoms of a cold. When you come to sing, however, the infection shows by mucus bubbling up and impeding the voice. If you continue regardless, it ends in an attack of coughing.

Sometimes when you are overtired and have taken on too much work, it seems almost providential that you catch a cold and have to stop. In the singing profession you cannot break a contract just because you are tired; signed undertakings have to be fulfilled. So you go to a throat specialist, who can confirm that you really are ill or overwrought.

I was in fact saved by a higher power in exactly this way as recently as October 1996.

Throughout my career my various agents have offered me engagements in Australia. I have always declined because, as we all know, the winter there is during our summer in Europe, and for all the money in the world I would never sacrifice my summer holidays in Sweden to sing in an

Australian winter season. I always thought that the coming summer might be my last.

In the spring of 1996 I received an offer of five concerts, four in Australia—Melbourne, Sydney, Adelaide, and Brisbane—followed by a final one in Auckland, New Zealand. I was to be there from mid-October to early November, in other words not during our European summer.

At the time this offer came the expenses on our house in Switzerland had begun to mount up. The old pipework needed replacing, for some vast sum, and the house was freezing cold and without hot water. So I accepted the offer, and by the time I signed the contract the arrangement had been extended to include three concerts in Japan (Osaka, Yokohama, and Tokyo), one in Taipei, Taiwan, and one in Seoul, South Korea. I hoped that the income from these engagements would cover our domestic expenses so that we could return to a warm home.

It might be opportune to mention here that anyone who assumes I must be a rich man is sadly mistaken. My last marriage involved such an enormously expensive way of life that it swallowed up all the income I had received from a lifetime of recording work. So I had no choice but to accept this contract.

I performed the concerts in Japan, Taiwan, and South Korea, despite the extremely taxing nature of the traveling. In Australia I left Aino in the hotel in Sydney, where we had our headquarters, so to speak, and went on my own to Melbourne for the first concert. Aino was totally exhausted after the long journey from Seoul. So was I. I decided to rest for a while in the afternoon before the concert, but I did not wake up in time, something that had never happened to me before in my forty-five years as a singer. I arrived at the theater just before the concert was due to start. My voice felt as if it was somewhere down in my shoes, but by some miracle I managed to warm up in the few minutes I had. The concert went well, but afterward I felt as if I had a throat infection. It was also freezing cold in Melbourne, a very different climate from Sydney.

My most important concert was two days later, in Sydney City Hall. I managed it by rearranging the program somewhat. The audience was very well-disposed toward me and applauded enthusiastically, apparently not noticing, thanks to my good technique, that I was not on form. But Aino, who knows my voice, realized that it was not sounding as it should.

After that I was dog-tired and fearful. I immediately told my agent, a kind and amiable man, that I would have to see a doctor the next day. I had the concert in Adelaide ahead of me, and the day after that a rehearsal with an orchestra in Brisbane with a conductor totally unknown to me.

My agent of course was horrified and said right away that we could cancel the Adelaide concert to let me rest before Brisbane. He also got hold of the most skillful throat specialist in Sydney. The three of us went together. The doctor, who was quite old and obviously very experienced, inspected my throat with the aid of all the newest medical technology. We could see my vocal cords on a TV screen, red and inflamed. After the examination came the verdict: "If you try to carry on singing with this infection, you'll never sing again."

I could see my agent staring out of the window with tears in his eyes. There were three concerts still to come, the one in Brisbane with a large orchestra. All the performances were sold out. I could sense him doing the calculations that added up to his own bankruptcy.

In desperation I asked the doctor whether there was anything he could give me that would cure it in a few days so that I could do the remaining concerts. He looked at me sternly and said, "No, the only medicine is absolute rest, absolute silence."

My agent now had the task of having to cancel all the fully booked concerts and send out my medical certificate to all the organizers involved and to the individuals poised to launch various receptions. Two days after the visit to the doctor, everything was arranged and we were able to fly home to Europe.

It took me two months to get my voice back and an equal length of time for Aino and me to overcome the exhaustion that resulted from the big time difference between Europe and Asia and Australia. The return flight was a pure nightmare. We were too old for such a long journey, and if my body hadn't broken at its weakest link, the throat, we both probably would have collapsed with heart attacks. We came home to Switzerland in a much worse state of health, which we will have to live with for the rest of our lives.

To round off the account of the last long journey in my life, I can say that apart from ten good days in Tokyo the trip gave me nothing other than utter exhaustion. The audiences everywhere were wonderful, but apart from the concerts in Japan there was no time for me to sign a single autograph. The evenings ended late and we had to get up early the next day to fly on to the following engagement.

Aino found time to visit a national park outside Sydney and hold a koala bear in her arms. I myself could not even manage to leave my hotel room. My experience consisted solely of endless traffic jams to and from various airports and concert venues. It could take a good hour to travel just a few miles by car. Going for a walk in a city in the East was completely out of the question: the air was thick with exhaust fumes, fatal for a singer. Seeing all that traffic chaos, a veritable curse, it was hard not to believe that the Day of Judgment was almost upon us.

Our house got its new plumbing—but at what a price!

Of course, a singer's private life can suffer from touring as well. When you are singing every evening it is not always easy to take female company with you. And the talk of a tenor having a girl in every town is just that— talk! No serious singer could live like that if he wanted to stay in his profession. It is not possible to live life to the fullest and at the same time expect your singing apparatus to continue functioning. Singers who take their work seriously are more likely to lead an ascetic life. After a performance the organizers will often issue a supper invitation, which I would accept only if I did not have to get up early the next morning to travel or did not have a new concert within a few days. If I had work before me, I always refused and went home to bed in my hotel. I have done that throughout my career. Nowadays I always decline such invitations after a performance. I have to get to sleep before midnight to protect my heart.

I must take the opportunity to direct some criticism at agents and organizers. In the six months prior to our departure for our tour of Asia and Australia in 1996 I had given about twenty interviews to the various media in order to avoid having a press conference in Sydney on arrival. Nevertheless I was met by a great crowd of journalists and photographers, the latter overwhelming in their excesses. We were not left in peace even at meal times and were interrupted by telephone calls, despite express instructions to the contrary. And the whole Australia schedule was very heavy. I had asked for at least two days' rest between a recital in Adelaide and the big orchestral concert in Brisbane. But no, that was impossible to arrange. I would have to travel across half of Australia the day after the recital to rehearse with an unfamiliar orchestra immediately on my arrival in Brisbane in the evening and then give the concert the next evening. The result: sleepless nights and cold sweats. On top of all that, in my free time I was expected to appear at lunches "given in my honor," where I would be interviewed by the city notables and paying guests. All of this was very kind and well-meaning, but despite my insistence that I could not take part in such events, no allowance was made for my seventy-one years at all. I had to disappoint the organizers and explain that I quite simply could not cope with their homage.

A word of advice here to all younger singers: Think first and foremost of your voice and your physical condition. If your voice is not in top form, no one will want to bother with you anyway, so you have nothing to lose by saying no. When I was young and inexperienced and making my own decisions, all too often I thought only that this famous conductor is conducting here and that famous director directing there, and obviously I have to sing now that they want me. But when performances followed one another too closely, at times it seemed a burden rather than a stimulation. On top of the performances themselves there are the journeys between the various venues; and the climate also could have a negative impact on one's vitality. As a result I sometimes would be overcome by a feeling of weariness and think that everything I was doing was pointless and tedious. I was afraid of not being able to achieve my absolute best.

My teacher Paola Novikova taught me how to choose and reject the various offers presented to me as my career started to take off. If I told her about a proposal I had received, she might respond: "No, no, that's come too early for you, it will only do you harm." On other occasions she would exclaim joyfully: "Of course you must sing that part, it's made for you." That is the kind of advice a young singer can get if he has a wise teacher. During my most active years I was often angry with myself for not having followed my teachers' well-meant advice more closely. With the experience of age I know that it is not so important where you sing or with whom. The decisive factor is *how* you sing.

In the days when my schedule included fairly long breaks I felt more secure knowing what I would be doing for several years in advance. Then I had a chance to prepare myself in a totally different way.

At the height of my career the thought frequently entered my head that no one, not even I, could remain young forever. I knew that vitality would gradually diminish, and the voice, after thirty-five or forty years of constant use, would become worn out, like any other part of the body. You have to take things easily, and I tell myself that even if I no longer have my youthful freshness, I have instead a greater experience of life and greater technical ability. Both often come to my aid now.

For many years of my career I suffered dreadfully from a fear of not being able to achieve my best every time; but I got through my difficulties without destroying myself with alcohol or excessive sexual activity. I slept quite a lot instead of hanging out in nightclubs attempting to overcome my nervousness. I saw all too many of my able and talented colleagues succumb to the excesses of alcohol and night life, and that deterred me.

I can well understand that such a healthy lifestyle may sound dreadfully boring to the young and energetic. When I was younger, of course, I did not live such an ascetic life. But at my age now it is a prerequisite for being on form during the day. This regimen is one reason why I am still able to sing so well and sound so good even in my seventies. You have to have the strength to recognize your limitations, even purely physically.

Even if your voice and body are in good condition, however, it is still not certain that you will always be in the right psychological state of mind to go on stage and face an audience. But you have to do it anyway, and on those occasions when you feel less inclined, you have to rely on your professional ability. This does not mean performing as if it were an automatic routine—that you must never do—but previous experience can be of the greatest assistance at times when you do not exactly feel inspired. Even if his private life is in turmoil, the artist must always erect a wall between that and his art. As Hans Sachs states in Wagner's *The Mastersingers*: "For an artist, art must always be paramount."

Immersing oneself totally in one's art can offer a form of salvation in chaotic periods of one's private life. When all is not right in the personal sphere and one does not quite know where to turn, having control over one's professional activities can at least provide a source of some strength. Devoting oneself to work is a way of forgetting problems at home. At least this has been my experience. Of course, it is just a temporary opiate; sooner or later one has to tidy up one's personal life.

As a young child I had no idea that I would be a singer when I grew up, nor in all probability had my parents. I have been asked on countless occasions where I got my tenor voice from, whether there was anyone in my family who sang. I can only answer that the gift of singing came from God. I have therefore always regarded my voice as something I have to hold in trust, and I have always endeavored to take care of it and develop it and to live in a way that would not damage such a gift.

Several colleagues of mine could be criticized for the frequent inadequacy of their voices. Yet the public loved them still because they were big stage personalities. Maria Callas was one such, as was Renata Tebaldi. The audience felt that they were giving their all, right from the heart.

In the first few years of my career I was irritated by newspapers' claims, especially in Sweden, that I was a direct successor to Jussi Björling, who died in the autumn of 1960 at the age of forty-nine. I regard the assertion that my style imitated his as simply foolish. I realized right at the beginning of my career that I would never be a popular national singer. Jussi came from the heart of Sweden, from the forests and lakes of Dalarna, from the sighs of the birch trees on summer evenings. He sang straight to the national soul of Sweden. As a man, I have heard, he was lovable, generous, and uncomplicated. Unfortunately he died so young that I had far too few chances to meet him.

I was never promoted as a purely Swedish singer, even though I actually have more Swedish than Russian blood in my veins. Since I grew up in my Russian foster-father's home, however, I was marketed as Swedo-Russian. From the point of view of my career abroad, this made no significant difference, but back home in Sweden it meant a certain distance between me and my public. Jussi was Jussi to the whole of the Swedish people, just as Birgit Nilsson has always been known to her audiences by her Christian name.

TWELVE

Europe

COMING HOME TO EUROPE after a long period at the Metropolitan Opera was always a superb experience. The feeling in New York of being dwarfed and diminished by the huge buildings stayed with me for many years after I first arrived there in the autumn of 1957. The seasons at the Met were really long at the beginning of my career, but eventually I was able to shorten them and even ask to be omitted from the spring tours to distant American cities.

Returning to Europe was like returning to a world of human proportions. In the 1960s the cities of Europe had not yet expanded to the extent they have today; they were cozy and enjoyable. Everything was clean and tidy and the traffic was not so dense, since in those days not everyone had their own car.

But occasionally even such a positive experience could have cold water thrown on it—literally.

In the summer of 1959 I was doing a guest performance at the Salzburg Festival in Mozart's *Così fan tutte*, directed by Karl Böhm. I was playing Ferrando, Irmgard Seefried played Fiordiligi, and Christa Ludwig was Dorabella. Salzburg's big Festspielhaus had not been built then; operas were staged in various courtyards. We were allocated the large courtyard of the Episcopal Palace.

We were singing under an open sky, and after my big aria in the first act it suddenly started pouring rain. The musicians were the first to disperse, because they had to protect their instruments. The audience was next and sought shelter in the Carabinieri Room, to which we also withdrew. The room could not accommodate everyone, however, and those who had to go home were given their money back. It was a long interruption in the performance and by the time the curtain went down on the last act it was past midnight.

The downpour continued. The little River Salzach broke its banks and flooded much of the surrounding countryside. Drowned animals were floating around in the swirling water, and almost the whole of Salzburg sustained damage. Many people contracted infections, presumably caused by the rotting animal corpses.

I sang my final performance in Salzburg only moderately well; I did not exactly have a cold, but it felt as if something strange was lurking in my throat. From Austria I went on to Scotland, where I had a contract to sing the Duke in Verdi's *Rigoletto* with the Stockholm Opera, which had been invited to the Edinburgh Festival. But the infection took hold in my throat with a vengeance—I had always had susceptible tonsils.

My first performance of Johann Strauss's operetta *The Gypsy Baron* came during my third season at the Metropolitan. I have always loved operetta music, and the fact that I have seldom sung operetta on stage is not because I regard it as a lower form of art than opera; it is rather because other singers are able to play operetta roles better than I can. Operetta is harder than opera. There is always much spoken dialogue, which demands good acting ability. Playing Danilo in *The Merry Widow* is a difficult task that can only be achieved by an artist who is both a proficient actor and a good singer. I have made recordings of a good number of operettas, but that is entirely different from singing and dancing the parts on stage.

My willingness to do *The Gypsy Baron* at the Met was due to the fact that it was such a rare event for them to put on operetta at all. It was normally just Strauss's *Fledermaus* that came up in the Met's repertoire, which was put on every New Year's Eve. But there was another attraction for me: the tenor role of Barinkay is quite difficult and demanding. Barinkay is a young and insolent gypsy baron, charming and personable and with a lively sense of humor, a role that is fun to play.

The Gypsy Baron was a great success for all concerned. Nevertheless I continued to turn down operetta parts, with the sole exception of a gala performance of Lehár's *Land of Smiles* at the Volksoper in Vienna in April 1965, in which I played Sou-Chong. *Land of Smiles* is an operetta that is close to the opera in form and contains a tenor role that is a real challenge to sing. I was back in Vienna for another production of *Land of Smiles* at the Volksoper in the autumn of 1988. My return was met with acclaim, and I was invited to give a further series of performances in the spring of 1989. My guest performances in Vienna ended in the festival weeks of May–June 1990.

Vienna, of course, is the home of operetta. It should be performed by the Viennese, who have their own unique dialect and authentic Viennese jokes that are found nowhere else in the world. Erich Kunz's performance in *The Gypsy Baron* was inimitable; he introduced his own jokes and was so amusing that the performance often had to stop for several minutes for the audience to finish laughing. Viennese operetta is far removed from slapstick, however; it is complete artistry.

Although operetta loses something in translation and in its atmosphere and style when played outside of Vienna, the melodies remain, and that undoubtedly is the most universally popular aspect of operetta. Who is not enchanted by Kálmán's "Two dark eyes and golden hair," from *Die Zirkusprinzessin*?

Vienna is also known for much more than its operetta. In June 1962 I was to sing Tamino in Mozart's *Magic Flute* at the Theater an der Wien, which had been reopened after substantial restoration. Herbert von Karajan was conducting. (This was when I decided never to work again with that conductor.) The performance was part of the Vienna Festwochen, which was attended by the Danish king and queen. King Frederick IX was a great lover of music and also an amateur conductor, reputedly an accomplished one.

The king and his Swedish wife, Ingrid, expressed their desire to attend the gala performance of *Der Rosenkavalier* at the Vienna Opera, preferably with Karajan conducting. Karajan had been head of the Vienna Opera since 1956, but he refused point blank to conduct for the king and queen. Although he was free that day, he felt that he needed the day for rest. There was a great fuss and the board of the Opera brought all their powers of persuasion to bear to get Karajan to conduct. He refused right to the last moment, but he finally agreed, and the Danish king and queen were able to have their Karajan *Rosenkavalier*.

After the performance Karajan and the soloists were called into a little room in the Vienna Opera to receive Dannebrogen, a Danish order, from the king. I remember King Frederick as a delightfully straightforward and natural man, and Queen Ingrid also as very charming and likable.

Herbert von Karajan at the Vienna Opera is, of course, a stormy chapter in the musical history of Vienna. Because he was a genius it was inevitable that people would conspire against him, but he also acted the part of dictator during his period in control, which lasted until 1964, when he left after a final rift.

Dissatisfaction toward Karajan among the singers grew throughout his tenure. He was accused of engaging too many Italians, though on that point I think he was right: Austrians have difficulty singing Italian opera correctly. They of course were unwilling to recognize that and became angry and jealous.

Karajan also took on an Italian prompter, a *suggeritore*. The Austrian prompters were beside themselves with anger, and Vienna society soon divided into two camps. The Viennese are immensely proud of their Opera House, and if something happens behind the scenes, every butcher and baker and all their customers are soon talking about it. They frequently have long conversations about opera without really knowing what they are talking about, as in the case of the Italian prompter. Some said, "Let Karajan have his *suggeritore!*" Others asked, "What the hell does he want to take on a *suggeritore* for?" They had read the Italian word in the newspapers but had no idea what it meant. Nevertheless they discussed the incident in heartfelt tones, because the Opera and its music and practitioners mean such an enormous amount to the people of the city. You can talk to everyone in Vienna about music; a girl behind a shop counter or a taxi driver is happy to discuss their favorites at the Opera House for any length of time. In Britain and the United States there is a similar passion for pop and rock singers, but it hardly reaches the levels of pride felt by the Viennese for their opera. This has made Vienna the stronghold of classical music for the entire world.

Herbert von Karajan had every right to bring in the absolute best exponents and to be extremely demanding. But that cost money, enormous sums of money, and the city councilors wanted to curb "wastefulness," which led to further arguments. Karajan believed that if they wanted him as manager they had to provide him with the resources to keep the Vienna Opera at the artistic level he thought necessary, cost what it may.

They did not agree with that at all. There were plots and aspersions against Karajan, who naturally felt both hurt and angry. He resigned and resolved never again to return to Vienna as a conductor. He held to that intention until 1976, when the Vienna Opera, after a period of severe artistic decline, at last got a competent administrator in the person of Dr. Egon Seefehlner, who had previously been head of the Berlin Opera. Seefehlner not only persuaded Karajan to come back as conductor, but he also convinced a number of singers who had turned their backs on the Opera in its years of decline.

Nevertheless Karajan went to Austria three times every year, at the Easter Festspiele, the Whitsun concerts, and for a summer guest performance in Salzburg. Much of the tourism in Salzburg was dependent on his pulling power: thousands of people came from all over the world to hear him and see him conducting, many of them not primarily great music-lovers, for whom it did not matter what he conducted; they just admired him as the foremost conductor in the world.

In general I enjoyed coming to Vienna, because they almost always had a repertoire that suited my voice. The city and its people are also very amenable. Vienna is at its loveliest at the end of April and beginning of May when all is in bloom, or during Advent when the whole of the central city area, including Kärntnerstrasse, Graben, and Kohlmarkt, is so prettily decorated for Christmas that you can imagine you are standing in a real Advent Calendar. Nor should autumn in Vienna be ignored: the weather can be warm long into October. I particularly remember the autumn of 1989. I was in Switzerland with Aino before going on to Vienna to rehearse *Hoffmann*. It suddenly turned terribly cold in Switzerland and, to cap it off, the central heating boiler broke down at home and the whole house was freezing cold. We decided to leave Switzerland a week early for Vienna, where we encountered the most wonderful Indian summer. We went on long bus and tram excursions to the beautiful outskirts of the city and ate at inns. I really got to know Vienna in quite a different way during that free week. Despite having been there many times I had never traveled by either bus or tram, I was always in taxis.

I had a similar experience in Rome in January 1993, when I had a concert with Victoria de los Angeles at the Teatro dell'Opera. We got to Rome in good enough time to look around for a few days. The weather was at its best, sunny and nearly 70°F at midday. Aino, who knew Rome well, insisted that we walk and take public transportation. I can heartily recommend that approach if you want to get to the heart of a city like Rome. Since I speak Italian I was also able to converse a little with people we met and find out things I otherwise would not have understood.

That visit to Rome in 1993 was a great triumph for both Victoria de los Angeles and myself, but it was also very nerve-racking because we did not know whether the concert would even take place. When we came to the Opera for rehearsal on the evening of the previous day, we were met by chaotic scenes outside the theater. We soon discovered that the evening performance of *La Bohème* was canceled because of labor action. It took some time for the angry crowds to be given their money back at the box office. The miracle was that the staff assisting at our concert did not go on strike.

What did go wrong, however, was the payment of my fee. The contract stipulated payment directly after the concert. We waited and waited, but nobody came. When after some difficulty I finally got through to the contracts office the next day by telephone, I was told that I should present myself in person. I did so, but there was still no money forthcoming. After endless furious telephone calls back and forth I was told to turn up at three o'clock in the afternoon at the Banco di Roma on the Via Corso, where I would be able to draw my fee from a special counter. I arrived exactly on time. There were indeed two smartly dressed men who had mountains of paper in front of them, but they took no notice of me at all. I reiterated my business repeatedly in the half hour I stood there in the bank; they just shook their troubled heads and said I should wait. Eventually a man arrived with a pile of documents that must have been three feet high. When I gave him my name, I learned that he had come direct from the Opera and that the bundles of documents contained everything that the bank was to pay out from the Opera's account. After much searching, my little slip of paper was found, and I finally got my money. I must admit that I felt angry and uncomfortable and was repeatedly on the verge of giving up, but it turned out to have been wise to wait there all that time: when I spoke to Victoria de los Angeles six months later she still had not been paid for her part in the concert!

Despite all the difficulties, singing in Italy is a marvelous experience. If you are in good form and everything works as it should, there is no more appreciative audience in the world. And it is wonderful to go out afterward and eat a superb Italian meal. All honor to French cuisine, but for me there is nothing to rival delicious Italian food.

A funny thing happened during that stay in Rome in 1993. I suggested to Aino that we cross the River Tiber and have dinner in Trastevere on the right bank. I remembered a special restaurant that had divine food. We arrived between eight and nine in the evening, we ate and drank, and everything was exactly as I had anticipated. Then as we sat there the house musicians came over to our table and asked us to name a piece we would like to hear. I proposed the well-known "Core'ngrato." The singer gave his all, but since he was totally lacking in proper breathing technique he ran out of breath and faltered on the high note. At that the devil got into me and I sang the song perfectly for him. His brow darkened and his companions had murderous looks in their eyes. I could understand what they must have been thinking: this bastard is trying to do us out of a job. When we left the restaurant half an hour later, they were all standing lined up at the exit; I half expected a dagger in my ribs—but luckily he must have faltered with that too.

In November of the same year I had the honor of opening the autumn season's concerts at La Scala in Milan. My agent wanted me to hire a claque, as is customary in Italy, but I refused, as always.

I was proved right. The evening was a huge success and I knew that the applause was genuine. It took a long time before we were able to leave the theater, and by the time we were out all the restaurants near our hotel were closed. The only food outlet that was open was a pizzeria, so we bought an enormous pizza and took it with us up to our room. We tore it in half, gorged ourselves, and then fell asleep, tired but happy.

The next day brought its own difficulties. This time I had my fee in my pocket and felt quite content in the taxi to the airport. When we arrived at the airport it occurred to us that it seemed incredibly quiet, with not a soul at the check-in desk, and that something must be wrong. After hunting around for a while I found a man who told me that there was a strike that afternoon. He was kind enough to advise us that if we hurried we could catch a bus to the small airport in Bergamo, northeast of Milan. We climbed into the bus at the last second and sat wedged in with all our luggage on our laps. At Bergamo a puny little aircraft stood waiting, and in this we wobbled home to Geneva in the thickest November mist. I was sure we would collide with the Alps at any moment.

I have experienced strikes at various theaters over the years; they can totally ruin life for the artists. I realize that strikes may be a necessary evil, and that stagehands, dressers, and make-up and wardrobe staff are as important for the theater as singers and dancers. But it is distressing that their trade unions should so often feel compelled to resort to such drastic measures. It can sometimes turn into pure farce. I remember one occasion in particular when I was singing Don José in *Carmen*. At the end of the first act Carmen runs out, but the soldiers bar her exit; Carmen beats them off and the intention is that they give way and let her go. But in this performance Carmen ran up to soldiers who were firmly fixed to the stage floor. She tried over and over again, but to no avail. The soldiers were walk-ons who had gone on strike. If they were to step aside for Carmen, they wanted more pay for moving.

When I did *Faust* at the Opéra in Paris in 1975 there were many unpleasant interludes. It began with the stagehands complaining that the scenery was too heavy, a fact I would agree with. But there was actually only one piece of scenery, and they only had to bring it in once to set it up on stage and then take it away at the end of the performance. They asked for more pay because of its weight. The management refused. The trade union called a strike. The theater responded by mounting the performances without scenery, and in fact the production was just as good.

The stagehands were disconcerted when they realized that the audiences came to listen to the music and singing, but they soon recovered the initiative. They lowered huge placards from above: WE DEMAND A SATISFACTORY SOLUTION TO OUR PAY CLAIM. The opera-house manager had trouble finding someone to take them down, since that was regarded as strike-breaking.

For many years of my career I could say that Munich was my second home. In March 1953, the year after my debut at the Stockholm Opera, I was in Munich to sing *Trionfo di Afrodite* in concert. I had sung the part at La Scala in Milan immediately prior to this. The composer, Carl Orff, honored me with his presence in person at the Munich performance. The director was Eugen Jochum.

The Opera House in Munich had been more seriously damaged by the war than the Staatsoper in Vienna. Parts of the facade were still standing but the rest was just one big ruin. Bushes and trees were growing where the auditorium used to be. The rebuilding of the devastated city after the bombing had not progressed very far by the early 1950s, but the Herkulessaal had been very tastefully restored, and that was where my concert took place.

When I returned to Munich in 1962 the Hofburg had been rebuilt, as had the center of the city around the Opera House. The architects had taken the greatest care, and many of the sixteenth-century houses looked once again as they had before. That of course cost big money, but Munich was in a good financial state because of its excellent beer. The breweries pour millions into the city's coffers every year.

The Munich Opera, or Bayerische Staatsoper as it is properly known, was the last of the prominent structures in the city center to be rebuilt. In 1962 I sang in the Prinzregententheater, a fine old building mostly used for Wagner productions. It is similar to the Festspielhaus in Bayreuth, only bigger. A strange feature of this theater was that you had to beware of a particular place on the stage where you could hear your own voice as an echo, which was very disconcerting. On this occasion I was singing in Mozart's *Don Giovanni*, a part I felt very confident in, so just to test it I moved across to the risky spot. My voice came echoing back at an interval of half a second. It was quite a shock. Such effects are caused by faulty construction. In the late 1990s the theater underwent further reconstruction.

The people of Munich are direct and easygoing; I made several friends on my first visit, and a couple of them are still alive. The relaxed Bavarian lifestyle and atmosphere appealed to me, and I have always enjoyed going back. I have had my greatest German successes down there, with tickets selling out in half an hour every time, months in advance. Munich is also the city where my records have sold best of anywhere in the world.

I have given countless concerts and recitals in Munich over the years, but I have not sung much in their Opera House, which was beautifully restored in the mid-1960s. I gave guest performances in *Don Giovanni, Rigoletto,* and *La Bohème,* and there were summer festivals too, which included *Don Giovanni* and *Der Rosenkavalier.*

The audiences at my concerts in Munich, Berlin, and Hamburg are so enthusiastic that I have always had to sing at least half-a-dozen encores. The Germans love all beautiful music: Germany may well be the most musically cultivated nation in the world, and for many people musical education begins in the home, where Schumann and Schubert are frequently played.

As a singer I have only one objection to German concert audiences: everything has to be so perfect for them, even to the extent that the songs and poems are printed out for performances. They sit there in a fully lit concert hall leafing through sheets of paper. When the song goes on to a new page, they all turn over their rustling pages simultaneously. If I make a mistake and sing a different word from the one printed, I see a thousand pairs of eyes glaring at me in reproach.

Most of my German recordings, particularly the operettas, were made in the Bürgerbräukeller in Munich. It is a huge beer-hall, and we used their large ballroom, which has exceptionally good acoustics. The Bürgerbräukeller has gone down in history as the place where the Nazis had their first meetings and where Hitler made his speeches to the Bavarians. So it has a disreputable past that makes the outside world recoil in horror; but the citizens of Munich try to forget the past, and Bavarians today never speak of the Hitler period.

I undertook a lengthy concert tour of Germany in February 1962, which included appearances in Munich, Hamburg, and Berlin. With half a dozen smaller towns in between, it was a heavy schedule. But I was young, so it was not particularly arduous. I remember I sang Beethoven, Mozart, Tchaikovsky, Gounod, Rimsky-Korsakov, and Miaskovsky, a program I still have in my repertoire. It was a very full program, but I sang the same pieces everywhere, and the towns I visited were not far apart. The experience was also made easier by the fact that I had the same accompanist for the whole tour, Werner Singer. He was married to my singing teacher, Paola Novikova, and I brought him with me from New York expressly for this tour. It was a great comfort having him there, because I had prepared my program with him and his wife. We also used to work together on my opera repertoire. I thus needed no extra rehearsals when I arrived in a new town, which one always has to do if constantly changing accompanists. Werner Singer was a good accompanist, if not in the same league as Gerald Moore or Geoffrey Parsons.

A tour such as that with a dozen places scheduled may not have been onerous then, but I never would have dreamed that at the age of sixty-one I would make an even longer tour through Germany, visiting forty-two places. It was with the Don Cossack Choir, which had been formed by Sergei Jaroff in the 1920s and then revived again under the conductor Misha Minsky. The choir entreated me to support their tour as a soloist.

It was incredibly tiring at that age to sing every evening and then travel by day between venues. Financially it was equally pointless; the whole tour paid no more than what I get today for a single concert. To imagine now that I sang for forty-two evenings in just six weeks with a couple of weeks' rehearsal beforehand seems pure madness. But all the other performers had to be paid too.

Why did I do it? Mother Olga had died at the beginning of 1985 and my uncle Harry had passed away in January 1986. Three years earlier I had left my second failed marriage behind me. I had been living separated since November 1983 and sending $9000 a month in alimony to America. I wondered the whole time how long the money I had in the bank in Switzerland would last. My lawyer declared that I would have to halve the payments if I was to avoid a financial catastrophe, but the suggestion brought an outcry from New York. To be able to think in peace—or rather, to avoid having to think about it all—I went on tour with the Don Cossacks.

Standing in the choir in various places in Germany, I began to feel a little calmer inside. I could see what an immense error I had made with my second marriage too, despite mother Olga's warnings. I was finally able to admit to myself that she had been right and that even in 1965, when I entered into this second fateful marriage, I was still inexperienced. My charity tour with the Don Cossacks was to be a homage to mother Olga, who had worked so hard and striven her utmost for me, and to my foster-father Michail Ustinoff, who was the first to introduce me to the wonderful world of song.

THIRTEEN

Back Home in Sweden

MY FREE SUMMERS, as I have mentioned, were always spent in Sweden. Stockholm meant freedom and relaxation after the long concert and opera seasons; back home I was the boy from Södermalm again, and it felt fantastic. I recall that in the summer of my thirtieth birthday I was still away singing in Europe when a telegram arrived from an old schoolmate. I will never forget the wording, in typical Stockholm slang: "Your thirty-year stretch is almost done, so hurry home and have some fun!"

My old friend owned a sail boat, and I can still remember as if it were yesterday the feeling of happiness when we put supplies aboard for a few days' trip. My friend, who was good with women, also made sure we had company, different girls every time. That was exactly what I needed after such an overprotected youth. When I got married in Paris I had had no experience with women whatsoever. I do not know whether I learned much then, either, during those short summer weeks: at least I did not become attached to any of the girls concerned. My principal joy was in being back home and experiencing again the delights of nature in the Stockholm archipelago, the most beautiful landscape in the world.

This yearning for my homeland has been with me all my life. When I was a child in Södermalm in Stockholm my parents often took me on fine summer Sundays to a café called Fåfängan, situated on an elevation from which there was a view across an arm of the sea to the fashionable district of Östermalm. Over on the other side was the amusement park with its whirling merry-go-rounds and the open-air folk museum of Skansen with all its animals and old Swedish farms and cottages. Skansen also had a popular open-air dance floor in summer. While my mother Olga unpacked the picnic basket that we brought with us (you could sit at Fåfängan's tables just by ordering a cheap soft drink), I would stand by the stone wall longing to be over on the other shore. The sounds of the amusements and the dance band wafted across the water.

When I had been working in a bank after completing school, reconciling the books with an old-fashioned adding machine, I longed for a different life in the artistic sphere. But then when I had flown out into the world on the wings of song and was living in Paris, I longed to be back in Södermalm with my old schoolmate who was such a success with girls. It was the same when I married for the second time in America: I wanted to rush home to my own country the moment my work at the Met was over.

Now in my seventies I feel I have come full circle. I have finally found happiness, finally found the woman of my dreams for whom I had been searching everywhere. With her I can speak my own language. And when we are out in the world together, whether in Switzerland or traveling abroad, we can share our yearning for our Swedish homeland. The most wonderful thing of all is that Aino's former husband, Arne Sellermark, is my best friend. He is always longing for us to come home again when we are gone, and he is always waiting for us whenever we return to Stockholm. But to think that it should take so many years to construct a proper life.

In August 1964, during one of my visits home in the summer between Met seasons, I was invited to take part in a concert with the conductor Claude Génetay at the National Museum in Stockholm and at Drottningholm Court Theater. Every summer since the 1930s the National Museum, directly across the water from the Royal Palace, had midnight concerts that were held in high esteem and very well attended, not least by foreign tourists. The atmosphere in the Museum is exceptional; a broad marble staircase leads up to the art galleries, and at every performance that too was full.

It was equally wonderful to sing at Drottningholm Court Theater, built in 1764–1766 under the patronage of the Swedish king Gustav III. It has been used for summer seasons since 1946, with opera productions always playing to a full house. As a tourist in Stockholm you can take a magical trip to Drottningholm on one of the hundred-year-old steamers that leaves the City Hall quay every hour. The hour-long journey through the landscape of Lake Mälaren is a beautiful prelude to the evening performance.

In the autumn of 1964 I was engaged to give some guest performances at the Royal Opera House in Stockholm. I had contracted with the new Opera administrator, Göran Gentele, to sing the Duke in *Rigoletto*, Lenski in *Eugene Onegin*, and Rodolfo in *La Bohème*.

At that same time the Royal Opera was preparing a new production of Puccini's *Tosca*. Gentele had called in the Italian Fausto Cleva as guest conductor; he was then at the Met, and I had already sung in a number of performances with him. He had been Arturo Toscanini's assistant for many years. As a conductor he was good without being among the greats, but he was respected for his expertise in Italian opera.

In Stockholm, however, the singers would not tolerate his behavior. Cleva kept a very strict regime. There was friction and discord, and the director fell ill and Göran Gentele had to take over. Ragnar Ulfung and Erik Saedén were totally shattered by Cleva's slave-driving techniques. They had to think about *A Masked Ball* as well, which was also going to be conducted by the explosive Cleva at the Royal Opera.

I sang my *Rigoletto*, and the next day Gentele telephoned me at home to say that both Ulfung and Saedén had dropped out of *Tosca*. Tosca herself, Aase Nordmo-Løvberg, coped with Cleva better than her male colleagues had, however, and was still in the cast. Gentele found it too painful to contemplate postponing the production, since it was the first premiere of the season and he rightly thought it was significant for him as the new administrator of the Opera. So he asked me to try to save the premiere.

I had never sung *Tosca* on the stage, only in concert. I stepped in at a rehearsal a few days after my *Rigoletto*. It was extremely hard work, since I had not had time to prepare the part and had no idea how it was staged. The female production assistant led me around the set showing me where to move, while Fausto Cleva directed, red and angry. I said to him very calmly: "Maestro Cleva, you must have a little patience, it is difficult for me to step in unprepared like this." He carried on shouting; he was the kind of man who just flails about thinking only of himself and could not care less about the singers' difficulties. But on this occasion he actually had to pay a little attention to me.

Against all the odds it was a scintillating premiere. I managed my role as Cavaradossi, Sigurd Björling played Scarpia, and we all received good reviews. Göran Gentele was extremely happy, and for once even Fausto Cleva was pleased.

Göran Gentele without doubt was of great significance for the development of the Stockholm Royal Opera. When I arrived as a student in the '50s he was there as a director, alternating the work with film directing. He had worked under three administrators of the Opera: Harald André, Joel Berglund, and Set Svanholm. When Svanholm fell ill, Göran Gentele succeeded him as administrator in 1963. Gentele's primary contribution was that he put musical theater on a firm footing in our opera house. His distinctive feature was that he exercised great influence and pressure on the singers not just to sing beautifully but also to perform well dramatically. During his tenure in office the Stockholm Royal Opera became world famous for putting on good theatrical performances.

A fine example of Gentele's influence in putting on strong dramatic productions was his *Masked Ball* in March 1970, in which he persuaded me to do a guest performance. We worked together on the role of the king; I did not want to make the character as obviously homosexual as he was in Gentele's original version. Instead I paid attention to the personal characteristics mentioned in literature about Gustav III. The tripping gait that contributed to the rumors of his homosexuality was actually caused by his having one leg shorter than the other and endeavoring to conceal it in public. His limp feminine gestures arose from his having been brought up surrounded entirely by women at the royal courts of Sweden and France, which also led to decidedly effeminate speech mannerisms. An excellent touch in Gentele's production was the king's frequent use of French—a language of course spoken at the Swedish court in the time of Gustav III. I had studied paintings of the king and attempted to adopt a similar posture: in the portraits he holds his feet almost in a ballet position, which he must have learned while working with the theater. He never missed an opportunity to participate when shows were put on at the Royal Palace or out at the summer palace of Drottningholm. I have always had sympathy for this Swedish king, who introduced our vernacular onto Swedish stages and founded so many institutions for the Swedish language and the promotion of art in our northern land. Before Gustav III Sweden was culturally an undeveloped country.

I consulted Gentele about all the troublesome details in the part. Even musically it was difficult, since Verdi's music is so passionate, especially where it has to portray the king's relationship with Amelia, the wife of his good (fictional) friend Holberg. (In other productions the king's friend is called Count Ankarström or, in the Boston setting, Renato.) According to his biographers Gustav loved to surround himself with beautiful women, mostly the wives of his courtiers. He is said to have delighted in clandestine meetings with these women, even if in all probability there was no sexual contact. An encounter like this occurs in the opera with Amelia on Galgbacken (Gallows Hill, actually situated on Södermalm in Stockholm). The difficulty for me was to express the spiritual feeling of love between the king and the woman, his enjoyment of being near her and enjoying her warmth, without the scene becoming too romantically loaded, which would destroy the atmosphere of refinement. Then Gentele had a brilliant idea. He had the king come in and introduce himself to the audience as if he were an actor in a play, making him theatrical and removing the emotion of love, turning everything into a game. I was thus able to sing Verdi's love duet without giving a false portrait of the king.

Another of Göran Gentele's accomplishments was to encourage contemporary composers, such as the Swede Karl-Birger Blomdahl, to write opera. Blomdahl's *Aniara*, based on the epic poem by the Swedish Nobel laureate Harry Martinson, was extraordinarily good theater. It was also performed outside Sweden, and I know it was successful in Hamburg and elsewhere. Under Gentele's management the Stockholm Royal Opera also put on Igor Stravinsky's *Rake's Progress*, directed by Ingmar Bergman with Ragnar Ulfung and Kerstin Meyer in the principal roles.

Gentele was widely known and could represent Swedish opera throughout the world. The Royal Opera's guest performances in his time included Edinburgh and Montreal, and they were always a success. He was equally good at getting high-quality international singers to do guest performances in Stockholm. To increase audiences he introduced matinees for young people, significantly cheaper than evening shows. It was under his leadership that the Opera started having full houses. To this day it is probably reasonable to say that Göran Gentele was the best administrator the Stockholm Royal Opera has had since John Forsell, who served from 1923 to 1939.

Of course Gentele was also the object of criticism. I remember older opera buffs complaining that bel canto operas were few and far between in Gentele's time; they wanted to hear their customary Italians and Frenchmen. In fact Gentele had a lot of Verdi and Puccini in his repertoire, as well as Wagner and Mozart of course. He largely ignored the French opera repertoire, however. Instead of Gounod's *Faust* he preferred to put on Ferruccio Busoni's version. Musically it is inferior, but it is more acerbic and suitable as musical theater, with more powerfully crafted roles. The choice of Busoni was typical of a theater man like Gentele.

As a person Göran was cheerful and good humored, and we soon became firm friends. We would go out to eat together after my guest performances back in Stockholm. We also developed a tradition of visiting the archipelago to eat crayfish one evening during the Swedish crayfish season in mid-August.

Göran was an expert at practical jokes. Once when I was having lunch with a group of serious elderly men from a charitable foundation in Stockholm, the waiter came up to our table and handed me a folded note on a silver tray. I opened it and read with mounting horror: "Aren't you ashamed of coming into an establishment like the Opera House Restaurant in that state? You look dirty and unkempt—you could at least have taken the trouble to wash your hair." I started to sweat, wondering what I actually looked like. And who had spotted me? Was it a member of the public? I tried to peer around discreetly in the restaurant. Then I spied Göran sitting at a table some way off; when he caught sight of my pale and startled face he nearly died of laughter.

He engaged in other practical jokes that I found less intelligible. On another occasion I had invited him to lunch, also at the Opera House Restaurant, and was just about to pay when he stuck his hand in my fairly full wallet and pulled out a large note, folded it carefully, and stuffed it into his breast pocket. He looked at me roguishly and said: "You have so much money that you won't mind my keeping this." Admittedly I was not exactly rendered destitute by his action, but even so I thought the joke in rather poor taste.

The great event in Göran Gentele's life was when he was offered the job of administrator at the Metropolitan Opera in New York following the resignation of Rudolf Bing. The board of the Met was frantically seeking a replacement, but one potential candidate after another declined or withdrew. I know that the administrator of the Hamburg Opera, Rolf Liebermann, was among them, but he chose instead to become head of the Paris Opéra.

Someone on the board of the Metropolitan had heard of the abilities of Göran Gentele and sent a representative to Stockholm to commence negotiations with him. The board agreed to make Gentele a concrete proposal, and he went over to New York in several phases to study the functions and activities of the Met, which was much larger in size than the Stockholm Opera. Nevertheless Göran was optimistic and thought it would be a positive step, and so in 1971 he accepted the offer to become the general manager of the Metropolitan Opera.

He was immediately popular because of his friendly and open manner; he went around greeting and talking to everyone, which is not all that usual among opera administrators. He began to organize his team and establish the repertoire, with the plan of taking up his post in the autumn of 1972. He intended to open the first season with *Carmen*, directed by himself and with Leonard Bernstein conducting and Marilyn Horne in the title role. The whole program of his first season was soon finalized. I was going to be there too, opening the second season with his own production of *A Masked Ball*.

Gentele had set up a fine, carefully selected team around him. First and foremost was Schuyler Chapin, a very proficient man whose previous experience included management positions at Columbia Artists, Columbia Records, and Lincoln Center. Another competent colleague was Charlie Rieker, whom Göran liked personally very much. He took Rieker out of the Met's costume department and promoted him to be his assistant. As music director he appointed Rafael Kubelík, whom he had known for years and for whose ability he had the utmost respect.

Then came the tragic fatal accident in Sardinia in July 1972. Charlie Rieker was the first to arrive on the scene. He found Göran's wife Marit in the hospital, where she was lying with slivers of glass in her face. She told him that the family had set out in the car for a swimming outing when they collided with a truck on a bad road. It was a head-on collision.

Göran and their two daughters in the front seat were killed. Marit was in the back seat with the eldest girl, who was Göran's daughter from a previous marriage. She escaped with a broken arm. Marit was thrown through the window and rolled down a ravine. She suffered back and arm injuries and abrasions to the face. Since the windshield had shattered into tiny fragments it took weeks to extract all the glass from her face.

The funeral for Göran Gentele was held in the Stockholm archipelago, and it was a deeply depressing occasion for all of us. Göran and his two little daughters were buried at Ingarö Church. They had a summer cottage out there that they had loved. Marit made all the arrangements herself; she must be a person of great inner strength.

The Met opened the 1972 season with *Carmen* in accordance with Göran's instructions. The production was a great success, as were all the others that Göran had planned for the opera house he never came to direct.

FOURTEEN

On Literature and Philosophy

LIKE MOST PEOPLE, I have frequently pondered the meaning of life. Why we live, why we all exist. And I have contemplated the nature of happiness.

At one period of my life I sought the answer from writers and philosophers. I read Aristotle's *Ethics*. He holds discussions with his readers, and the answers we find to our eternal questions are so logical that we cannot doubt them. He says that happiness is different for different people, that the concept is relative. For one person the greatest happiness might be eating a good meal at the end of a working day; for a doctor it might be a successful operation that saves a patient's life.

For me, strangely enough, a triumphant opera performance or concert has never inspired the greatest happiness. Of course evenings on which I have felt in top form and given a good performance, rated highly by both audience and critics, are very satisfying. But that feeling is more gratitude than true happiness. The satisfaction is extremely limited and soon passes; it never moves me really deeply. I suspect that the surgeon may feel something similar after the successful operation, wondering how it will go the next time, whether it will be equally effective then.

If on the other hand I have done something good for another person, completely spontaneously, without exhortation or pressure or appeal from others, I may feel a sense of happiness of a higher order, bringing a glow to the heart. I also find joy nowadays in simply waking up in the mornings and hearing the birds singing out in the garden, being able to get up still feeling fit and healthy. It is a happiness that was not present before, since I took all that for granted.

Everybody all over the world strives to be happy, nobody—regardless of religion, race, or nationality—wants to be miserable. Is it perhaps mankind's natural state to be happy?

But there is so much that threatens to undermine the fulfillment of our happiness. Not least in the artistic world there is envy, which in my opinion is a very serious affliction. We all have to fight to suppress feelings of malicious pleasure at a colleague's defeat or of mortification at his success. If you cannot overcome envy you will never be happy.

It is development, not just from child to adult but also psychological growth, that gives meaning to our lives. I began reading Leo Tolstoy's books when I heard that he had devoted the last decades of his life to religious writing. His thoughts on the church and dogma were so controversial that his religious works were banned by the censors in Russia at the time. I chanced upon a Russian edition of Tolstoy's *The Kingdom of God Is Within You* in a secondhand bookstore in Paris. They said that the book had once belonged to the Russian dancer and choreographer Serge Lifar and was probably one of the fifty copies that Leo Tolstoy had printed clandestinely at his own risk and distributed among his friends.

Tolstoy maintains in his book that Christ's teaching does not demand that we should reach perfection within a certain time; he argues that we can never reach such a supreme state in a single lifetime. What is most vital is that we strive toward the ideal during our life on earth. Tolstoy points to the repentant thief hanging next to Jesus on the cross, taking him as an example in that he begs forgiveness for his sins. Each one of us must try to recognize our own faults, pray for forgiveness, and do everything possible to improve ourselves if we want a good start to a better life.

I agree with Tolstoy's view that church dogma has nothing to do with true Christianity. Tolstoy goes so far as to say that most dogmas are pure misunderstandings or conscious distortions by the church or other social or religious communities for their own advantage. Rituals are often invented to keep people in order, to frighten them into obedience.

Tolstoy stresses that Christ never laid down these dogmas; he only gave us guidelines as to how we should live to become ideal human beings, happy human beings creating a happy existence. What is of value, according to Christ, is "the path toward the ideal," to make some progress during one's earthly life.

If I examine myself, have I made any progress? I no longer feel envy of my colleagues and am not guilty of calumny. If things go badly for any of my colleagues, I feel sorry for them; I know how hard this profession can be.

I am not particularly keen nowadays to see other singers socially, because the conversation so easily turns to comments on colleagues who are not there to defend themselves. I can no longer bear to sit gossiping for an entire evening. Why should I waste my short life like that?

Naturally, after a career spanning more than forty years, I know a great number of singers as colleagues, but I do not have a single colleague as a friend, someone to whom I can completely open myself in all life's situations. That is not because I do not respect any of them but simply because we have all gone off in different directions after our work was over. Besides, my human curiosity has always been directed toward those outside the theater, in ordinary life. I have met many really fine people in other fields, though sadly many of them are now dead.

By socializing with people outside the hothouse atmosphere of the theater I have found it easier to understand the roles I have to create on the stage. I see how ordinary men and women react, what makes them happy and what causes them sorrow and suffering.

When I was young I was very inquisitive about people, especially those who were unusual, leading unusual lives. I sought them out in the world of books. We had no books in my childhood home, of course, so my mother would go to the Old Town and borrow some for me from the Nobel Library in the former eighteenth-century Stock Exchange building. I devoured *The Surgeon's Stories* by the Finno-Swedish writer Zacharius Topelius, and all of Pushkin's works, including *The Captain's Daughter*, which depicts the time of Catherine II and the revolt of the Cossack leader Pugachov. I also read Pushkin's dramatic poem *Eugene Onegin*, which would be of great benefit to me later in life, since I sang the role of the poet, Lenski, dozens of times in Tchaikovsky's opera based on Pushkin's poem. I am able to appreciate Russian literature to the fullest, since I can read it in the original language.

The Russian Church on Birger Jarls gatan in Stockholm had in the 1940s a small library of Russian books on various subjects, not exclusively religious. There I found exciting adventure stories of travels in Africa and other exotic parts of the world. It was that reading, combined with sexual fantasies, that contributed to my failing my final year at school and having to repeat a year in order to graduate and be able to wear the white cap awarded to all pupils who pass their school-leaving examinations.

This acquaintance with literature was worth the price, however. Apart from Tolstoy, the Russian author who fascinated me most for a long time was Dostoyevsky. He is an author who can be read again and again at regular intervals and who constantly provokes new human awareness. He exposes the naked soul in its isolation like no other writer. He shows us characters who can be both angels and devils in the same body, and he demonstrates how extremely hard it is to be a human being.

Ivan Goncharov is another Russian author I enjoy, but for years I had read only one of his books. His novel *Oblomov* is one of the pearls of world literature, and I actually read it quite early on in my life. It was not until the 1990s that I was encouraged to read his other two novels, *The Precipice* and *A Common Story*. Together the three novels form a unity. I think Goncharov was a great writer who was unfortunately overshadowed by his contemporaries Ivan Turgenev and Leo Tolstoy.

Because during the height of my career I was constantly having to learn new parts for roles I was doing, it is only in recent years that I have been able to read fiction regularly. When I read the nineteenth-century French classics such as Balzac and Zola, to name but two, I am surprised to find that people seem not to have changed one little bit for the better. We human beings have always been avaricious and egotistical; however far back in literature you go you come across these unsympathetic traits.

When I was to perform the title role of Benvenuto Cellini in Berlioz's opera I read the autobiography of the great sixteenth-century Italian artist. Cellini's memoirs are an invaluable reference from a historical point of view, since he portrays life in the sixteenth century in great detail. This is true not only in his interesting studies of princes and popes like Clement VII but also in his depictions of the lives of ordinary citizens. He tells of how the powerful pope who ruled during that time would promise the Italian sculptor and goldsmith fantastic sums of money and other privileges if he carried out his wishes, but when the work was completed such promises were never fulfilled; there were always cardinals and subordinates who seized every opportunity to appropriate the greater part of Cellini's reward. According to Cellini, everyone tried to cheat him, and that may well be true, given the new knowledge we have today about those in power who were supposed to be the saviors and champions of their subjects but instead impoverished and sucked dry the countries they controlled.

Benvenuto Cellini, the opera, was from the start meant to be performed at a comic-opera theater so that the spoken dialogue could be heard throughout. The problem is that the music is written for grand opera. Berlioz also had great trouble trying to shorten portions of the work after the singers had refused to sing such long and difficult parts. The French piano arrangement available nowadays is the abridged version. Unfortunately Berlioz failed to resolve the structure of the drama, and the first act in particular is too long. Cellini has an interminable love duet with Teresa (a fictional character), and his rival Fieramosca stands concealed behind the curtains listening throughout. It makes for a ridiculous effect. The fact that the opera is worth putting on despite its faults is primarily due to its wonderful music.

The staging has always been a major problem for any director. The first time I did *Benvenuto Cellini* was during the Holland Festival in Amsterdam in the summer of 1961. The French director Marcel Lamy put on a traditional production, just as it had been done at its world premiere in Paris in 1838.

In 1966 I was called upon to do a guest performance as Cellini at Covent Garden. They had unearthed the music that Berlioz had cut from the original score. Sir John Pritchard was conducting and John Dexter was responsible for the new production, his first opera commission. Even today John Dexter speaks with some reverence of that *Benvenuto Cellini*. He has been kind enough to say in interviews that working with me then at Covent Garden inspired him to continue with opera. We met again when he put on Verdi's *Sicilian Vespers* at the Met in 1974.

The production of *Benvenuto Cellini* in December 1966 at Covent Garden was a great success, even if it was absurdly long. Dexter was asked back in 1969 when they were planning to stage it again, and he agreed to go; but then a play intervened and he turned Covent Garden down, which is hardly decent behavior. When the opera was being put on for a third time, in 1976, I asked the management whether they intended to ask Dexter to direct, since he was the original director for the production. Their response was that since he had left them in a difficult situation before, they preferred their own director, John Copley.

By the 1976 staging, half of this very difficult opera had been deleted, but the production was still not perfect. When we took it to La Scala in Milan in March we were greeted by wild Italian applause. Sir Colin Davis conducted, and almost all the principal roles were sung by British singers: Teresa by Elizabeth Harwood, Ascanio by the mezzo-soprano Anne Howells, and Pope Clement by the old Covent Garden veteran David Ward, a very fine Wagner bass. Fieramosca was sung by the French baritone Robert Massard; that role, with so much spoken dialogue, has to be played by a Frenchman.

Another opera with a literary libretto that seldom has perfect productions is Gounod's *Faust*. There of course it could be said that the fault lies in Gounod's sugary and romantic music, which ill suits Goethe's play. In the operatic version the old and learned Faust, dissatisfied with life, rejects all Mephistopheles' offers of happiness and declares that youth is the only thing of value. At the price of his own soul, Faust buys back his youth and experiences love for the pure young Marguerite. The meeting with the Devil and the love story with Marguerite are what is featured; Goethe's profundities are omitted entirely.

I have sung Faust so many times and taken part in at least half-a-dozen different productions. I have been really pleased with only one of them, the one that introduced my ninth season at the Met in 1965, with Jean-Louis Barrault directing and Georges Prêtre conducting. The production had extremely beautiful stage sets of the Middle Ages, and at times you felt as if you were standing in a Brueghel painting, so overwhelmingly naturalistic was the scenery. The stage designer for this successful enterprise was Jacques Dupont.

The Walpurgis Night scene, on the other hand, provoked a huge scandal; it was unmitigated pornography throughout, though very well done by the Dane Flemming Flindt. Of course Hell is imaginable as one long sexual orgy with little male and female demons engaged in eternal intercourse, but the conservative opera-going public protested vociferously, and so Hell was gradually toned down until it finally disappeared altogether.

Barrault was a good man to work with. I had seen many of his now-classic films in my youth and admired him immensely. In general, choosing film directors for productions by a theater like the Met is pure speculation in well-known names; in many cases their effectiveness is only on paper. Film directors usually know nothing about opera and its many facets. Choruses in particular often drive them mad. An opera chorus is used to standing still and singing, and they have no idea how to move. Film directors have tried to get choruses to run and sing at the same time—it is hardly attractive.

One must be knowledgeable about music to be able to produce an opera. Of course a film director will listen to the music first, but he does not understand the essence of music and therefore cannot hear what movements it demands. Instead of working with the music he will often work against it.

A sad example of that mistaken technique was by the great French film director René Clair. He put on Gluck's *Orpheus and Euridice* at the Paris Opéra with Jeannette Pilou as Euridice opposite myself as Orpheus, a part I had played once before in Aix-en-Provence in the 1950s. I arrived in Paris for rehearsals in the spring of 1973. We started immediately on stage, which is the worst thing imaginable at the Opéra, where so many people are constantly rushing around in chaos (at least they were in those days).

I remember René Clair greeting me, and saying something about where I was to come in and where Euridice came in. Then, before I knew it, Euridice was dead and I was lamenting her! That was about all the instruction I received. Throughout the rehearsals I had to make inspired guesses as to what I was supposed to do. Once or twice Clair came over to me and said: "You can take a couple of steps to the left here, and you can stand there when you sing this phrase." Clair himself wandered around the stage looking a little lost and gloomy, when he was not immersing himself in sketches for the scenery or chatting with the assistants and their assistants.

Day after day passed like that and I kept thinking that the next day we would come to a discussion of the director's concept of the opera. But I was told nothing, nor was anyone else. One day during a musical rehearsal the conductor Manuel Rosenthal remarked to Jeannette Pilou and me that René Clair was unfortunately not up to the task. Rosenthal apparently had asked him: "What do you think Mr. Gedda should do now, Maestro?" René Clair replied: "Gedda should *sing*, of course; what he *does* is entirely a matter for him!"

René Clair as an opera director was a profound disappointment for me, especially since I had always so admired his films. I had been looking forward to working with him ever since the head of the Opéra, Rolf Liebermann, came to me with the proposal.

In fact *Orpheus and Euridice* is an opera that needs the greatest amount of direction. Gluck wrote it as a *Gesamtkunstwerk* with song, music, drama, dance, and painting. The famous George Balanchine had been engaged as choreographer, and for some reason he was especially eager to direct me. He tried to get me to take tripping dance steps. But I refused. Orpheus appears in this play as a real man, and that is how he should be portrayed.

When he stands by Euridice's grave and laments her death, I did nothing but let my voice express the deep grief he felt. For the scene in which he turns to the gods to ask for help, I tried to write my own "movement plan" in a way that seemed realistic.

One enchanting element in the production was to be the showing of slides of Gustave Moreau's paintings. Unfortunately most of such finer points were lost, since René Clair had no more understanding than anyone else at the Opéra about effective technical application.

On the first night hardly anything worked, not even the lighting. As far as the singing was concerned, Orpheus was perfect for me, and the premiere was a great personal triumph. I realized later that René Clair had imagined *Orpheus and Euridice* as a series of beautiful film scenes. He did not understand that opera singers, singing the same thing for perhaps half an hour, have to move around to put some life into the action.

Jean-Louis Barrault was also no great musical expert. He may have succeeded with *Faust* in 1965, but his *Carmen* at the Met two years later was a complete disaster. I had never before witnessed anything so terrible as when he went out on stage alone after the performance and was greeted with boos from four thousand mouths.

A new production of *Faust* at the Paris Opéra in the spring of 1975 was also not a happy story. The director wanted to do something fresh and had Faust and Mephistopheles going around in ghastly gray morning dress. I tried as much as I could to make the best of the situation. Throughout my career I may have been mistaken in preferring to remain silent rather than challenging what I felt to be wrong. It is hard, almost impossible, to sing when you can feel the audience's disapproval of the costume and stage set the whole time.

Faust is a difficult enough role with which to do anything sensible and credible anyway, but I have nevertheless sung the part more than any other in my life. Now I have cast the old boy aside forever; I really cannot share his foolish belief that happiness is congruent with youth.

For me personally it has been the converse: happiness comes with maturity.

FIFTEEN

Grand Old Conductors

I WAS TOO YOUNG to have had the opportunity to work with Arturo Toscanini, Bruno Walter, Wilhelm Furtwängler, or Leopold Stokowski, which is a matter of personal regret to me. The first of the older star conductors I sang with was Sir Thomas Beecham for a recording of Bizet's *Carmen* that he conducted in Paris in 1959. He was a jovial man with chalk-white hair, a goatee beard, and a gleam and sparkle in his expressive eyes. He was very ironical and never slow to reprimand the singers. Unfortunately some took him seriously and then there would be tearful scenes during rehearsals. They did not realize the man had a sense of humor.

Beecham would often severely try the patience of the singers by his unconventional rehearsal methods. In the recording of *Carmen* the title role was sung by Victoria de los Angeles, who as I have already mentioned was the mildest and calmest woman imaginable. Sir Thomas, however, pushed her to the brink of desperation by jumping back and forth through the opera. De los Angeles is a singer who prefers to sing a musical work in sequence, from beginning to end. During one such disjointed rehearsal she suddenly closed her score and said in a pleasant but determined manner: "I've had enough of this."

No one took her particularly seriously, but the next day she did not turn up. On further inquiry it turned out that she had been so angry that she returned home to Barcelona. Since she had other engagements immediately afterward, the recording could not be resumed until the next summer. When we then came together to try again, I was anxious to redo the recordings that I had been involved in, so I appealed to Sir Thomas: "I am afraid that my voice has changed since last summer." He looked at me in his superior way and asked in a refined Oxford accent: "For the better or for the worse?"

Another odd tactic of Beecham's came up during the recording with regard to unusual (to say the least) placement of the singers: Sir Thomas stood facing away from us, conducting the orchestra. The only part of him that we could actually see was his broad back. So when we started singing, we could not follow him in the right time, which made him break off and bellow: "I am not here to accompany, I am here to conduct!"

The recording of *Carmen* was a major undertaking, with technical staff from both England and France. The work was a bestseller and is still holding its own today. The high quality was in large measure due to Sir Thomas Beecham. Carmen, of course, was also an attraction: Victoria de los Angeles was then at the peak of her career.

During the recording session Sir Thomas and I were both staying at the Hotel Raphael on Avenue Kléber, and one day his valet knocked on my door with an invitation. I went across to Sir Thomas, who received me in yellow silk pajamas, which made him look like a gigantic chicken. He took his seat in a dignified manner, asked me to sit down, and then began to speak about me in friendly and laudatory terms. He liked my voice and wanted us to do a series of recordings together. He mentioned in particular the orchestrated songs of Grieg and Rachmaninoff, both of whom were among his favorite composers.

We began our cooperation with a public concert at the Lucerne Festival in the summer of 1959, where we performed Handel's *Messiah*. Elisabeth Schwarzkopf had the soprano part and I was the tenor, and we sang it in English since the original text was taken from the English Bible.

When we were about to commence rehearsals we had a long wait for Sir Thomas. He had succumbed to an attack of colic and was in the lavatory. It seemed that the afflictions he suffered always verged slightly on the ridiculous. He arrived very late for rehearsal and the run-through was bad.

The concert itself had attracted a full house, and it went well until we came to the point that we had not had time to rehearse. There is a chorus part between two short solo recitatives; I sang one solo and then the chorus came in—but chorus and orchestra were out of step. Before I fully realized what was happening, I heard Sir Thomas bang down his baton, interrupt the whole concert, and yell at the top of his voice: "Chorus, will you sing in time, please! From the beginning."

The audience did not react at all, but Wilhelm Pitz, the choirmaster, said afterward that he could have murdered the famous conductor.

Unfortunately our plans for further joint projects did not come to be. Sir Thomas went to South America on tour, taking his sick wife with him. When he returned to England a few weeks later a big reception committee was awaiting him at the airport, as always. Inside the VIP room someone inquired discreetly after Lady Beecham, since she was nowhere in sight. Sir Thomas pointed down to the luggage and calmly replied: "She is in that bag." His wife had died on the South American tour; she had been cremated and her ashes were going to be buried in England. Sir Thomas himself passed away not long after, advanced in years but active to the end.

Another older conductor with whom I worked successfully was Sir Adrian Boult. In the summer of 1975 I did a recording of Edward Elgar's *The Dream of Gerontius* with the then eighty-six-year-old Sir Adrian. He had been personally acquainted with Elgar, who was a wonderful composer of church music, and no one could interpret that music better than Sir Adrian.

I succeeded with Elgar's difficult piece probably because it is an oratorio, and I have been very familiar with that form of music ever since childhood. Sacred music always inspires me, and I try to immerse myself in it as deeply as I can. Over the years that ability has increased, thanks to both greater life experience and better developed musical skills.

The Dream of Gerontius is about an old man, who, on the verge of death, has a conversation with God. After death his spirit is heard speaking. I attempted to establish a contrast between the dying man and his spirit, and it seemed to be reasonably effective.

The record went over well with the critics, and I received an extremely kind and appreciative letter from Sir Adrian. He wrote: "I can only say that your performance exceeded all our expectations, whether your flawless English or your absolute immersion in the spirit of the part— or rather . . . the spirit of the two separate parts—or your understanding of the work as a whole." These were words written by a grand old man.

Herbert von Karajan, on the other hand, merely grew old and never became a grand old man. I did a comprehensive tour of Germany in 1966, which included a guest performance as the Duke in *Rigoletto* in Berlin. For the first time a real effort was made to publicize me. By then I had more than sixty recordings on the market—opera, operetta, lieder, and oratorios.

The publicity surrounding me in Berlin in 1966 took on such proportions—with interviews, television appearances, and shop-window displays—that there was a reaction from His Highness von Karajan. We had not worked together for some years, but his secretary rang me at my hotel to say that Karajan would like to have a chat, adding that I should bring my wife with me.

We turned up at the stipulated time at the Savoy Hotel. Karajan came over to greet us and congratulated me nicely on my success. Then he threw out a recommendation that I should sing Schoenberg's *Gurrelieder*, a work for soloist, chorus, and orchestra. I replied that I had never sung Schoenberg. "Take a look at it anyway," he said.

The whole encounter lasted at most two minutes, after which the god rushed off to all the others who were awaiting an audience with him. His behavior toward me was pure insult, one of his prima donna acts. He wanted to show me that I should not make any false assumptions. He was the star, not I. That was the last time I met him.

A conductor whom I do count among my grand old men is Karl Böhm. At the age of eighty he still looked a youthful sixty-year-old. My earliest work with him was in *Don Giovanni* and *Der Rosenkavalier* during my second season at the Metropolitan and then *Così fan tutte* in Salzburg the following year. I always felt a great respect for Böhm's ability, which came from having worked directly with Richard Strauss. In his youth he was also assistant to Clemens Krauss, the great Strauss and Wagner conductor of his day.

I first met Karl Böhm in 1959. He was friendly but authoritarian and demanding. He knew exactly how he wanted things. He approved of my voice and seemed to like me personally because I had twice saved his productions of *Der Rosenkavalier* at the Met. On one occasion they had engaged no fewer than three Italians for the role of the Singer. It is an incredibly difficult part to sing and the tenors fell by the wayside one after another, so I had to take on the part and help Böhm out of his dilemma. Since I do not sing Richard Strauss or Wagner, Böhm and I did not work together very much. Karl Böhm, too, has now departed this world, having died in 1981 at a ripe old age.

Another conductor whom my voice suited was Igor Markevich. I worked with him on several occasions in the late 1950s. At the Montreux Festival we did *The Damnation of Faust* as a concert, and also Haydn's *Creation* in Montreal. We worked together in Paris on Verdi's *Requiem*, and we made a very fine recording of Glinka's *A Life for the Czar*.

I worked with Sir Georg Solti at the Metropolitan, in *Boris Godunov* among other things. We did *The Damnation of Faust* as a concert at the Edinburgh Festival in 1963. Solti was not then the famous conductor he later became, but he achieved magnificent performances. In his ten years of conducting at Covent Garden he turned that theater into one of the foremost opera stages in the world. He had a preference for conducting orgiastic music like *Tristan and Isolde*, where the musical climaxes follow one another in a never-ending stream. Even in his eighties he was still at the peak of his artistic prowess.

Solti, the Hungarian, made an undeniably virile impression; the same can be said of the Indian, Zubin Mehta. We first encountered one another in *Carmen* at the Metropolitan in 1967. Mehta is a very skillful conductor and a delightful person, friendly and kind.

One of my favorite conductors is Carlo Maria Giulini. Sadly he does not conduct much any more. He is a perfectionist and thinks, as I do, that there are far too few rehearsals, both for productions and recordings.

I remember that Giulini was seldom satisfied. When he agreed to do a recording, however, he would be really top rate. In August 1970, he recorded *Don Carlo* for EMI with Montserrat Caballé, Shirley Verrett, and Plácido Domingo at Covent Garden, and it is absolutely fantastic. I sang Verdi's *Requiem* with Giulini in London in the early '60s, and experts maintain that this recording is the best there is. The other singers were Elisabeth Schwarzkopf, Christa Ludwig, and Nicolai Ghiaurov, with the Philharmonia Orchestra and their chorus. Conductors often forget what Verdi's *Requiem* is: it is an invocation of God, but an invocation that is one great enthusiastic roar from the Mediterranean peoples. Most conduct it as if it were a variant of *Aïda* and turn a religious work into opera. But not Carlo Maria Giulini—he succeeded in bringing out its spiritual nature. I also thought Giulini himself looked like an angel, a tall, thin angel with a face like an icon.

André Cluytens is a conductor that I worked with a lot. He conducted my first opera in Paris, Weber's *Oberon*. As a person he was very kind and considerate and never elbowed his way forward in his career. He has been dead for a long time now.

Among the younger personalities, Sir Colin Davis is a conductor with whom I sang frequently in the late '60s and '70s. He really explores the depths of the music when he rehearses with his singers, and he thus brings out nuances of expression that other conductors pass by. We had a wonderful time together recording *Benvenuto Cellini, The Damnation of Faust,* and *Così fan tutte* for Philips during the early 1970s—all are now available on CD. Another memorable encounter with Davis was in Covent Garden's triumphant guest production of *Benvenuto Cellini* at La Scala in Milan in March 1976. He had recently become director of music at Covent Garden, following after Solti.

Sir Colin Davis and I have always felt a mutual friendship. In October 1969 we were doing a recording together in Paris. Davis arrived with his wife and little children, and I could see immediately that he looked rather lost in a very British way, so I decided to invite him out to dinner. He accepted enthusiastically, and since we were staying at the same hotel we arranged to meet in the lobby before going out into the melee of Paris traffic. As we were about to cross the street, I spontaneously took him by the arm to guide him between the hooting cars and cursing Parisians.

Sir Colin later told me that my helpful gesture had done him a world of good. He admitted that he felt paralyzed and confused in the noise and bustle of Paris. It is splendid and refreshing to know that there are people who are not afraid to be so open and direct.

Sir Colin Davis is a genuinely good man. He is entirely devoid of prima donna behavior and has a natural modesty. When we had breaks during rehearsal he would come over to his soloists and ask if he could get us coffee. Only in my most fevered dreams could I imagine Herbert von Karajan standing before me with a coffee tray!

My most recent meeting with Sir Colin Davis was in February 1997 when we bumped into each other at the entrance of the Royal Academy of Music in London. As kind and unpretentious as ever, he had promised to conduct the Academy's spring-term production of Mozart's *Così fan tutte.* The reason for my own presence at the Academy was to provide some instruction for the six singers who were given the biggest parts. My encounter with Davis was warm but very brief, since each of us had to hurry about our business. Time enough, however, for me to note that my friend had retained with age all the charm that his good nature had endowed him with.

Many amusing stories are related about the great conductor Otto Klemperer. My first work with him was in *St. Matthew Passion* and *The Magic Flute* in London at the beginning of the 1960s. He was delighted with me and we made a series of recordings. Klemperer was probably the most popular of all conductors at that time; he was liked because he always had such brilliant things to say. He had a gentle and refined nature, though I have heard that he had a violent temper in his younger days.

A classic Klemperer story comes from Zurich. He was taking a walk with a representative of HMV, whose name happened to be Mendelssohn. They came to a record shop and Klemperer went in to see which of his own recordings they had in stock. Did they have, he wanted to know, Beethoven's Fifth Symphony conducted by Otto Klemperer? The assistant went off to look but came back empty-handed. "I'm sorry, we haven't, but we have one by Bruno Walter." "No, no," said Klemperer, "I'm only interested in the one by Klemperer." The assistant searched again and then informed him: "We also have Furtwängler's version." That was no good either. The assistant went on hunting and, in the end, he was extremely sorry but he could not find Beethoven's Fifth by Klemperer. Klemperer became annoyed and revealed who he was. The assistant, tired and irritable by now, looked at him and said: "If you're Klemperer, I suppose this is Beethoven?" "No, no," Klemperer replied, "that's Mendelssohn."

Otto Klemperer did not like modern composers, other than Gustav Mahler, whose works he often conducted. Klemperer was once in a town in Germany where Paul Hindemith was lecturing on his music, and he went to hear the composer speak. There was discussion afterward and Hindemith, who had talked ardently about his own music, was now keen for the audience to ask questions about modern music in general. Klemperer put up his hand. Hindemith, recognizing him, was flattered. "It's splendid to see you here, Professor Klemperer. What is it you'd like to ask or add?" Klemperer replied: "Where's the toilet?"

I did my last work with Leonard Bernstein in December 1989. He asked me whether I would like to do three small but demanding roles in his musical version of Voltaire's *Candide.* I was enthusiastic about the idea and went over to London at the beginning of December. An influenza epidemic was raging in London and the whole of England was hit by a violent hurricane that lasted several days. On top of all that, there was a strike by ambulance staff. London seemed to consist of nothing but coughing and sneezing. When I arrived for the recording Bernstein had a heavy cold, but he had taken antibiotics and was carrying on working. His soloists soon fell ill one after another. I was all right because I had been inoculated, and I finished my part just before Christmas and returned home; but the rest of the recording had to be postponed because of all the illness.

I guess Leonard Bernstein never recovered from his influenza. He continued working with his body pumped full of antibiotics without allowing himself any rest. On the contrary, he was planning a long tour of Japan, but he unfortunately had to cancel. He did complete his 1989 revision of *Candide*, which was originally produced in 1956. Everyone is familiar with his hit musical *West Side Story*; *Candide* too was very well received, and even Sweden was treated to a television broadcast in 1993.

I am glad that I accepted the offer of singing with Bernstein. His death considerably diminished the ranks of great conductors. It is with great sadness now that we listen to the recordings of these masters; I do not believe they will be surpassed in the future.

SIXTEEN

Accompanists

FOR MY OWN CONCERTS I am responsible for the results myself, and I therefore always choose accompanists who suit me. I audition them first and never engage them unseen, even if I have heard very good reports of them.

It is hard to find the ideal accompanist, but I have worked with one. His name was Gerald Moore. He was already advanced in years when we started our collaboration, and he contented himself then with a recording from time to time and a little teaching. Moore was a personality who knew what he wanted but was nevertheless very adaptable, and he had wonderful technique. He could truly create the atmosphere that each individual piece demands. He introduced a new era for accompanists: before him there had been just pianists who sat and struck the keys, slavishly following the singer. Moore succeeded in keeping a balance between following and making himself heard; his contribution was equal to that of the singer. That is how it should be, of course. Just think of Schubert's songs, where the piano part is quite as significant as the vocal. That is always the case with German lieder, where a whole world of mood and color is enshrined in the piano part. The difficulty is expressing as much of that as possible without drowning the singer. It is after all the singer's concert the public has come to hear.

To create the right ambiance around the piano the singer and the accompanist must feel respect for each other and for their undertaking. During a concert it is almost a question of a loving spiritual relationship between the two of them.

In rehearsing before a concert it is also important to be able to inspire one another to find new insights into the rendering of a song. You may have sung a song perhaps a hundred times but still suddenly discover something new. Then you feel enormous pleasure in realizing that art seems to be without limits. You can never achieve complete perfection, not even an ideal performance. You can work endlessly on a Schubert song, always uncovering some new aspect. The older you are, the more you are able to discover, because you mature in both spiritual and human terms, and what was hidden in youth suddenly becomes clear and obvious. This is the splendid feature of all art, that every time you come to the work again you find new shades and levels of expression.

I enjoy analyzing a piece with my accompanist, as long as I know the discussion is based on deep mutual good will. To show my appreciation of Gerald Moore I made a recording with him in the late 1960s, the English edition of which bears the title *Tribute to Gerald Moore* and which was recorded in honor of his seventieth birthday.

Moore's heir as my accompanist was the Australian Geoffrey Parsons, a worthy successor. In November 1971, I did a program called "Songs of the North" with him at the Queen Elizabeth Hall in London. The British audience very much enjoyed that concert, which comprised works by Russian, Swedish, Finnish, and Norwegian composers, including of course Grieg and Sibelius. Their appreciation was due not least to the fact that Scandinavian songs so seldom feature in my repertoire.

I had quite a lively program of work with Geoffrey Parsons in the early '90s, partly in my own concerts (including one at the Wigmore Hall in London) but particularly in recitals all over Europe with Victoria de los Angeles. In the spring of 1993 we gave three concerts together in and around London. Geoffrey Parsons was kind, calm, and sensible, with a large measure of humor in his character. We shared many a laugh in the past, but sadly Geoffrey also passed away a few years ago. Our last concert together was in Wales in October 1994 with Victoria de los Angeles.

The Austrian Erik Werba is the pianist who has probably accompanied me most often in Europe, usually in German-speaking countries. He knew his job extraordinarily well. Werba's particular strength was his tremendous versatility in changing from one musical work to another. His weakness was that he was inclined to pound on the instrument when he came to something he found technically difficult. But he was a great personality at the piano, and that is very important when performing lieder. He also had a relaxing effect on an artist's often tense nerves. Always in a good mood, full of funny stories, he was at the same time a gentle and pleasant man with an air of modesty about him.

I have used many other accompanists throughout my career simply for financial reasons. Commissioning managements frequently prefer to engage a pianist who lives not too far away, as budgets have come to assume an ever greater importance for concerts over the years. But none of those random accompanists stands out significantly from the others. They have all been more or less good. One very capable pianist I used for several years met with a terrible misfortune. Since he was rather plump he decided he ought to slim down, so he took a preparation that made him lose weight with immense rapidity. The cure had unfortunate side effects, however: as soon as he came to play, his hands would start to sweat, his fingers would slide all over the keyboard, and he would hit every note except the right one.

I have been asked on several occasions why some pianists become accompanists and others soloists. The reason lies in the time invested in training at the instrument. A piano soloist must begin early, as a small child, and then practice six or seven hours a day—and continue thus throughout his whole career.

Accompanists have not had time for that, often because other interests have intervened and taken over. For Erik Werba it was teaching and his work as a music critic; he was also a composer and served as chairman of a number of different music societies. Gerald Moore gave lecture tours around the world and wrote books on the art he had made his own. Geoffrey Parsons was both an accompanist and a respected soloist in his own right. The same applies to the world's foremost living cellist, Mstislav Rostropovich. Slava masters almost everything as well as he plays the cello. He was, for many years until 1993, the conductor of the Washington Symphony Orchestra, and he has accompanied his famous wife Galina Vishnevskaya on the piano with great success.

I sang with Rostropovich on 27 May 1993 during his festival week in Evian, directly across Lake Geneva from where I live. He had devoted that year's festival to Russian music and I gave a concert that included arias from Rimsky-Korsakov and Tchaikovsky. That orchestral concert was not conducted by Rostropovich; he contented himself with being the festival's artistic director.

Rostropovich was the conductor of a recording in London in 1978 of Dmitri Shostakovich's opera *Lady Macbeth of Mtsensk* (or *Katerina Ismailova*).

Galina Vishnevskaya sang the unfaithful miller's wife and I the insuffer-able farmhand. We worked together again in Paris in 1986 in a concert version of Prokofiev's *War and Peace*, also with Vishnevskaya as soloist. In Washington in 1987 we gave a concert at the same time as recording Mussorgsky's *Boris Godunov*, in which I sang the role of the truth-telling village idiot.

Rostropovich and his wife were expelled from Russia in the days of the Communist regime, but after its fall they were warmly welcomed back. They traveled to Russia and were given a triumphal reception, which I saw glimpses of on television.

Mstislav Rostropovich has a strong personality, warm, open, hearty, and spontaneous as a child. He embraces everyone with hugs and kisses. I find it hard to imagine that the man could have a single enemy.

Since I have devoted this chapter to accompanists I will answer a question that has been put to me many times: what do the soloist and accompanist do after the concert is over? We frequently just thank each other and go off to our respective hotels because we are traveling on to dif-ferent destinations the next day. But sometimes we have time to go out for a good meal together, to switch off from the music entirely and swap hu-morous anecdotes instead. Comic stories are relaxing after a cultural eve-ning; one comes back down to earth, so to speak.

I will conclude with a true and tragi-comic example of such an anec-dote. A young singer was on her way home from a concert in Germany. She took a berth in a sleeping car, and in order to sleep with peace of mind she stuffed her evening's fee into her tights. She woke up in the middle of the night and groped her way sleepily to the toilet in the corridor. She pulled down her tights—and moments later was shocked into full con-sciousness as her thousand-mark notes fluttered down beneath her onto the track! Unfortunately this story is true, but tact precludes mention of the somnolent singer's name.

SEVENTEEN

Roles and Preparation

I HEARD at an early stage of my career that *The Mastersingers of Nuremberg* was a kind of bible for singers. In this opera the character Hans Sachs sings about how for an artist art must always come first. That became an important credo for me, and meant that whatever other personal misfortunes might strike me or my family, nothing should be allowed to affect my art. An artist must concentrate on his vocation; everything else is secondary. That is how it has been for me throughout my career, for better or for worse. It was good for my professional career, since this single-mindedness has enabled me to be active as a singer so late in life.

A young singer coming to a series of parts for the first time cannot be expected to have a full understanding of all the secrets of operatic art. Indeed, one should be able to discover greater depths even on the second or third occasion of singing a role, and thus such development should continue throughout one's entire career. That was what I noticed every time we came back to a particular role when I was studying with Paola Novikova. Something had happened to me, and I was able to draw out stimuli to develop a new understanding from my subconscious. It is comparable to reading a classic work of literature: in youth you follow the plot but not much more; if you read the book again a few years later you also comprehend something of what is not directly expressed but lies between the lines for the reader to discover. It is the same with music. When you first work on a part, so much time and energy are spent on learning it that even the finer points that you already understand tend to get lost.

There is a whole world to discover and conquer in every role, not least in Lenski, the poet in Tchaikovsky's *Eugene Onegin*, which has always been my favorite role. It is so typically Russian, with its jealousy, passion, resignation, and lost poetic happiness. Lenski's great aria expresses all of that. Melancholy at the disappearance of youth is mingled with a premonition of the approach of death. Lenski dies shortly thereafter in a duel.

Eugene Onegin was written by Alexander Pushkin, and the extraordinary thing about Lenski's aria is that it bears such a close resemblance to Pushkin's own life. He was by nature jealous and passionate. A man paid court to Pushkin's beautiful wife, and perhaps she may have replied to one of his love letters. That was reason enough for Pushkin to challenge his rival to a duel, a duel that he lost. He was only thirty-seven when he died in 1837.

When I was preparing to play Lenski for the first time, at the Metropolitan in December 1958, I consulted a Russian actress in New York. She was a friend of Paola Novikova, and she told me that she had been a celebrated actress at the Moscow Art Theater before the Revolution, which was the most renowned of all the theaters in the Russian capital. This Russian lady taught me Stanislavsky's techniques, going through the dramatic aspects of *Eugene Onegin* bit by bit. I think it was very useful for me to have had those lessons, and both the director I was working with and the critics were much impressed.

My *Eugene Onegin* at the Met was staged by Americans, and although they had misrepresented almost everything about the Russian context and Russians' reactions, I was pleased to receive praise from the critics and warm approbation from the public. The other performers were George London as Eugene Onegin, Lucine Amara playing Tatiana, and Rosalind Elias singing the part of Olga. Dimitri Mitropoulos conducted with great sensitivity.

The role of Prince Tamino in Mozart's masterpiece *The Magic Flute* is another one that I came back to several times in my career. In addition to the awful spectacle at the Paris Opéra under Maurice Lehmann's direction in 1954, I was in an old and unattractive production at the Metropolitan in 1958. In 1962, with Karajan's version at the Theater an der Wien, I at last participated in a worthy production, with full artistic consistency. The administrator of the Munich Opera, Rudolf Hartmann, directed it, and the performance was fabulous. I am sad that television was not advanced enough at the time for any of the performances to be filmed. It would have been an audio-visual document of great significance for the future.

The Magic Flute is a fairy tale, and it has to be approached with innocence and without pretension. Some directors have tampered with it, transposing the plot to Egypt and making it a kind of variation on *Aïda*; others have embroidered it in a variety of ways. Whatever they did, it was a flop. But Mozart is no flop. I have taken part in many productions of *The Magic Flute* and have seen many others. Only Rudolf Hartmann and Ingmar Bergman really understood what the opera is about. In his world-famous television version of the opera Bergman has the overture circling around the faces of the listeners and returning to a young girl's face and sparkling eyes, expressing the idea that *The Magic Flute* is so simple that it can only be correctly understood if we approach Mozart's music as naive and innocent children.

Good and evil engage us constantly, and tests such as those that Tamino and Papageno are subjected to are not uncommon experiences. Some of us, like Tamino, hold higher ideals and are able to overcome more severe hardships; others do not set their sights so high and are more like Papageno. That is not to say that Tamino's elevated love for Pamina is in any way better than Papageno's uncomplicated love for his girl.

We had a wonderful and fitting Papageno at the Theater an der Wien in the person of Erich Kunz. Not even the original player, Emanuel Schikaneder (director of the Theater an der Wien when Mozart's opera was first staged in 1791), could possibly have been better. Pamina was played by the outstanding soprano Wilma Lipp, and the whole production had a real Viennese atmosphere.

Unfortunately the same cannot be said of the later version at the Metropolitan that premiered on 19 February 1967. The conductor for that production was Josef Krips, who was then conductor of the San Francisco Symphony Orchestra. Günther Rennert was the director, and they had gone to the expense of engaging Marc Chagall for costumes and scenery.

We were all full of great expectations about the boost the program would be given by Chagall's renown, but the disappointment with the results was greater, not least on my part. He had designed for me a dreadful white costume that made me look like the American wrestler "Gorgeous George," an enormously fat man in a kind of fluffy shirt. When the stage manager first saw me dressed in the Chagall costume he burst into laughter, as did everyone else. I felt so embarrassed I just wanted to sink through the floor; I hardly knew where to hide.

I was terribly miserable at the dress rehearsals, so miserable in fact that the administrator of the Met, Rudolf Bing, came to my dressing room afterward to ask what had happened to me. I replied, "My dear Mr. Bing, I am supposed to represent a handsome fairy-tale prince. A prince who faints in the first act when he sees the idiotic serpent, a serpent that is then killed by three tiny little girls. It is bad enough to have to portray such a hero in America, where people still have their childhood concepts of heroes accomplishing heroic deeds. If on top of that I have to appear in this ridiculous costume, I'm going to break off my contract."

Bing was rather shaken by my justifiable outburst and arranged for the costume to be altered to look reasonably presentable. But the entire production was fatuous. Chagall had his own vision of us in our costumes merging into his scenery so that the whole stage became like a single Chagall canvas. Instead the result was one big jumble of color. Of course there was a large snobbish and stupid element in the audience who cried out when the curtain rose: "Ah! Chagall, Chagall!"

After the performance the soloists were given posters of their costumes signed by the great man, but I was so angry that I refused to accept mine. Chagall could keep it himself, as far as I was concerned.

Prince Tamino is by no means the most rewarding part in *The Magic Flute*. The Queen of the Night and Papageno are better. One has a feeling that Mozart was being malicious toward the tenor. Tamino has nearly all his most beautiful songs at the beginning, such as the wonderful aria he sings while holding Pamina's picture in his hands—the aria vanishes without trace as the action progresses. Musically the end is also ignominious for Tamino: he has very little to sing as he and Pamina go hand in hand through fire and water.

Other operas too have their best tenor arias at the beginning. It is often the case with Verdi: in *Aïda* Radames has his famous aria "Celeste Aïda" right at the start, so people hardly remember that piece by the time they leave the theater, despite the fact that it is so complicated and demands so much of the tenor. Part of the difficulty is that the singer must be in top condition to manage the aria since he has no chance to sing himself up to it during the course of the performance, as he might in other operas.

Nor can you warm yourself up in the role of the Singer in *Der Rosenkavalier*, who comes on stage right away. As an additional problem, the part is incredibly difficult for the voice. Legend has it that Richard Strauss was annoyed at the Italian tenors, who always held long notes right to the last and at such an immense volume. He is reported to have said, "Now I am going to write an aria that will give the tenor one high note after another to struggle with." And that is what he did. Thankfully that part has never given me any difficulty: I have always been able to step straight onto the stage and fire off the aria without mishap. The last time I did it was the spring of 1989 at the West Berlin Opera.

It is not unusual, however, for an opera to have a tenor role that surpasses all other feats of singing in the work. By that I mean a tenor part that is beautiful and rewarding, with long arias and many high notes. In Donizetti's *L'Elisir d'Amore* the tenor cannot fail to have great triumphs if he possesses a good voice. At the end there is a very famous long aria, in which singers seldom fail if they have their voices under control. That is the aria audiences remember and perhaps even hum as they leave the theater.

Nemorino, the farmer's boy in *L'Elisir d'Amore*, is a comic role, something that I have otherwise avoided after my successful debut in the comic opera *Le Postillon de Longjumeau*. The *Elisir* at the Met in 1965 was perhaps my greatest success at that theater; the opera, directed by Nathaniel Merrill, played at full strength for two seasons to packed houses. Robert O'Hearn's set was very colorful, childlike, and charming, without seeming garish or vulgar.

Nemorino seemed then as far from my own personality as was possible to imagine. I had to suppress my own nature completely and still had a hard job transforming myself into this clownish lad. The strange thing is that I was able to come to grips with the comic side of my nature much later in life. Many of those who know me privately say nowadays that it is a shame I did not make more of my comic potential.

Nemorino is in love with Adina, played in this production by Mirella Freni, a young and absolutely delightful performer. The other parts were also perfectly cast. It is vital in comic opera that everything be precise, both dramatically and musically. Comedy must never seem slack and careless; it is terribly difficult to do a hilarious comic opera right, but this production succeeded.

Puccini is another composer who was fair to each and every voice, and *Tosca* is a truly rewarding opera for the tenor. Although Cavaradossi is not the most interesting of characters psychologically, Scarpia is, and he runs through practically the whole range of human behavior: he is in turn considerate and good, devilish, cunning, and jealous. Just as human beings are.

I have always regarded opera as the greatest of all the dramatic arts; its aim is to create an experience of beauty through a combination of music, song, dance, and drama. And the quality of an opera production should be such that the audience can enjoy all the forms of art employed.

I have the same rigorous expectations of myself when I give a concert, and I have therefore worked on training my voice throughout my entire career (and still do today), refining my technique to produce beautiful sounds. I also try to express various states of emotion with my voice, to convey those feelings to the audience and touch their hearts.

It is hard to analyze why an audience becomes captivated and entranced by a performance. Perhaps it is an appeal in the voice for communication, perhaps an interpretation of longing that is common to us all, or the accentuated art of performance. When a good singer presents Scarpia in *Tosca* he can enlist the sympathy of the audience despite the basically unsympathetic nature of the character. If he is effective in arousing the hatred of the audience, then he has succeeded in evoking the feelings he is meant to evoke.

It is not enough merely to have a good voice. You have to supplement it with an inner strength and a spark that will kindle the imagination of the people in the auditorium and make them believe in what you are trying to convey. The worst thing that can occur is for the audience to sit there unmoved. To establish contact you have to offer the personality you have. In my own case I know I am not an ebullient figure who incites the audience to applause the moment he appears on stage. There are stage personalities like that, who do not even need to open their mouths to create a kind of ecstasy.

What must an artist do to maintain his charisma, and what happens when he loses it?

I myself try to withdraw into tranquillity for several days before a concert. On the actual day of the performance I talk very little and then only with the person closest to me. By keeping oneself in this state of peace and quiet one accumulates energy that can then be released on stage. On the other hand, it is all too easy to dissipate such personal presence by throwing oneself into a life of superficial pleasure—alcohol, women, and late nights.

To generate something that radiates on stage and excites the audience, there must also be internal tension, but it has to be a nervousness that is positive in nature. Even if I have sung a romance or a song-cycle a thousand times, I still feel a certain anxiety when I come on stage and meet the expectant gaze of the audience.

On one occasion in my career I remember my nervous state transforming itself into a sense of impassivity. It happened in the summer of
1976 at Drottningholm Theater and at the National Museum in Stockholm. I was asked to sing *Fredman's Epistles*, written by the eighteenth-
century Swedish poet Carl Michael Bellman, with a chamber orchestra
conducted by Claude Génetay. Bellman's songs were originally written
for the lute and were sung and played by Bellman himself.

As soon as I heard the proposal I felt that the idea of orchestrating the
work was wrong, but I let myself be persuaded. I was frightfully nervous as
I sang, but the audience applauded nicely and I thought they were with
me. A critic in one of our leading daily papers had a different view, however. She wrote after my Bellman concert: "Is he really bothered that he
sings so beautifully?"

I understood immediately what she meant. My nervousness had
changed in nature and to her sensitive ears gave the impression of impassivity. In fact it was the complete reverse: I cared too much about what I
was singing and how I was singing it. Rendering those almost holy Swedish
ballads caused me to suffer so much pressure that I could feel nothing of
the reaction of the recipients.

Normally, if there are rest periods in which to recharge between
engagements, a singer can stay on form. Then when he faces the audience
in a full house, the spark is ignited. That kind of nervous tension is creative
and induces an immediate rapport with the audience, who can feel the
singer's commitment. On occasions such as those the singer achieves great
satisfaction, albeit fleetingly. If one were just to go in, feel self-assured,
and simply sing one's songs, it would become routine. That should never
happen and that is why, despite my advancing years, I still work constantly
on developing my singing. The personal reward for me is not least that
I find it more enjoyable if I do not sing every song or aria in the same
manner.

What I find interesting is that I am able to adapt easily to different
styles. The best thing I can read in a review is the sort of remark written by
one critic after a concert in Vienna in 1976, which went approximately
thus: "Gedda's versatility is something completely unique. When he
moved on in the program to Spanish songs his voice was suddenly Spanish." I could not expect finer words of praise. Achieving such a pure and
genuine presentation is what I seek to accomplish in my singing, and I
bring all my imagination to my aid. If I sing something French, I want to

get as close to French as possible; I want to give expression to its clarity and transparency.

I attribute my ability to sing well in various languages partly to the fact that I had to learn to speak several different languages as a young boy: Russian, German, and Swedish. Over the course of my singing career I did performances in all the languages of opera. The languages I most enjoyed singing in were Italian, French, and Russian. German is not a language that is pretty to sing, but it can be wonderful in a lied if the words are conveyed well. The worst languages in which to sing are English, Dutch, and Danish. Swedish is quite good, with the exception of certain vowels.

In March 1997 I gave a lieder recital at the Deutsche Oper in Berlin. I sang in four different languages: French, German, Czech, and Russian. It was a joy to see the opera house practically full, and the audience was with me from the very beginning with long, warmly welcoming applause. When the program was over I gave an encore of half a concert. It was very rewarding to still be able to give the public something that they took to their hearts. Unfortunately the weather was so cold that I could not stand outside to sign autographs. It seemed as if half the audience was waiting for me as we left for our hotel, and I had to ask them with a few brief words to excuse me. They did, with no fuss at all.

There was one period, in the 1970s, when I became nervy, restless, and exhausted in my professional outlook. It was probably because of a lack of patience; when I studied something new, whether an opera, a romance, or a concert part, I wanted to master it quickly. I could no longer labor over the same thing for months. Of course I polished it tirelessly, but above all I wanted a speedy overview and an immediate command of whatever new item I took on.

This is no longer the case, since I have stopped learning new material. I have given up opera roles entirely, though in 1996 Covent Garden inquired whether I would sing a small but significant character in Pfitzner's *Palestrina*. It was intended to be a major production, one of the last of the 1997 season before the theater closed for renovation. The reason for asking me was that I had sung the title role of Palestrina on a recording in the early '70s with Kubelík in Munich. The principal part is extremely demanding, not something I could cope with nowadays, and Thomas Moser had been engaged to play it. The role I was to sing on the opening night of 28 January 1997 was Archbishop Abdisu of Assyria.

I was on stage for forty-five minutes, and of that I sang for only about seven minutes in total. It was not an exacting task, and even though Covent Garden does not pay so well, it was a good engagement in that the theater paid travel and accommodation expenses for myself and Aino. And I enjoyed being with English and German colleagues. My rehearsal period was very short, only amounting to one week in total, since the part was so small, nor was it difficult to memorize.

I did not think for one moment that I would be mentioned in the reviews at all. Imagine my surprise when my confused little archbishop became a success in his own right.

Aino and I had a lovely and relaxing time in London over the course of the month in which the six performances took place. We went for walks in the parks since the weather was so wonderful, we went to the zoo in Regent's Park a couple of times, and we crisscrossed London in the red double-decker buses. We found ourselves in places we would never otherwise have visited. We could look from our height atop the buses down on the Sunday crowds in the East End. On other days we would take a taxi, visiting, for example, Dickens House and the fantastic Wallace Collection. These were two places neither of us had been before. Otherwise we were able to live quietly and peacefully as if at home, because we had a splendid apartment at our disposal in a block in Mayfair.

Covent Garden was planning to send this production to America in the summer of 1997, and they tried to persuade me to go. But that I definitely had to refuse: my doctor has strictly forbidden me to fly on long journeys with big time differences. You never know in advance how a journey will turn out, so it is just too great a risk. Besides, the guest performance was scheduled for July. I have never been in New York in the summer months when the humidity can reach ninety percent; that along with the air conditioning is a combination that can be deadly even for a young singer.

Our return trip home to Switzerland was not without a little adventure, however. Despite the fact that we had enjoyed ourselves enormously in London we were longing to get back home. When the day came to fly back to Switzerland we set off happily for the airport and arrived in such good time that we were able to take an earlier flight to Geneva, so we hastily changed our tickets and rushed through the various control points. Just as we were about to board the plane I noticed that I no longer had my bag over my shoulder. It contained my whole month's fee, my credit card, my passport, and our tickets.

Where could the bag be? I froze with horror, mainly because I thought I must be going gaga if I could not keep track of my possessions. The kind staff quickly unloaded our luggage from the plane that was waiting to take off for Switzerland. We then had to walk back through all the control points looking for my little bag. Our good fortune in adversity was that the police had taken charge of it to check whether it contained a bomb. I got the bag back with its contents intact. The reason I forgot it was that a small chocolate cake I had in my breast pocket was wrapped in aluminum foil and set off the security alarm in the metal detectors. In the process of fiddling about going back-and-forth several times I completely forgot the bag.

I was not so forgetful in my younger days. I also had infinite patience then with my singing training. I worked on it assiduously for fifteen years and found it equally enjoyable, exciting, and rewarding the whole time. I knew that the development of a singer or artist often consists of many successes in a row followed by a period of stagnation. Then you have to continue to work unfalteringly just the same, until you get over the threshold.

Offers for commissions might come either from the head of the opera house or from my impresario. At the Metropolitan, the opera house where I have sung the most, my involvement usually began with a meeting as soon as something was being planned that was considered to suit my voice and character, and I would be invited up to the general manager's office to talk to the conductor and director of the particular opera. In most cases I accepted, since they were stimulating engagements. In Germany the opera house almost always went through my agent, and the same was true in Vienna. The impresario would then check who was conducting, directing, and singing the other parts. In the later stages in my career I could say no without offending anybody, especially if the soprano part was to be sung by someone with a rich voice and I knew she would sing to her fullest extent.

At the beginning of your career you want to say yes to whatever is offered. You think it is imperative to sing at an important theater, and the invitation might come from the Met, Covent Garden, or La Scala. You fear the chance will never come again. But if you are not entirely sure that it is the right commission or that you will be able to carry it out brilliantly, it is better to decline. For if you fail, the opportunity will not be repeated: opera-house management is completely indifferent if a singer's career is wrecked. They just look around for a new voice.

I was always booked at least four years in advance, because opera houses frequently plan their productions that far ahead. Before I accepted other invitations I always waited to find out in which periods the Met wanted me to sing. They unfailingly let me know in good time. When I had booked my season there, I would tell my impresario that I was free for other times during the year. Then European theaters were fitted into my program, though I always left a few gaps in case something came up that I really wanted to do.

If I accepted two operas at the Met, it meant about two months' work, including rehearsals and performances. We would rehearse the one opera first for several weeks, and then came the performances; between performances we fitted in the rehearsals for the next production, followed by the new performances. If I had planned to go on to Europe afterward, I had to have at least a week's breathing space. When I was young and confident, and physically very strong, I would take on commitments that followed very closely upon one another. With fast air connections it is possible to sing at the Met one evening and at a theater in Europe the next. Many singers do so, without even bothering about rehearsals but just landing in a place and going on stage an hour or two later. If you do that regularly, to earn as much money as possible, you shorten your career by at least ten years.

Having accepted a new production, I would start by learning the work as a whole, both the music and the text. The quickest way of doing that is to sit down at the piano at home and sing it phrase by phrase, scene by scene, repeating it until the music and text become one and are fixed in the mind. I used to carry the work around with me, even on trips, and I would look at the piano score before I went to bed at night. In the end I would know it by heart.

In my experience many singers come to the first stage rehearsals without knowing their part at all and try to learn it during rehearsals. I loathed that method, partly because it made me even more nervous and partly because it never turned out well. One could of course ask for separate rehearsals with a coach; he would know how the conductor wanted it and could give tips on the director's particular traits and wishes. Rehearsals with the whole cast would normally take two weeks before the premiere, or three or four weeks if it were an especially complicated work.

All rehearsals are accompanied by music, at the beginning just with a pianist. At that point you do not sing, which certainly spares the voice; but even if you are only rehearsing the movements it is important to sing aloud a few times to check that the vocal apparatus is working. I used to select one little scene each day during rehearsals in which I would sing properly. It was useful because there was always so much else to think about when going out on the stage.

Some directors actually demanded that the singers sing at all rehearsals—Walter Felsenstein, for instance, at the Komische Oper in Berlin. He achieved fantastic results: his *Tales of Hoffmann* became world famous and was filmed; his *La Traviata* will also go down in operatic history. I never worked with Felsenstein, but I am sure he was right: when you act and sing simultaneously through all rehearsals you achieve as true an expression as is possible to obtain. But singers soon wear their voices out, so the question is which to sacrifice: the singers' voices or the quality of the production.

As far as the movement pattern for an opera is concerned, it is not as strictly confined as for a ballet, and certain movements can be made within a particular radius. The pattern is first outlined as a skeleton and the director states in broad terms how he imagines the whole. As work progresses he then adds in the details and builds up the movement pattern to what he hopes will be a fully harmonious entity. That, I believe, is the most constructive way to work. Unfortunately there are always some capricious directors who suddenly get it into their heads to change everything after you have learned the staging. That is one of the worst calamities that can befall you in learning a part.

The costumes are a drama in themselves, and inevitably they are not ready until the last minute. That is not the fault of the tailors or seamstresses but rather is due to the fact that the studios are always understaffed. I remember they were always completely hopeless at the Paris Opéra, where we sometimes had no opportunity to rehearse in costume at all, nor with scenery for that matter.

The final stage of rehearsals is with the orchestra. For complicated works this will begin a week before the premiere. In a three-act opera the rehearsal with orchestra would be done one act at a time, without costumes. The fourth day would be in costume but without make-up; on the fifth day a preparatory dress rehearsal in both costume and make-up. That fifth-day rehearsal can be without orchestra, for reasons of cost, since a full orchestra is an expensive business.

The sixth day is for the final dress rehearsal. The scenery is in place, everyone is in costume and full make-up, and the orchestra plays. In my time at Covent Garden they used to invite the Friends of Covent Garden, and at the Met the Metropolitan Opera Guild. Both societies consisted of people who had donated money to the theaters as sponsors. These opera fans also went to the first night, but they were especially keen on dress rehearsals, since so much could go wrong. The true enthusiasts thoroughly enjoyed that!

For me personally, the real nervousness would begin when I heard the musicians tuning up their instruments at the first orchestral rehearsals. The week before a premiere I would be among colleagues who were equally nervous, and the conductor and director would probably have come to blows several times already. Under the most trying circumstances I would have to remind myself that thankfully it would not last forever; one day soon it would all be over. It was an attitude that kept me calm, and I could go home after rehearsals and relax with something entirely different.

Once I got going in rehearsals the nervousness would disappear, and I would not be tormented again until the dress rehearsal and first night, when the public was in the auditorium. That was when you suddenly realized it was serious—here were people who had paid good money to see the production, and we had to do our very best in the almost fatalistic atmosphere that now pervaded the theater.

On the day of the premiere I always slept long into the morning so as to be completely rested. I warmed up my voice at home before I left for the theater. If I was staying in a hotel, I would take a walk to the theater around one o'clock and warm up there. Then I would go back and sleep for a few hours. I always got to the theater in good time to warm up again before make-up. When I was working at Covent Garden or the Vienna Opera I usually rented an apartment, which would sometimes have a piano. If there were no piano, I could manage anyway; my ear is so well trained that I can begin low and then go higher and higher, and that is how I would go through what I had to sing. I do the same today before my concerts.

You could usually tell after the first act on the first night whether it was successful. Then everything would flow with delightful ease. Friends would look into the dressing room and express their pleasure, which was gratifying.

After the first performance was over I would go out and eat with friends. It was always hard to sleep when I returned home later, of course, because I was still so wound up. But I would never lie awake to wait for the newspaper reviews.

The situation was often quite different when I came to an opera production as a guest artist. Time could be so short that it was only possible to discuss the most important points with your opposite number; we would go through the entire performance musically but the rest would have to fall into place of its own accord. If your partner suddenly did something totally different from what had been agreed, you had to remain icy cool.

Personally I did not like working under such conditions. I would prefer it as it was at Covent Garden, where there was always time for proper rehearsals. Unfortunately few theaters could offer that, even a theater as good as the Vienna Opera. After being in the profession for many years I was able to insist on having at least a couple of rehearsals. When I was in Vienna in 1976 to play the Duke in *Rigoletto* I recall the resident Rigoletto protesting loudly, since he thought it was too tiresome to have to attend a rehearsal with me. I had to beseech him and explain that I had not sung the Duke in the Vienna Opera production for more than ten years. He took pity on me then and I got my rehearsal. I was thus able to feel more or less secure, since I had at least had one decent run-through.

In this context I must mention something else that has an impact on artistic activity in the theater. There is a craze nowadays for group work, with everyone in the collective making the decisions. My experience is that the only thing that happens in such collective endeavors is that you waste masses of time on unproductive discussion and the result is an inadequate performance.

I am actually rather concerned about the future of the theater. If this fashion continues to spread, it will have an adverse effect on quality. It is very easy to impair the delicate art of the theater.

I have often been asked what I think of the future of opera. Will the public want to see the classical works even into the next millennium? I am convinced that classical music will survive. And I hope that in the future directors will cease experimenting with opera staging and controversial concepts, such as making the Duke in *Rigoletto* a gangster boss in New York. That violates the original. The emotions that music conveys are indeed timeless and can be applied to any period in history, but I still prefer to see a production of *Carmen*, for instance, in costume and scenery of Bizet's time. Perhaps I am old-fashioned, but so too are most opera audiences. Whenever a director and stage designer have brought in newfangled ideas, the public has generally responded by booing, which is particularly hard for the artists who have to stand there and face the disapproval. So I hope that the era of experimentation is at an end.

We who work with such a fragile art as opera must always remember that the public audiences who pay money to see and hear us are also very demanding. As ready as they are to praise a singer to the skies, they are equally keen for the opportunity to knock their idol down. That is the pressure we artists live under. I have to say, however, that it requires both courage and strength to try to persuade agents, opera managements, and others involved that you cannot take on a particular commission. You have to take all the responsibility yourself, but you are able to do it because you know what the alternative is.

The public can be merciless enough even when you do well. There are, or were, theaters in South America that had offensive audiences who came and went as they pleased throughout the performance. They used the theater, a holy place for us artists, as a salon for private conversation. Their presence seemed primarily to be an occasion for the ladies to display their jewels and expensive dresses. Such behavior in a theater is not only extremely uncouth but manifests a total contempt for both the art and the artists.

EIGHTEEN

Saying Good-Bye to the Theater

THE READER may wonder whether I miss the theater nowadays. I can honestly answer that question in the negative. I began to discard roles such as Romeo quite early in my career, because it is ridiculous for a man past his sixties to play a first lover. Even if my voice was as fresh as possible, I knew that my lack of youth would show in gesture and movement. Bit by bit I stripped away everything that could spoil the visual illusion for the audience. I retained only one youthful role for a long time, and that was Lenski in *Eugene Onegin*. I had great difficulty giving that up because it suited my voice and my personality so well. But now I have even taken my leave of Pushkin's poet, many years ago, although I have often been asked to play the role despite my age. As recently as 1996 the Zurich Opera asked me to be their Lenski, but I refused. Hoffmann was the part I kept longest, since Hoffmann was a man who had been through a lot in life, and if he looked aged beyond his years, it was appropriate for the character.

A particular production of *Tales of Hoffmann* that I look back on with pleasure is the one at the Opéra in Paris in 1974. Patrice Chéreau, then a young genius, was the director, and he made the principal role a drunken, impoverished poet living in squalor and decay. When Hoffmann sang the Kleinsack song in the Prologue, he entered in a torn suit and dirty shirt, unshaven, yet with a trace of past elegance. It was obvious that he came home so drunk every night that he fell asleep fully clothed.

I liked Chéreau's interpretation of the Hoffmann character very much; it was extremely well delineated. It was also a great success for me personally, not just as a singing role but dramatically too.

Hoffmann was my last really successful role in the theater. I think I performed it well at the Volksoper in Vienna in 1989 and again in the Stockholm Opera production in the autumn of 1990 and spring of 1991.

I should have stopped there, but regrettably I let myself be persuaded to appear in the Stockholm Opera's anniversary production of *Gustaf Wasa*. The libretto of this opera was written in the eighteenth century by the Swedish court poet Johan Henrik Kellgren on the basis of a draft by King Gustav III. The music is by Johann Gottlieb Naumann, a German who was in the employ of the Swedish king at that time. *Gustaf Wasa* became the national opera and played very successfully in Stockholm throughout the eighteenth and nineteenth centuries. It was to be brought back anew to celebrate the 250th anniversary of the composer's birth.

The opera has two major tenor parts: the Swedish king, Gustaf Wasa, and the Danish king, Christiern II. The part of the young blond Gustaf Wasa was given to a completely unknown Swedish singer, and I was offered the role of the irascible and bloodstained Danish king. Christiern II is known in Sweden as "Christian the Tyrant," and at the time at which the opera takes place, 1520, he also ruled over Sweden.

I resisted the offer most emphatically. I had never played such an unsympathetic role in my whole career, and it felt quite contrary to my own personality. I absolutely did not want to do it. But persuasion came from all quarters and I felt it was my duty to my debut theater to take on the task. It would be an interesting contrast to my earliest role as the happy young Postilion of Longjumeau.

The director was promised to be one of the biggest names in what was then East Germany, but the Berlin Wall came down during the planning period, bringing about numerous changes even in the world of theater. When rehearsals began in Stockholm, Detleff Rogge, an unknown director from a small province in Germany, was appointed instead.

I remember Aino in tears begging me to refuse the role of the bloodthirsty Christiern. She could sense that it was all wrong. In negotiating my contract Aino increased my fee to triple the amount of the previous one, with the intent that they would thus be unable to afford to engage me, but they agreed to it without protest. And despite Aino's warnings and presentiments I signed the contract.

We left our home in Switzerland at the height of summer, when the garden and nature were in full bloom, and when we would have been able to enjoy another good six weeks of swimming and sunshine. It was wonderful summer weather in Stockholm too, and it felt really perverse to go in to the dusty and badly ventilated rehearsal rooms at the age of sixty-six. I remember wondering if I would live to see another summer.

The weeks dragged on. Even when I saw the costume sketches I considered withdrawing from the whole enterprise. I had thought that the opera would be performed in period costume and that I would be able to parade in a fine velvet suit. I was dressed instead as a ridiculous carnival figure roaring out threats of blood, disgrace, and cruel revenge. But I had already signed a contract for twenty or so performances, and, most important of all, the theater had invested heavily in the project. Nor did I have an understudy. So I had to struggle on.

At the 16 October premiere, I sang well Christiern's extremely beautiful aria that comes at the end of the first act, and I received warm applause. The Danish king does not appear at all in the second act, but he comes on again in the third and final act. My scenes were dreadful. I stood there swathed in the Swedish flag that I was frantically attempting to hold around me. I was painfully aware of how ridiculous I looked.

The curtain descended on a premiere that I had known in advance would be a total disaster. When the actors came on stage at the end we got loud, if not overwhelming, applause, even for the main players individually. Then the director and choreographer stepped onto the stage—and we all stood there as the audience broke out in wild booing, enveloping us all. Not in my worst nightmares had I sweated with fear as much as I did when I saw the director, Detleff Rogge, jump up and join the line of singers on stage. I later read in the papers that, along with one of the critics, the chorus of boos had been led by a female colleague of mine who had been at the Stockholm Opera at the time of my successful debut in 1952.

The initial reactions from the critics the next day likewise spared the singers. It was the director who was subjected to the most devastating criticism, but even the costume designers and the choreographer received their due share. The criticism in the morning newspapers was quite balanced, but the evening press was to follow. One paper had the bad taste to single me out in order to put an individual face on the fiasco. I was on placards and front pages. I could understand their presentation to some extent. I was the only well-known name and the press regarded it as a great triumph and achievement to bring me down. They persecuted me for months, despite the fact that after the third performance my nerves were so frayed that my doctor declared me sick and forbade me to continue. I could not sleep at night, which was not surprising since journalists were standing on my doorstep for weeks on end, ringing the bell in the hope of getting an interview. They even turned to my friends and acquaintances to try to wheedle out information about me and my "great debacle."

Being singled out as the name and face attached to the fiasco was too much for me. I could not sing a note for several months. Even today I am puzzled how I could receive such treatment in my native country. Could it possibly have been the black abscess of envy bursting and spewing out its stinking purulence? Although the Swedish newspaper critics were united in their view that the singers emerged from the debacle with honor and that it was the direction and stage design that were total failures, the one who had to bear the brunt of the humiliation was Nicolai Gedda himself.

I also took it as my own personal failure, and I could not forgive myself for not listening to my own intuition—nor to the advice of my confidante, Aino—when it told me the part was wrong for me.

But what was done was done. After three performances *Gustaf Wasa* was taken off permanently. The Stockholm Royal Opera actually attempted to continue with a new young tenor asked to learn the part, but it did not work. The role was too difficult to sing, and I was probably the only one who could manage it. So it was decided that the opera should be performed in concert and I was asked to sing the part. Since there was nobody else, and since I wanted to show that I could do it, I agreed. The reviews were very favorable and the newspapers expressed their regret that it had not been done as a concert from the outset.

The original contract had specified that we take *Gustaf Wasa* to the Semper Opera in Dresden in May 1992. I had signed for that, and now that the production was changed to a concert I was happy to go along with my commitment. Earlier in January I had fulfilled another clause in the contract by making a recording of the opera for the English record label Virgin. So the engagement was not a total failure, but nevertheless my final opera appearance left a bad aftertaste. I resolved not to sing in opera productions any more.

I still wonder about the irresponsibility of the head of the Stockholm Opera at the time, who did not turn up once to watch the rehearsals. As far as I remember, his first appearance was at the dress rehearsal, when it was far too late to change anything. He must have given Detleff Rogge carte blanche as director, and the same for the stage and costume designers.

The part of Gustav III in Verdi's *Masked Ball* was one that I kept right up to the mid-1980s, when I performed it in a new production at the

Stockholm Opera House. The director was Göran Järvefelt, who died a few years ago. He wanted to experiment with new ideas, and he transposed the greater part of the plot to a rehearsal room at Drottningholm Castle. The king had loved theater and enjoyed playing principal roles himself, and Järvefelt based his production on that known historical fact. It premiered in mid-December 1985, to mixed reviews. I came out of it well as far as the singing was concerned, but both director and designer were thoroughly criticized.

People often ask why Verdi chose the events surrounding Gustav III as the setting for his passionate music. The original libretto by Eugène Scribe was entitled *Gustave III ou Le Bal Masqué*, and was written not for Verdi but for Daniel Auber. That version was first performed in Paris in 1833. Verdi became interested in the subject, but at that time the murder of a king would have been considered scandalous on the Italian stage; in response to the demands of the censors, Verdi's librettist, Antonio Somma, transposed the setting to Boston, and the main character became an English governor. It was not changed back to the Swedish court until 1935, for a production in Copenhagen.

Another opera that I discarded later in life was Massenet's *Werther*, which has a wonderful tenor part in the title role. I was first offered the part in 1956 at the Opéra-Comique in Paris, but my American debut intervened and I had to turn *Werther* down. I also thought I was too young. The difficulty with this opera is that it is very long and you have to be a chamber singer to manage the various ranges of musical expression. You have to sing pianissimo and yet express feelings with the greatest intensity. You need both technique and experience for that, not least experience of life.

A few years later I had an offer of the same part at the Met, but I rejected it on the grounds of not wanting to sing solely French opera there. So the part of Werther went to Franco Corelli, which led to a violent reaction from the public, so violent that I was utterly embarrassed by it. They demonstrated at the first night with placards and threw leaflets into the auditorium: GEDDA FOR WERTHER! Corelli sang the part excellently, but the public had got it into their heads that it was I and not he who was the expert in French opera.

The next time I encountered Werther was in a concert production in Carnegie Hall in November 1965. It was organized by the Friends of French Opera and their president Robert Lawrence. The performance was done "semi-stage," meaning that we did not sing with scores in our hands but there was some scenery and we made limited gestures and movements. We wore evening dress rather than full costume. The concert was a great success.

In 1968 I made a recording of *Werther* with Victoria de los Angeles, which is still classed as the "definitive" version. The conductor for the recording was Georges Prêtre.

In the spring of 1977 I had the good fortune to work on *Werther* with George London as director. London was then manager of the Washington Opera in the Kennedy Center, which comprises both a concert hall and an opera house with 2000 seats. Despite the large size of the auditorium it still manages to feel intimate. We had begun thorough preparations the previous summer in Switzerland, where George London was a near neighbor of mine just outside Lausanne. The role of Charlotte went to Joann Grillo, an American of Italian origin, and London brought her over for a few weeks for us to rehearse together. Massenet's almost static opera contains little movement, but on the other hand there is a strong emotional interplay between Werther and Charlotte. The duets on the theme of deep and unfulfilled love demand solid work to bring out all the torment the two young people suffer. The preparations seemed to pay off, as the production went very well.

I think I was successful with my Werther; at least I received consistently positive reviews. By this time I had the necessary personal experience for this difficult role and a voice that though apparently light was able to express strong emotions. All the critics thought I had the figure for the part, and of course I had the help of a skillful make-up artist—Goethe's Werther is twenty-three years old, and I at fifty-two was somewhat over-mature.

The Metropolitan is the theater where I have sung most, participating in twenty-four seasons, though in the 1970s and '80s for shorter periods than I had previously. Above all, I have the former general manager of the Metropolitan Opera, Rudolf Bing, to thank. My performances were broadcast on the radio and I gradually rose to command top fees. Bing was a consummate businessman and very demanding in regard to the artists, but there are many who think that the Met lost much of its old reputation during his time there. People remembered the period when Giulio Gatti-Casazza was in charge, from 1908 to 1935, which was the era of Caruso and Toscanini. Admittedly Gatti-Casazza had the resource of those two great artists, but that was not the only reason why the Met became the world's foremost opera stage at that time. For many decades the Met represented the pinnacle of a singer's career.

Rudolf Bing's amateurishness and lack of judgment caused the theater to decline. He did not understand voices, for one thing. His gravest mistake lay in engaging good and able singers for inappropriate parts. He also had no visual sense.

In October 1963, we were about to do a new production of that most French of all operas, Massenet's *Manon*. So Bing engaged Günther Rennert as director, a specialist in Wagner and, to some extent, Mozart. For the stage design he brought over a German from Berlin, and the conductor was American. Instead of a Parisian setting, the opera was enveloped in the atmosphere of Munich and the Hofbräuhaus. I was very unhappy to be taking part in it. Bing dented the Met's reputation by errors such as these.

The farewell gala for the final performance at the old Met building on 39th Street took place in the early spring of 1966. The program lasted four and a half hours and consisted of twenty-five opera excerpts with sixty soloists under the direction of eleven conductors. I sang the trio from *Faust* with Jerome Hines and Gabriella Tucci. Tickets cost an average of $200 each. A lot of people wanted to be present at that gala night to witness the closing of an era in opera history. Older singers who had sung at the Met were in the audience, and they were brought up on stage and accorded a lively ovation. Speeches were given and the tributes rounded off by our all singing "Auld Lang Syne." One of the older Italian singers, Licia Albanese, bent down and kissed the floorboards. And the curtain went down for the last time in the eighty-three-year-old opera house.

The new Met is in Lincoln Center. To the right of the Opera House is Avery Fisher Hall (originally Philharmonic Hall) and to the left the New York State Theater. The Juilliard School of Music also forms part of this beautiful cultural complex. The Met is built in semi-classical style, and the interior is decorated with enormous Chagall panels in the huge windows of the entrance hall. The auditorium is bigger than the one in the old Met, with 3800 seats and 200 standing places. For the performers on stage the auditorium still feels intimate.

The factor of supreme importance for a singer is the acoustics of a theater. The acoustic conditions at the Met are ideal, and that was one of the reasons why I sang there for so long. Another reason was that the atmosphere among colleagues was always so friendly and open.

The move from the old building cost so much that I am not sure whether even now all the bills have been paid. The opera house itself is said to have cost fifty million dollars. The 1975 season was extremely hard financially, and we singers had to put on gala performances to raise money to ensure the Met's future. The budget shortage that year was four million dollars. It was not the singers' fees that swallowed the money but the enormous administration.

The inauguration of the new Met was unfortunately a resounding fiasco. Samuel Barber had composed the opera *Antony and Cleopatra* specially for the occasion, and it was staged by the Italian film director Franco Zeffirelli. He was given free rein over the revolving stage and its new machinery, so he brought in heavy scenery and huge numbers of people and animals, even cows, onto the stage. The whole lot sank down to the basement during the first performance, and the machinery was out of order for the entire season.

Avery Fisher Hall was also a catastrophe: because of a fault in construction the orchestra sounded like an old scratched gramophone record. I have sung there, and it is an absolute nightmare; even if you breathe in as deep as you can, the sound only travels a few yards before fading away. They had to spend another five million to put matters right. It is said to be better now, but far from ideal.

To my great delight my fans followed me to the new Met. My most devoted admirer was probably Sandra, a girl who must have weighed about 300 pounds. She always wrote to me to ask for the dates of my appearances far in advance. She lived a long distance from New York and had a two-hour train journey each way to come to my performances. But she never failed to turn up—what dedication!

A male admirer who was constantly loyal to me over the years was a tramp, who I think missed not one single performance at the Met. He was there in his standing place night after night. We artists paid for his spot for him. He would come backstage after the performances to greet us and thank us for the show. Not many people are allowed in behind the scenes at the Met, but we always let in this little man in his tattered rags who looked as if he slept in the gutter. He was the theater's living mascot. He had only one tooth in his permanently smiling mouth, and he cleaned it so well that it shone like a beacon. I think it is wonderful that there are people quite low down in society—or even right outside it—who love music, who perhaps actually survive because of music.

In the autumn of 1983 I took part in the Met's 100th anniversary celebrations. I sang in the first section, and then there was a long break. Since I was not participating in the second and final sections of the gala performance and also felt very tired, I went home to watch the rest on television with my second wife, who had not been at the theater. The anniversary performance ended with all the artists involved lining up on the stage to receive the audience's ovation. My wife gave me a long wondering look and said: "Why are you sitting here? You should be there being applauded!" I got up without a word and went to my bedroom to try to sleep.

Later that season I made my final appearance at the Met, playing opposite Kiri Te Kanawa in Verdi's *La Traviata*. Many people may well have wondered why I suddenly disappeared from the Metropolitan Opera and the United States, since I already had an agreement with the Met to work on several more operas after that. I can disclose the reason now. Because of the severe discord in my marriage, the constant arguments and quarrels that went on for years, I had taken quite a pounding both psychologically and physically and it had brought on dangerously high blood pressure. I did not feel well when we began rehearsals for *La Traviata*, so I went to see the theater nurse. "Your blood pressure is real crazy," she said, and she sent me straight to a doctor. He confirmed that my blood pressure should be treated immediately, and he gave me tablets so that I could go on working at my own risk on the performances I already had booked.

When I finished *La Traviata* in November 1983 I went home to Stockholm and contacted a heart specialist. He was horrified and started treating me immediately. By then I was so bad that I felt giddy and had a buzzing in my ears. I had trouble keeping my balance as I went along the street and kept bumping into walls. The first advice my Swedish doctor gave me was to cancel all the work I had ahead of me in the U.S. The long flights and the time difference of six to seven hours were not good for me, and also my domestic situation was dangerous for my health. I initiated then the separation from my second wife that led eventually to divorce.

After I had been in Sweden for a while everything calmed down and I was able to sleep normally again. My blood pressure stabilized with the right combination of drugs. But the damage that was done will be with me for the rest of my life; I will always have to take tablets and have regular medical check-ups.

Over the years since then I have had many invitations to return to the Met and to other theaters in the United States, but I have decided not to endanger my life by traveling there. I also feel a great reluctance because of what happened in my private life. The constant traumas of my second marriage have made me susceptible to high blood pressure even by just thinking of New York. That does not mean that I have forgotten my devoted American public. I have seen some of them over the course of the years in Europe, music-lovers who were on holiday or had other business in cities where I have been giving a concert. They often come to greet me after the concert and it is always a pleasure to see them.

In the spring of 1989 I was telephoned in Vienna by an Austrian conductor, Eric Binder, who suggested that I go to Tokyo, where an admiring public awaited me. The proposal was that I share the concert platform with a Japanese singer. I discussed it with Aino and we decided to accept. We had met the singer, Hiroko Hiraishi, and her husband, a pianist, before and liked them.

In Tokyo we stayed in a splendid hotel on the edge of a famous old imperial park. I gave four performances in two weeks there and in Yokohama. The Japanese audiences were marvelous. Whenever we came down to the hotel lobby during the day to go out and look around the city, I was always met by a whole crowd of people sitting waiting with their record sleeves and CD cases to ask for my autograph. I heard from the hotel staff that my fans had sat there waiting patiently for hours. No Japanese would ever dream of ringing and disturbing me in my hotel suite.

Almost every year I receive offers to do guest performances in the most distant places on earth. I was invited to sing in South America, either solo or with their favorite, Victoria de los Angeles. Australia and South Africa both tried to tempt me over. And the Japanese were soon asking me back again, an offer I chose to accept.

The flight from Europe this next time was a miserable experience. Our sleep was totally ruined by a single cigar-smoking German. He chain-smoked from take-off to landing for ten to twelve hours in a first-class cabin that mixed smokers and nonsmokers. So we arrived dog-tired and bad-tempered. We stayed in the same wonderful hotel as on the first occasion and felt at home, and on the whole, the time we spent in Tokyo was very pleasant. My concerts were also successful. The Japanese are splendid audiences; they are considerate not only of the singer's time but also of one another. None of them would start a conversation with the singer about their own problems when standing in a long queue waiting for an autograph—and there are indeed fans who take the liberty of doing just that, which is a nuisance both for the artist and for the others who want an autograph before rushing off to catch their train to the suburbs.

My last trip to Asia in the autumn of 1996 was in many respects a great disappointment, though not as far as the audiences were concerned—the music-going public is for me something holy. People who sit quietly listening to music are at least not doing any harm while they do so, which is a good thing in a world so full of violence. My disappointment stemmed rather from the exploitation of Asia. As a child and young man I had read travelers' accounts, and now it was an unpleasant experience to see that the East was no longer the East. The East has been raped by the West, not least by that curse of the West, the car, polluting the atmosphere. And those skyscrapers everywhere.

In 1984 I made a trip to South Africa. It was a journey I should not have undertaken. The offer came through a Swedish singer who was married to a Swiss conductor, both of whom worked regularly in South Africa. When I told Aino of the proposal she advised me emphatically against it, being well aware as a journalist of South Africa's apartheid policy and of Sweden's attitude toward it. Since I am obstinate by nature, however, I refused to believe there would be any harm in accepting an offer to sing there. As an artist I was quite keen to perform for both white and black audiences. So I set off—alone. It was not long before I received a telephone call in my hotel in Cape Town from a Swedish journalist. He wanted to know whether I was politically illiterate and had never heard of the United Nations' blacklist. I had, but I justified my actions on the grounds that our Swedish tennis players went there. That would not help: if I did not want to end up on the blacklist I should pack and go home immediately. Nor would that be enough: back home in Sweden I would have to make a public apology for my blunder.

I was quite shaken and realized that the best course was to comply. I rang Aino and asked her to send a telegram to say that my mother was very ill—which was true.

Back in Sweden there was a great outcry in the newspapers, on television, and on the radio. I had to admit everywhere to being a political idiot. That too, unfortunately, was true. Part of the truth was that I needed the money. Now there was no money, only shame and ignominy.

Since then I have had regular invitations to go back to South Africa. There is a new regime now, but I balk at the thought of flying so far once again, even though it is in the same time zone as Europe.

Now we have decided definitively to stay in Europe and limit ourselves to flights of no more than two or three hours, preferably without intermediate landings and changes of aircraft.

Shortly before Aino and I put the final touches to these memoirs, I had the good fortune to participate in a truly momentous occasion. EMI was celebrating its centenary and they asked whether I would agree to be Master of Ceremonies for the jubilee gala evening. I was immensely gratified, and I regard the invitation as the highest honor.

I received a typescript outlining what I was to say: my function included the presentation of EMI's new artists. I also had the opportunity to point out that I had been with EMI for nearly half of their hundred years. I was very proud and happy at this honor, or rather privileged duty. The centenary celebrations were held in the new auditorium at Glyndebourne on 27 April 1997, and the gala included many notable performers who have recorded with EMI.

Aino and I were provided with splendid accommodation in a former manor house that had once been owned by the family of the poet Shelley but which after numerous vicissitudes had been converted into a hotel in the 1930s. It was a typical English hotel with floral wallpaper, masses of cushions on its soft sofas, a tea tray on the lounge table, and a plate of homemade cakes.

Aino looked very elegant in a simple long black dress, and I wore my professional dress-suit. We were very happy. Everyone was looking forward to seeing us at the late-evening banquet that was to follow; marquees had been erected in the park for the occasion. Unfortunately Aino and I had decided in advance that we would not be taking part in this aspect of the festivities, which was also to include a huge fireworks display. We had to travel all day the following day, and at our age it is of utmost importance to get to bed before midnight, which is what we did even on this gala occasion.

Nevertheless, the evening was one of the highlights of my career.

NINETEEN

Loss and Gain

MY MOTHER OLGA often used to say to me: "I always knew you would do well with your singing, Nicolai." Yet my parents could never have suspected that my breakthrough would be such a triumph. Nor would they even have dared dream that my career would be such a long one, largely thanks to the solid grounding I had from my father in my childhood and youth.

It saddens me, however, that their delight in my success was so soon tarnished by that fact that I had to leave Sweden almost immediately after my debut and was constantly away from them for long periods. It is some consolation to me, therefore, that I did not get an apartment of my own in Stockholm when I began earning money. In fact I lived with my parents in the little family home in Södermalm until I was twenty-seven; even after the failed marriage with my Russo-French wife I stayed in my parents' home whenever I visited Stockholm.

During my first few years abroad I felt very emotional every time I flew home. In those early days all flights to Stockholm landed at the tiny airport of Bromma. My parents lived at that time in a larger apartment in Hässelby Strand, not far from the airport, and they always met me with hugs and tears of joy.

Even though they missed me and expressed their feelings both verbally and in their letters, they were naturally thrilled about my successes abroad. I used to send home all the reviews and cuttings I came across so that they could follow the development of my artistic career. My father took the greatest care of them, pasting them into a splendid album for me once they had been attentively perused. I found it touching that he would sit listening to the radio and tuning in to foreign stations that broadcast classical music in the hope of hearing me, and he was often lucky, since I started to be featured on gramophone records. He told me how proud he was of me, how pleased and grateful he was that what he had taught me had developed so much further. Neither he nor my mother ever missed a single occasion when I was broadcast on Swedish radio.

As my income increased it was only natural that I should take over complete responsibility for my parents' financial well-being. In any case they were now so old that they were not able to earn anything themselves and all they had was a miserably small old-age pension. I had in fact given them financial support from the day I left school and started working at the bank and earning extra money singing at weddings and funerals.

Once the foreign engagements began bringing in money, I was able to make better provision for them. My mother was a good cook and had attended a culinary school when she was young; the sad thing was that for so many years she did not have the chance to prepare the kind of food she was capable of due to their strained financial situation. Now I made sure that she could buy whatever she wanted to put into the pot.

I also acquired a little summer cottage out in the Stockholm archipelago and had it renovated, and I think my parents liked their summers there. I tried to enjoy myself there with them too, when I had some weeks free in the summer. I use the word "tried" since the summers during the 1960s generally were very cold and rainy. We called the summer our "green winter": the same conditions recurred year after year. I was busy working hard on my foreign engagements in June, when the weather in Sweden was at its most magnificent. I just longed for the work to come to an end so that I could go home to the archipelago and experience the beauty of the Swedish summer. When the time eventually came for me to get the plane back to Stockholm, I opened my eyes on the first day of my holiday to see the sky covered by thick clouds and the rain pouring down, and so it would continue until the day I went back to America again!

On the few isolated days in those summer weeks when the weather was more or less good, I would go sailing with my old school friend in his splendid boat; we would stock up with provisions and set off out to sea, anchor in a quiet spot, swim, eat, and sunbathe. I can still see us even today, in his car on our way out to the moorings and the boat, with him humming the same old song: "Silver moon over the mountains." The song and the happy mood were also an expression of our anticipation of finding an open-air dance floor and meeting some pretty Swedish girls. Sometimes it even happened.

But for the most part it seemed as if there was a curse on my holidays. I sat imprisoned in the little summer cottage lamenting the passing of the days, knowing that I would soon have to leave for a new season at the Met in America. Then it would be a whole year before I was back in the Swedish archipelago again. It was a very painful experience and the approach of autumn still generates a mood of melancholy. In fact as soon as midsummer has passed and most of the flowering season is over I begin to feel sad.

Of course the autumn can often be beautiful, with its clear translucent days, but I am nevertheless unable to rid myself of the sense of something around me dying. It has become a little easier over the years as I have spent more and more time in my home in Switzerland. The villa in a pretty country village on the shore of Lake Geneva has a large garden and I can experience the fruit-picking and the scent of making apple and plum jam in the kitchen. The autumns there are usually warm and beautiful and we can sit out in the garden well into October listening to the crickets. That is a new happiness that has developed over the years.

When I returned home to Stockholm as a young man I suffered quite a lot from my parents' overprotectiveness. Of course I appreciated my mother's fussing and concern, but it often seemed an excessive love, a love that just caused me distress and pangs of guilt. With the passing of the years I have come to realize that they meant well and that they missed me very much when I was abroad. They were both foreigners in Sweden and I was the only one they had, so their thoughts and emotions were always focused on me. I do not think it is wise for parents to live through their children, however; parents should have their own interests to fall back on. It is not just children who need to free themselves from their parents but also parents from their children.

Many of my school friends had very casual relationships with their parents, and I envied their ability to do what they liked. They did not have to telephone home every hour to report that they were still alive as I did. If I arrived home late at night, I would have to be told that they had sat up worrying the whole time. And that was when I was almost forty!

I am still mortified when I recall getting so angry one summer evening at my parents' concern for me that I could no longer restrain myself and exploded with rage. I cannot recollect now the furious words that poured forth: it was probably a complete list of unjustified accusations against them. But what I do remember is my mother's hysterical attack of weeping. She sobbed and sobbed for hours without ceasing. I have realized since that I probably damaged my father's health with my inability to control myself. While my mother wept he just sat there chain-smoking nervously. My father's anxiety on my behalf was understandable, because he was a singer himself and knew how delicate the apparatus in the throat actually is; the slightest excess of late nights could have a detrimental effect. My mother's chief worry was that I would fall into the company of undesirable women. Both she and my father continued to be haunted by the specter of my unhappy first marriage, and it was easy to imagine that I might repeat the mistake. Nevertheless I should have contained myself on that occasion and explained to my parents calmly and rationally that I needed commitment-free relaxation to counterbalance the tensions of my hard work abroad.

I can see now that my parents were overprotective simply because I was not their own child, and because the adoption had not been recognized by the Swedish authorities due to their poverty. Now they were afraid that the person they had taken such good care of would come to no good out in society. It never occurred to them that the child was now grown up; on the contrary, in their eyes I was still a weak, helpless little boy who could not defend himself against the evil and cunning of the world.

I understood my parents' reactions more fully after Olga's death in 1985. Among her papers I found their application, submitted shortly after their marriage, for my adoption, and the hurtful reply from the authorities. Nevertheless they had the courage to keep me illegally. They had become attached to me and loved me as their own child, and that was the great good fortune of my life. What would have become of me had I been placed in a children's home? As it happened, I had exactly the right home. They may have been extremely poor, but my father was able to develop the gift with which God had endowed me.

As some small expression of gratitude for that I still sing as often as I can with Orthodox choirs. In the last few years it has most frequently been the choir of the Uspensky Cathedral in Helsinki, a fine body of people with whom I really feel at ease, and it has become something of a tradition that we give a concert together every summer in the Old Church at Espoo on the outskirts of Helsinki. We have also gone on tour together; the Uspensky Choir has sung in Stockholm and in the Russian Church in

Copenhagen that was built on the instructions of the Danish Princess Dagmar, who was married to Czar Alexander III.

I have also accompanied the Russo-Finnish group to both the new Finnish Valamo and to the old Valamo Monastery by Lake Ladoga near St. Petersburg (at the time still known as Leningrad). We did a guest performance at the old Valamo Monastery for a few wonderful summer days in August of 1990. The weather was perfect. The countryside there has a fairy-tale quality; there is probably none more exquisite in the whole world. We began with a concert in the newly renovated Smol'nyy Convent in St. Petersburg, singing to an audience that listened to the old hymns in tears. The crowd was so huge that we barely made it by taxi to the boat that was to take us across Lake Ladoga to Valamo, the beautiful monastery, which had once been Finnish, spread over a number of islands. All the monastery buildings were demolished, however, and the Communists had even used the chapel as a potato store. Dampness and mold had spread unimpeded and destroyed all the wonderful frescoes that once covered the walls. We gave a delightful evening concert in aid of the restoration. The audience was as large as the one in St. Petersburg: the news that we were going to sing in Valamo Monastery had spread like wildfire and several big boatloads of people came to listen. That visit to Valamo at Ladoga stands out as a highlight in my memory, and I am pleased that we had the opportunity to make the journey.

Reverting to 1960 and my parents, as I mentioned before my father Michail smoked too much, especially when he was nervous. In the winter of 1960 he began to feel tired and complained that his winter clothes were too heavy. The doctor revealed that my father had lung cancer. He was operated on by a leading specialist at Sophiahemmet Hospital in Stockholm, and he felt quite well again after a period of convalescence.

To improve life for my parents, I decided to have a house built for them in Danderyd, one of Stockholm's prettiest suburbs. My wish was for them to enjoy life in old age, to breathe fresh air and have a beautiful garden in which to putter around. I had no idea what work a garden can entail!

The house was built and my parents moved in. It was then two years after my father's operation and he still felt full of energy. But in the spring of 1963 he fell ill again; the cancer had spread to his liver and he was in critical condition. One day as I was touring abroad I received a telephone call from his doctor, Professor Clarence Crafoord (whose name I mention because he was well-known even outside Sweden), to say that the X-rays suggested my father only had a few months to live.

Upon returning home in the summer of 1963 I arrived to find my father sitting in a chair in the garden, and I could see him fading away even in the short period I was there. His condition was so bad that there was no question of another operation, and it was perhaps a blessing that he was able to be at home.

The weeks of summer passed gloomily, until it was time for me to depart once more to take up my contractual obligations in America. I suspected that I would never see my father again. When I left he had moved from diet food to baby food, but even that he could not keep down.

I knew from my mother's frequent letters that his condition was worsening. From once having been a big, strong man he was now just skin and bone. In despair I tried to find any preparation that might postpone death. I managed to get hold of a new medicine and sent it to my father's doctor. He felt intermittently a little better after that and was able to sit up in bed for brief periods. He was optimistic and convinced he would defeat the illness. Or perhaps he pretended to be, just for my mother's sake.

I received a letter from my father himself that autumn saying that he realized his days were numbered and that his strength was diminishing further. He gave me a lot of good advice that he asked me to think about, including his opinion that I should bring my bachelor days to an end (it was then almost eight years since my first marriage had failed, and the divorce had recently been finalized). He told me he thought I should look around for a good woman to marry, preferably one brought up in the same religious faith as myself.

In October 1963 I had a telephone call to say that my father's health had deteriorated drastically. I took the next flight home but nevertheless arrived too late. He had died at home just a few hours before, calmly and peacefully in his sleep.

My father's advice in his last letter took root in my mind, and in March 1964 I met a young woman of the Greek Orthodox religion whom I married a year later, firmly convinced that this time it was right.

What a terrible mistake that was. My mother was unhappy when she saw my choice, but I myself was obstinate and would not admit that I had again made a mistake.

I will not go into any details about that marriage since I was probably as wrong for her as she was for me. She was certainly as unhappy as I was, not least because as soon as we were married I flew home to Stockholm to see my mother, now a widow and complaining of loneliness. I also wanted to be with my Swedish friends. My wife came with me to Stockholm from time to time in the first few years, but it usually resulted in quarreling between her and my mother and the whole atmosphere was very disagreeable.

On paper the marriage lasted quite a long time, despite the fact that we grew further and further apart. I realized the marriage was untenable, and frequently I thought of getting a divorce. But I was also cowardly and afraid, a fear that stemmed from memories of the exhausting legal process of my first divorce. I always had so much work that I had no time or energy for further battles.

That second marriage was eventually dissolved, but only after we had been totally separated for almost ten years.

I do not blame my marital failures on either of my two wives. They were the people they were, and both of them asserted at the time of the divorces that they had done what they thought right and proper as good wives. The fact that their intentions did not correspond to my needs was probably my own fault. I should have realized, especially on the second occasion, that you do not propose to a woman after only a few meetings over a good meal in a romantic candle-lit setting. Above all, you have to know yourself and know what sort of woman it is that you want to live with. And not the least important factor is whether you are both sexually compatible in the long term. But none of this occurred to me either the first time or the second. In my stupidity I thought that infatuation was the same as love.

Anticipating events somewhat, I can say that I now have a happy, peaceful, and harmonious private life. I first met Aino in December 1971; she was working as a journalist for several Scandinavian newspapers. She was to conduct a series of interviews with me, which resulted in the publication of an earlier version of these memoirs in Sweden and Russia in 1977.

Over the years I came to know better Aino and her husband, Arne Sellermark, the latter becoming my best friend. Arne is an expert on film and a good friend of the Swedish director Ingmar Bergman. Arne became for me a kind of elder brother, and we share an interest that provides an inexhaustible topic of conversation—film. I have been passionately interested in the cinema ever since my childhood. Arne owns a fantastic collection of texts and pictures that I in fact have helped him put in order. He has suffered for many years from a chronic kidney disease. At Christmas in 1996 he was so desperately ill that he could not make his way to the hospital by himself: I had to go with him and take him in a wheelchair. The hours I spent with Arne at Danderyd Hospital gave me an insight into a world hitherto unknown to me—the wonderful work done for humanity by doctors, nurses, and other health-care workers. Arne is considerably better now, his dialysis is functioning well, and we have good times together. Arne has a splendid British sense of humor—but I also know he realizes that he is incurably ill, and he worries about Aino.

In January 1997 I plucked up the courage to ask—in case the worst were to happen to Arne—whether he would have any objection to my marrying Aino. He not only gave us his blessing but suggested that we get married as quickly as possible—and he even made himself available as witness at the wedding on 26 May 1997. (The divorce between Arne and Aino was announced in the beginning of March 1997.)

Aino is my third wife but the first real love in my life. I have a feeling that my mother Olga and father Misha sent her to me from their heaven. She has been in my life for more than twenty-six years—quiet, reliable, helpful, and loyal. She was born in rural Sweden and is thus very down to earth. She has something of my mother Olga's suspicion of people who she thinks are trying to exploit me, but she also has extremely good relationships with our neighbors in our little Swiss village. Having been born in the countryside herself, she can talk to country people in their own terms, and she is the same with everybody, whether high or low. She loves working in the garden among the plants and flowers and all the little creatures that find their way to us. We have hedgehogs and squirrels living on our land, a family of foxes have their den on an overgrown part of the hillside, and we are woken in the mornings by a multitude of birds.

I am reminded of the words that Johan Movinger, the old priest from Högalid, had written on a photograph of his wife, Marianne, that he kept on his desk: "My one and all." That was the finest thing I had heard a husband call his wife, and it illustrates as well as anything the kind of person he was. For me, it is not until now, in my seventies, that I am able to say that of my wife. I can say it of Aino, the only woman, except for my mother Olga, who has lived selflessly with me and for me. She is my beloved wife, my lover, my sister, my mother: My one and all.

Without becoming too sentimental, I can honestly say that I have never been so happy in my whole life. Of course it hurts when Aino and I think of how long it took us to find each other, and that is why we are so careful with the years that we have left. When we are together with Arne in Sweden we are actually quite a little family group.

I think my personal happiness has been reflected in my work. Why else would the critics be so united in their view that my artistry is now in its third flowering?

When I gave a concert in Berlin in March 1997, the critics were rapturous. As all music-lovers know, German music critics are extremely competent and impossible to deceive. I will take the liberty of concluding this chapter with an extract from a review by Manuel Brug in the Berlin paper *Tagesspiegel* (30 March 1997).

> Expression is the enemy of singers, as we have seen in the case of Maria Callas and Ljuba Welitsch, who burnt out like comets. We would not want to forego such unadulterated tones, incandescent in their fervor and aimed directly at the gut. But there are other ways. Emotion as art that has become second nature: technique perfected not simply to demonstrate control of the vocal cords and fluent functioning of the throat muscles, but used with intelligence and skill to produce emotions in the head of the listener. The artificial nature of song as an art form is transcended by style, taste and creative eloquence instead of directness and raw beauty.
>
> A singer who has embodied this ideal like no other since the war is Nicolai Gedda. He also has an incomparable extra element in his repertoire and a magnificent command of language and idiomatic sensitivity, gifts that make him exceptional, a lyricist of the highest rank who still has complete mastery of the riches of his medium, even at the age of seventy-two, when others have been living off their pensions for decades. And we are given not just *les beaux restes* of his now graying or fading vocal resources, with which many a former idol seeks to entertain us, but we hear the timbre, grace, ease of the *voix mixte* and of the flowing piano of the eternally young Gedda whom we know from so many of our favorite recordings. . . .
>
> Of course it is no longer the scintillating brilliance of earlier days; he holds back, but shines all the more radiantly when he needs to. His breathing is shorter, yet exemplary, his vibrato restrained, his tempo controlled. . . . Seldom have we heard Strauss's delicacies sung with so little pretension, with such clear diction, so palpable and yet noble in phrasing. The refined pianissimo climax in the serenade

from Lalo's *Roi d'Ys* would have brought honor to any Radames who could only bellow his "Celeste Aïda" high b. The tender melancholy of the Rimsky-Korsakov pieces, the robust gaiety of Dvořák's gypsy melodies, the *emphase* in Giordano's "Amor ti vieta": an evening etched in silverpoint. The artistry is complete: focused, a little less incisive perhaps, but more than compensating in spontaneity—and always the master.

TWENTY

Peace and Happiness in La Chaumière

AFTER MY FATHER'S DEATH my mother Olga complained increasingly about how hard it was for her to live alone in the big house in Danderyd on the outskirts of Stockholm. I decided to sell the house and get two separate flats in the center of the city, a larger one for her and a smaller studio for me that I could use for my overnight stays whenever I came to Sweden.

At the time that I was selling the Danderyd house I was also beginning to think about taking up residence abroad. My good friend George London had a house built for himself just outside of Lausanne, and he inspired me with enthusiasm for Switzerland. I had attained such levels of income from my engagements that it was becoming necessary for me to consider moving away from Sweden—if I continued to be registered there for taxes, I would have to be prepared for double taxation. I also detested collecting all the receipts that the Swedish authorities demanded for approval of expense claims. It was the same nightmare every year: I had to go home from America to submit my tax declaration, and there would be my mother Olga surrounded by papers and receipts with a tax adviser making the calculations and writing everything down. In fact the accountant who helped me with my declaration was the person who suggested that I do as everyone else in my situation did and register myself as a resident in Switzerland. So that was the course I took, and the search began for a suitable house to buy.

I was then newly married for the second time, and we drove around the Lausanne area with George London and his wife, eventually deciding on an old farmhouse in the canton of Vaud. La Chaumière had originally

191

been a small dwelling-house built in the Swiss country style. The interiors of the cozy little rooms on the upper floor were paneled and extremely pretty, and the only thing that spoiled the idyll was the primitive and dilapidated farmhouse kitchen. The road passed rather close by, but that helped to make the house and its enormous garden affordable. There were no neighbors in the immediate vicinity, and once the house was thoroughly renovated and extended it was very attractive indeed. I registered myself as a resident in Switzerland in 1968, though for many years I used La Chaumière only as a summer cottage when I was on leave from the Met.

I have now been living in Switzerland year-round for the last thirty years, with regular trips home to Sweden. Aino, my third wife, fell in love with the area as soon as she arrived here with me for the first time. She was born in the Swedish countryside and the surroundings remind her of her childhood environment on the shores of Lake Vättern in southern Sweden. The nearest community is the little medieval town of Morges, which holds a market on Wednesday and Saturday mornings. It is so nice to see the local farmers come in with their produce, everything from vegetables to bread and cheese, meat and fish. The people here are kind and friendly, and no one bothers about a world-famous face in the crowd. That was probably the reason my late neighbor Audrey Hepburn also bought and restored an old farmhouse here. Now she rests in the picturesque tranquil churchyard, just a stone's throw from her beloved home.

We have the most wonderful view over Lake Geneva (or Lac Léman, as they say here in French-speaking Switzerland) from our windows in La Chaumière. Weather permitting, we can see right over to the French Alps and the summit of Mont Blanc, like a white sugar loaf, with the Jura range on the other side.

The days pass peacefully and congenially. Living down here month by month, we can follow the changes of the seasons. Our garden is wonderful when all the fruit trees are blossoming and the lilac, jasmine, and honeysuckle are in bloom—not to mention the thousands of roses.

Previously there was no one here to enjoy either the fruit trees in blossom or their harvest. Now we can take delight in nature's rich gifts. Sitting in the shade of a cherry tree weighed down with juicy fruit and hearing the joyous song of the birds on a warm afternoon is one of God's blessings. There is also a large swimming pool in the garden, which is a great pleasure on hot summer days. In the summer when we are on our own and the weather is good we eat our meals out in the garden—I love barbecues.

I also enjoy reading aloud to Aino when we have some free time. She, like me, is interested in the classics and, again like me, read all the Russian classics long before we met. What we enjoy together nowadays are the great French writers: Balzac, Flaubert, Maupassant, Anatole France, Zola. We also read English-language and German authors, and we do not neglect our own Swedish writers such as August Strindberg and Selma Lagerlöf. Reading has also made me watch less and less television, whereas before in America I could sit in front of the TV set long into the night. We go to bed early now, almost like the farmers in the district, and we get up quite early, if not exactly at first light.

In the spring of 1994 a splendid thing happened in our life down here. Aino was in the habit of taking a walk almost every day to get to know the surrounding area. She usually went as far as the village with the beautiful medieval castle, about the right distance from the point of view of exercise. But sometimes she was forced to turn back because of a dark brown Gordon Setter lying on guard outside a farm; he would jump up and put his paws on her shoulders and she thought he did not want to let her pass. One April day I happened to be free and went with Aino on her walk. We met the dog and I called out "Bonjour." He wagged his shaggy tail in pleasure and ran along happily at our side all the way up to the castle. There was a grocery shop nearby so I went in and bought a sausage for the dog, who of course was overjoyed. We christened our new friend Tolly, and so he remained until we discovered his real name. He is called Blackie, and he belongs to a wonderful Swiss wine-growing family with four delightful children. The father's parents also live on the farm. The maternal grandmother lives nearby, and she is a leading light in the local music society. We have really enjoyed all the convivial evenings we have spent at the home of this charming family. It is a marvelous feeling for two people on their own like Aino and me to sit in the huge and homey country kitchen eating dinner while the children rush around noisily, full of health and vigor.

Our private life both here and in Sweden is simple and natural. I do not have a busy social life; we only meet people we really get along well with. Despite having lived in La Chaumière since 1968, it is only recently that I have made friends with genuine locals. And strangely enough it was through our meeting Blackie, the cleverest of dogs, who waits for us excitedly every day.

It is thanks to this healthy country life that I have managed to preserve my voice. Of course I sing nowhere near as much as I used to, but I still do concerts now and then. Those who listen to me, and particularly reviewers, express surprise that my voice continues to sound so young and fresh. That has led to requests for numerous radio interviews to explain the phenomenon, while the interviewer plays my records to illustrate my career.

I also have students who come to me from all over the world. I put a lot of myself into teaching and am thus unwilling to take more than two pupils a day and for not more than two or at most three days a week. As a responsible teacher you have to be alert the whole time and observe the slightest little fault. I have given a dozen master classes over the years, but I avoid them now because I do not think it profits the students at all. In the course of a week or ten days each student gets perhaps just a couple of lessons, because the number of participants is so great. If students want to work with me continuously, I am happy to have them both at my home in Switzerland and in Stockholm. As a teacher I feel a great sense of responsibility for my pupils, and I try to ensure that they do not lose their skills because of too lengthy intervals between lessons. I know there are plenty of charlatans among singing tutors, and many of them charge sky-high fees. I have seen the lamentable effects in students who have been to numerous such teachers and are totally confused by so many incorrect ways of singing.

I have said before that I have always regarded singing as a vocation. Throughout my life I have been convinced that my own voice was a gift from God, and I believed that this meant that I had to tend it carefully. I have often thought that, despite being born to impecunious parents, I was not badly off. Obviously in an artistic career such as mine there is a strong element of asserting oneself through singing to compensate for other shortcomings and difficult experiences in childhood. I think I strove not so much to win everyone's love as to gain attention for myself as a person. I have certainly had the feeling that without my voice I would have been a nonentity. When we are young we do not understand that it is enough simply to be a good and kind human being; the desire to make something of ourselves in some way is inherent in us all.

I am glad to be able to assert now that my success has not spoiled me. All the parts I dreamed of singing came to me without my having to ask for them. I have thus never been guilty of conspiring against colleagues by proposing myself for certain roles. That is a comforting thought as you get older. I have also striven to remain true to my origins and to regard myself as the same private person I used to be. Returning to Stockholm at regular intervals and seeing old friends from my school days helped to keep me the simple boy from the working-class district of Södermalm. I have also retained my shyness and have never been one to go up and slap people on the back and be on first-name terms with everybody. Many people have interpreted my shyness as arrogance, especially when I became famous and started earning significant money. Charitable foundations would be annoyed with me when I did not have time to sing at all their events, both in Sweden and in America. If I had agreed to everything I was asked to do, my voice would have been totally worn out several decades ago.

I have also not fallen victim to the greed that frequently accompanies success and large earnings. I made no effort to invest my income in profitable companies. Despite having worked in a bank I have never bought and sold pieces of paper or moved capital around. I have been content with a normal return, even if it was small compared with the prospects promised by speculation in stocks. I realized that that way of life would upset both my work and my sleep, since nobody can predict losses in business.

I have employed the vanity of artistic creation as the motivating force in my work. As a private individual I lack all desire to be conspicuous. I love going around in my old clothes, and the fact that I am nevertheless relatively well-dressed is not something for which I can take personal credit. I regard all purchases for myself as unnecessary. The same applies to status symbols such as cars and boats. In my second marriage I had to get a big solid Volvo for my wife, who thought that an "opera star" should have a limousine in his garage. When we separated I sold the car, and now there are two bicycles in the garage.

I like keeping our house comfortable, since my wife Aino and I spend most of our time at home when I am not giving concerts abroad. The beauty of the home is for our own enjoyment, not for show.

I am extremely satisfied with my present agreeable life. What has happened is that I have become friends with myself. I was convinced for many years that I was unable truly to love another person, a feeling that emanated from my unhappiness with my own situation and my inability even to love myself, since I could not be my real self. At times my sense of inadequacy took on such proportions that I saw suicide as the only way out. I would fantasize about taking the train right up into Swedish Lappland, getting off somewhere and just walking straight out into the wilderness, walking and walking until I collapsed and froze to death.

Of course I made an effort to analyze the origin of that self-loathing, and what I concluded was that my birth as an unwanted child continued to haunt me. Even being aware of that, however, I still could not control the depressive moods that came over me at the most inconvenient times. It only took somebody saying good-bye on the telephone too abruptly and banging the receiver down, or someone knocking too hard on a door. The causes of this feeling of worthlessness were thus often very childish. If there was a row in the family, I would sink into the blackest despair. I once heard a member of the family say that I might have a fine voice, but that was the only thing that was good about me. Such an utterance completely annihilated me. It strengthened my conviction that had it not been for my voice not a single person would have bothered about me, not a single one of all those who now flocked around me.

My mother Olga's unhappy youth in Russia made her view everybody very critically. She had seen families selling out their own relations or denouncing them so that they ended up in prison camps, just to win some little privilege. She thus came to rely on hardly anyone else, and she retained this cynical attitude all her life. When she saw how people thronged around me in my success she thought everyone was trying to cheat me or lead me astray. To some extent she was right, but I was hardly ever willing to admit it to her. I preferred to defy her, and the ostensible friends of mine whom she detested most were the very ones I chose to associate with. That was how I was indeed cheated, not least financially, by those I imagined to be my best friends. And had it not been for my defiance of my mother, my second marriage would have come to an end after a year. But I wanted to show her that I had done the right thing. I would get furious with her whenever she maintained that she was the only one I had to thank for my career. If I tried to point out that I had also worked and studied hard myself, she did not want to listen. Everything I represented as a singer was due to her and my father Misha.

I shall remain deeply grateful to my parents for as long as I live. I have said that before, but it deserves repeating. I must add, however, that it was not entirely good for me to see only those two as my benefactors and not to credit myself for any part of the way I turned out. It had a negative impact on my self-confidence. And this feeling that I was worth nothing unless I sang was the main reason that I devoted all my energies to my art (my second wife used to yell at me when we quarreled: "Don't say anything, just sing!").

Even if I sank to the depths of despair, that depression could soon be driven away if I got some pleasurable work that also involved associating with stimulating people. My character was fairly much the same as that of many other artists: I was free and uninhibited on stage but very shy in private. That was one reason for my persistent refusal to appear on American television talk shows, where the interview victim had to be prepared to bare his soul. Perhaps Peter O'Toole suffered the same fear when he was persuaded to do a talk show: he turned up drunk, collapsed, and had to be carried out.

It was almost equally hard for me to go to parties; I could never be completely natural because I am totally dependent on feeling rapport with others. In general I am not a good socializer. Even though I usually will not directly refuse an invitation if I am free, I nearly always regret it later and prefer to stay at home rather than stand in a corner with a glass in my hand making small talk about the weather. So on such occasions I may seem cold and reserved.

The fact that I avoid social life nowadays does not mean that I lack self-confidence. I am aware now of my worth both as a person and as an artist. I can look at myself with humor, self-criticism, and indulgence. The path to that insight has of course been mainly through experience of life, but literature has also been a great help. And last but not least through my wife.

I no longer allow myself to be exploited by others. This does not mean that I am uncooperative, but I go no further than I wish to, both privately and professionally. If I do not want to sing in a particular place, then I do not sing there, and if I do not want to see a certain person, then I do not do so.

My present psychological equilibrium and greater sense of self-confidence should not suggest that I regard myself in any way as perfect. As an artist I will always retain my self-criticism, and as a person I know that not even a long life is enough to develop perfection. One can only strive toward it daily.

When I started out on my career as a singer I was very poor, and many people believe that financial hardship makes for a good beginning. To some extent it can spur an artist—why did Rembrandt paint his best pictures when he was so poor that he had to struggle to get enough food to survive?—and by no means is it certain that an artist's best achievements will be produced in the years of greatest material comfort. But whether that also applies to singers I am not at all sure: a starving singer cannot make his abdominal muscles function as they should.

Nevertheless other kinds of suffering can in my opinion improve a singer's artistry. Singing while having to contend with personal problems is dreadful, but after living through a crisis you notice that you have in fact developed in human terms, assuming of course that you have not snapped under the strain. Overcoming a crisis gives increased life experience that enables you to see more clearly the larger significance of the musical work you are performing. Difficult personal experiences can have a positive effect on artistic performance. Your maturity as a human being is made manifest in what you achieve as an artist.

Many people think that life is so short that we cannot afford to suffer any hardships or difficulties. They would rather go around in a constant state of intoxication and turn to alcohol or drugs to achieve the desired effect. Fortunately I do not count myself among them. Of course even I realize that we have a very short time here on earth, and it is pitiful that so much of it has to be spent in anxiety and torment. I have often woken at night and worried about the mistakes I have made in life. Why did I waste so many years on two failed marriages? But then comes the sensible reflection: if things had not been as they were, I might not have the happiness I have today.

Nowadays I am grateful for every morning that I wake up and hear my wife singing as she putters around the house. I know that we cannot continue as before, looking forward to future events, because I am only too aware that the future is one day closer to the inevitable end. All we can do is humbly hope for another sunny day, perhaps another spring.

TWENTY-ONE

Final Reflections

IT BECAME SOMETHING of an *idée fixe* with me that if I had not had God's gift of a voice, I would have been completely worthless. That is why I concentrated every day on improving the details of the musical works I had learned, and I have continued thus for more than forty years.

By keeping up this constant polishing of my voice I was able, in the autumn of 1993, at the age of sixty-eight, to record two CDs for Philips-Polygram in Munich. One consists solely of Russian Orthodox church music, the other of Russian folk music. To assist me I had an ensemble of five male voices (all with their roots in Orthodox music) and a conductor who doubled as a tenor. I was the soloist in this fantastic little choir, which is based in Munich, where the young conductor, Vladimir Cielkovich, is also responsible for the singing in the Russian Orthodox Church on Salvator Platz. For the folk music we had a little instrumental ensemble consisting of balalaika, guitar, bass, and Russian accordion. The whole recording took two and a half days, plus two rehearsals. I heard from Polygram that they thought both recordings were little gems; there are not many singers nowadays who can manage that kind of music.

The financial reward would not be large, but that was not important. The main thing as far as I was concerned was to document the music that now lies closest to my heart. For me it was a song of praise and of gratitude to Providence, which arranged for me to come into the right hands when I was a baby. The circle is completed as I increasingly sing the hymns and songs that I began with as a little boy in the Gedächtniskirche in Leipzig under the direction of my good and kindhearted foster-father Michail Ustinoff.

I am happy to share my many years of musical experience and solid technical ability with younger singers. I began teaching on a small scale in the 1980s and continue now to the extent that my time allows. I take great pleasure in working with young people who have a will to learn and improve themselves. No young singers should think that their careers are mapped out before them simply because they have fine voices. You also have to be free of anxieties and pressures and open to what a tutor has to give.

A good example of this was an English teacher who was one of a dozen pupils taking part in a ten-day course I gave for young male singers in the summer of 1988 in Morges. His voice was not what one would call beautiful and he knew nothing of technique, least of all the control of breathing. After the first lesson he burst into tears and asked to continue as a passive student, just sitting and listening while the others sang. I persuaded him not to give up so easily, and he stayed on as an active pupil. Even in those ten days I noticed that none of the others with their superior voices assimilated what they were learning as easily as he. I had before me an intelligent person with a strong will to learn to sing. This student was lucky because he lived in Lausanne, ten minutes by car from my home. He continued with regular lessons, quickly improved in technique and confidence, and remarkably his voice also took on a new timbre, perhaps not the most pleasing in the world but nevertheless of high enough quality to audition with an agent and give his own concerts. He is sensible and has followed my advice to specialize in the kind of music to which his voice is suited. Since he has a family and three children, I have advised him against giving up his secure post as a teacher and becoming a freelance singer—which he understands. The important thing for this young man is that he should enjoy his voice. The money he has paid out for tuition will be recouped partly through his concerts and partly through taking on pupils himself. I have sent him some young people whose ambition is simply to sing for their own pleasure. He has enough knowledge now to teach them all they need. It gives me great satisfaction when I succeed in instilling in a young singer knowledge that is readily absorbed.

I am frequently asked nowadays how long I intend to go on singing. I usually reply that I will do so for as long as my voice continues to sound fresh and undamaged.

Some people also wonder whether I would have wished for more from my profession or from life. As far as the former is concerned, I have been able to do everything I have wanted, without even having to propose or persuade. I am therefore very content and grateful for the career that has been granted to me. I have never been a singer for the masses, which probably has something to do with my introverted nature and dislike of any fuss made about me personally. One of my fans once wrote rather beautifully in a letter that my voice was loved by good people. Perhaps that is one reason why I have not been able to fill big arenas!

What more do I want of life? Only that my wife and I retain for a few more years the health and physical vitality we have now. If we are granted a long life with our health intact, then I would most wish to keep my sight so that I can continue reading the treasures of world literature to her.

If a fatal illness should befall me, I do not think I would want to subject myself to pointless operations. I know how overworked and pressured doctors are today and how vainly many sufferers struggle to live for just a short while longer. I believe time for all of us is somehow measured, so why resist when that time has run out?

I have had a lot from life, even if not all of it has been good. I have sought to atone as best I could for the personal mistakes I have made. I have never consciously tried to deceive anybody close to me, even if I myself have been deceived. Through my reading of Dostoyevsky and Balzac and others I have come to understand, and am able to see through, the mechanisms that motivate the majority of individuals.

I believe in God with a sincere and childlike faith; I believe without questioning. I always have a little icon with me on my travels, a triptych that I keep wrapped in an old Russian handkerchief. When I arrive in a hotel room I set it up on my bedside table. For many years I carried the little cardboard icon that I was given by my father Misha when he came home from a tour with the Kuban Cossacks in southern Italy. On the back he had written that the saint's picture had been blessed in the cathedral at Bari. That little piece of cardboard was my guardian angel right up to the mid-1980s; I lost it on a journey from Stockholm to Hamburg when I was taking out my flight ticket. I was deeply distressed and hunted for it all over Europe, but to no avail. It was totally valueless for anyone except myself and had probably been swept up as rubbish.

Aino proffered consolation, telling me that the power of the icon lay in my faith. She urged me to replace my loss with the little triptych I travel with now, and which stands on my bedside table even when I am at home.

It is wonderful to have belief in a higher power.

Opera, Oratorio, and Operetta Repertoire

The dates given for the operas in Nicolai Gedda's repertoire indicate the first occasion on which the work was performed by Gedda at the particular venue.

OPERA

American

Barber

Vanessa (world premiere)	January 1958	Metropolitan Opera, New York	Dimitri Mitropoulos

Bernstein

Candide (concert)	December 1989	Barbican Centre, London	Leonard Bernstein

Menotti

The Last Savage (U.S. premiere)	January 1964	Metropolitan Opera, New York	Thomas Schippers

French

Adam

Le Postillon de Longjumeau	April 1952 (opera debut)	Stockholm Opera	Kurt Bendix

Auber

Fra Diavolo	November 1968	San Francisco Opera	Mario Bernardi

Berlioz

Benvenuto Cellini	June 1961	Holland Festival, Amsterdam	Georges Prêtre
Benvenuto Cellini	November 1964	Geneva Opera	Louis de Froment
Benvenuto Cellini (concert)	March 1965	Alice Tully Hall, New York	Thomas Scherman
Benvenuto Cellini	December 1966	Covent Garden, London	Sir John Pritchard
Benvenuto Cellini	March 1976	La Scala, Milan	Sir Colin Davis
Benvenuto Cellini (concert)	May 1983	Carnegie Hall, New York	Eve Queler

Berlioz

La Damnation de Faust (concert)	June 1953	Cours du Palais Royale, Paris (debut)	Pierre Dervaux
La Damnation de Faust (concert)	September 1959	Montreux Festival	Igor Markevich
La Damnation de Faust (concert)	August 1963	Edinburgh Festival	Sir Georg Solti
La Damnation de Faust (concert)	January 1969	Rome (RAI radio)	Georges Prêtre
La Damnation de Faust (concert)	October 1969	Théâtre des Champs-Elysées, Paris	Georges Prêtre
La Damnation de Faust (concert)	July 1973	Royal Festival Hall, London	Sir Colin Davis

La Damnation de Faust (concert)	June 1975	La Scala, Milan	Georges Prêtre
La Damnation de Faust (concert)	January 1983	Boston Symphony Hall	Seiji Ozawa
La Damnation de Faust (concert)	January 1983	Carnegie Hall, New York	Seiji Ozawa
La Damnation de Faust (concert)	October 1984	Salle Pleyel, Paris	Daniel Barenboim
La Damnation de Faust (concert)	June 1986	Tivoli Gardens, Copenhagen	Michel Tabachnik

Berlioz

Les Troyens	May 1969	Rome (RAI radio)	Georges Prêtre

Bizet

Carmen (concert)	October 1954	Musikverein, Vienna	Herbert von Karajan
Carmen	April 1964	La Scala, Milan	Georges Prêtre
Carmen	December 1967	Metropolitan Opera, New York	Zubin Mehta
Carmen	April–May 1968	Metropolitan tour	Alain Lombard

Bizet

Les Pêcheurs de Perles (concert)	January 1974	Carnegie Hall, New York	Eve Queler
Les Pêcheurs de Perles	April 1977	Atlanta Concert Hall	William Noll
Les Pêcheurs de Perles	October 1988	Utrecht Radio Hall	Henry Lewis
Les Pêcheurs de Perles	October 1989	Stockholm Concert House	Michel Plasson

Boieldieu

| *La Dame Blanche* (concert) | November 1964 | Concertgebouw, Amsterdam | Jean Fournet |

Debussy

Pelléas et Mélisande (concert)	March 1958	Carnegie Hall, New York	Jean Morel
Pelléas et Mélisande (concert)	June 1960	Stockholm Concert House (radio)	Jean Fournet
Pelléas et Mélisande	December 1962	Metropolitan Opera, New York	Ernest Ansermet
Pelléas et Mélisande (concert)	November 1971	Herkulessaal, Munich	Rafael Kubelík

Delibes

| *Lakmé* (concert) | April 1981 | Carnegie Hall, New York | Eve Queler |

Gounod

Faust	February 1957	Monte Carlo Opera	Jean Fournet
Faust	March 1957	Pittsburgh Opera (American debut)	Richard Karp
Faust	November 1957	Metropolitan Opera, New York (Met debut)	Jean Morel
Faust	April–May 1958	Metropolitan tour	Jean Morel
Faust	April 1963	Geneva Opera	Jean Fournet
Faust	June 1963	Staatsoper, Vienna	Georges Prêtre

Faust	January 1966	La Scala, Milan	Georges Prêtre
Faust	September 1969	Budapest Opera	Miklós Erdélyi
Faust	May 1971	Teatro Colón, Buenos Aires	Gianandrea Gavazzeni
Faust	February 1972	Teatro dell'Opera, Rome	Georges Prêtre
Faust	June 1975	Paris Opéra	Michel Plasson

Gounod

Mireille	July 1954	Aix-en-Provence Festival	André Cluytens
Mireille	June 1956	Opéra-Comique, Paris	Jean Fournet

Gounod

Roméo et Juliette	April 1968	Metropolitan Opera, New York	Francesco Molinari-Pradelli

Lully

Armide	May 1957	Bordeaux Opera	Jean Fournet

Massenet

Manon	October 1959	Metropolitan Opera, New York	Jean Morel
Manon	November 1960	New Orleans Opera	Renato Cellini
Manon	December 1963	Philadelphia Opera	Anton Guadagno
Manon	September 1971	San Francisco Opera	Jean Périsson

Massenet

Werther (concert)	November 1965	Carnegie Hall, New York	Robert Lawrence
Werther	March 1977	Kennedy Center, Washington, D.C.	Jean Périsson
Werther	March 1982	Miami Opera	Antonio de Almeida

Meyerbeer

Les Huguenots (concert)	February 1971	Konzerthaus, Vienna	Ernst Märzendorfer

Meyerbeer

Le Prophète (concert)	July 1970	Turin (RAI radio)	Henry Lewis

Offenbach

Les Contes D'Hoffmann	November 1958	Metropolitan Opera, New York	Jean Morel
Les Contes D'Hoffmann	October 1961	Stockholm Opera	Herbert Sandberg
Les Contes D'Hoffmann	October 1974	Paris Opéra	Georges Prêtre
Les Contes D'Hoffmann	January 1980	Miami Opera	Antonio de Almeida
Les Contes D'Hoffmann	December 1982	Hartford Opera	Antonio de Almeida
Les Contes D'Hoffmann	April 1983	Houston Opera	John De Main
Les Contes D'Hoffmann	November 1989	Volksoper, Vienna	Franz Bauer-Theussl

Rameau

Platée	July 1956	Aix-en-Provence Festival	Hans Rosbaud

Italian

Bellini

I Puritani (concert)	April 1963	Carnegie Hall, New York	Richard Bonynge
I Puritani	December 1970	Teatro Comunale, Florence	Riccardo Muti
I Puritani	March 1971	Teatro di San Carlo, Naples	Mario Rossi

Bellini

La Sonnambula	February 1963	Metropolitan Opera, New York	Silvio Varviso

Cimarosa

Il Matrimonio Segreto	June 1964	Vienna (Austrian television)	H. P. Adler

Donizetti

Don Pasquale	December 1978	Metropolitan Opera, New York	Nicola Rescigno
Don Pasquale	April–May 1979	Metropolitan tour	Nicola Rescigno

Donizetti

L'Elisir d'Amore	January 1961	Metropolitan Opera, New York	Fausto Cleva
L'Elisir d'Amore	May 1973	Theater an der Wien	Silvio Varviso
L'Elisir d'Amore	January 1981	Covent Garden, London	Claudio Scimone

Donizetti

Lucia de Lammermoor	February 1969	Metropolitan Opera, New York	Carlo Franci
Lucia de Lammermoor	June 1977	Zurich Festival	Nello Santi
Lucia de Lammermoor	February 1980	Budapest Opera	

Puccini

La Bohème	October 1964	Stockholm Opera	
La Bohème	February 1965	Staatsoper, Vienna	Argeo Quadri
La Bohème	December 1969	Metropolitan Opera, New York	Fausto Cleva

Puccini

Madama Butterfly	January 1961	Metropolitan Opera, New York	Jean Morel

Puccini

Tosca	February 1964	Staatsoper, Vienna	Argeo Quadri
Tosca	September 1964	Stockholm Opera	Fausto Cleva
Tosca	April 1972	Boston Symphony Hall	Sarah Caldwell
Tosca	1980	Belgrade Opera	
Tosca	January 1984	Warsaw Opera	
Tosca	January 1987	Nice Opera	Emil Tchakarov

Tosca	July 1989	Savonlinna Festival	Sixten Ehrling

Rossini

Guillaume Tell	May 1972	Teatro Comunale, Florence	Riccardo Muti

Verdi

Otello (role of Cassio)	June 1957	Paris Opéra	Georges Sébastian

Verdi

Rigoletto	April 1954	Covent Garden, London (debut)	Sir John Pritchard
Rigoletto	September 1956	Paris Opéra	Pierre Dervaux
Rigoletto	December 1956	Stockholm Opera	Kurt Bendix
Rigoletto	June 1960	Reykjavík Opera	Václav Smetácek
Rigoletto	June 1962	Staatsoper, Vienna	Francesco Molinari-Pradelli
Rigoletto	February 1966	Deutsche Oper, Berlin	Giuseppe Patanè
Rigoletto	March 1966	Stuttgart Opera	Josef Dünnwald
Rigoletto	March 1966	Staatsoper, Munich	Arrigo Guarnier
Rigoletto	October 1966	Metropolitan Opera, New York	Lamberto Gardelli
Rigoletto	November 1969	Belgrade Opera	Bogdan Babich

Verdi

La Traviata	August 1956	Paris Opéra	Georges Sébastian
La Traviata	November 1956	Stockholm Opera	Herbert Sandberg
La Traviata	January 1960	Metropolitan Opera, New York	Fausto Cleva
La Traviata	October 1970	Civic Opera, Chicago	Bruno Bartoletti
La Traviata	December 1971	Staatsoper, Vienna	Josef Krips
La Traviata	June 1972	Covent Garden, London	Carlo Felice Cillario
La Traviata	March 1981	Budapest Opera	István Dénes
La Traviata	October 1983	Metropolitan Opera New York (final Met performance)	Sir John Pritchard

Verdi

Un Ballo in Maschera	February 1965	Staatsoper, Vienna	Argeo Quadri
Un Ballo in Maschera	March 1970	Stockholm Opera	Silvio Varviso
Un Ballo in Maschera	October 1975	Metropolitan Opera, New York	Henry Lewis
Un Ballo in Maschera	February 1977	Covent Garden, London	Edward Downes
Un Ballo in Maschera	December 1985	Stockholm Opera	Eri Klas

Verdi

I Vespri Siciliani	January 1974	Metropolitan Opera, New York	James Levine

German

Gluck

| *Alceste* | December 1960 | Metropolitan Opera, New York | Erich Leinsdorf |

Gluck

| *Iphigénie en Tauride* | October 1956 | Cologne (Radio Köln) | Joseph Keilberth |

Gluck

Orfeo ed Euridice (concert)	July 1955	Aix-en-Provence Festival	Louis de Froment
Orfeo ed Euridice	April 1973	Paris Opéra	Manuel Rosenthal
Orfeo ed Euridice	February 1975	Rome (RAI radio)	Manuel Rosenthal

Haydn

Orfeo	May 1967	Theater an der Wien	Richard Bonynge
Orfeo	August 1967	Edinburgh Festival	Richard Bonynge
Orfeo (concert)	February 1968	Carnegie Hall, New York	Richard Bonynge

Liebermann

| *Die Schule der Frauen* | August 1957 | Salzburg Festival | George Szell |

Mozart

| *Così fan tutte* | July 1955 | Aix-en-Provence Festival | Hans Rosbaud |
| *Così fan tutte* | July 1959 | Salzburg Festival | Karl Böhm |

Mozart

Don Giovanni	January 1953	La Scala, Milan	Herbert von Karajan
Don Giovanni	December 1953	Teatro dell'Opera, Rome	Herbert von Karajan
Don Giovanni	July 1956	Aix-en-Provence Festival	Hans Rosbaud
Don Giovanni	November 1956	Stockholm Opera	Bertil Bokstedt
Don Giovanni	November 1957	Metropolitan Opera, New York	Karl Böhm
Don Giovanni	April–May 1958	Metropolitan tour	Erich Leinsdorf
Don Giovanni	August 1961	Salzburg Festival	Herbert von Karajan
Don Giovanni	June 1962	Staatsoper, Vienna	Josef Krips
Don Giovanni	September 1963	Cuvilliéstheater, Munich	Karl Böhm
Don Giovanni	June 1971	Staatsoper, Hamburg	Bernhard Klee

Mozart

Die Entführung aus dem Serail	July 1954	Aix-en-Provence Festival	Hans Rosbaud
Die Entführung aus dem Serail	November 1956	Stockholm Opera	Herbert Sandberg
Die Entführung aus dem Serail	August 1957	Salzburg Festival	Joseph Keilberth
Die Entführung aus dem Serail	October 1979	Metropolitan Opera, New York	James Levine

Mozart

Idomeneo (role of Idamante)	January 1957	Stockholm Opera	Herbert Sandberg
Idomeneo (concert)	February 1971	Rome (RAI radio)	Sir Colin Davis

Mozart

Die Zauberflöte	December 1954	Paris Opéra	Georges Sébastian
Die Zauberflöte	December 1955	La Scala, Milan	Herbert von Karajan
Die Zauberflöte	November 1956	Stockholm Opera	Herbert Sandberg
Die Zauberflöte	November 1958	Metropolitan Opera, New York	Erich Leinsdorf
Die Zauberflöte (concert)	May 1961	Royal Festival Hall, London	Otto Klemperer
Die Zauberflöte	June 1962	Theater an der Wien	Herbert von Karajan
Die Zauberflöte	January 1970	Staatsoper, Hamburg	Horst Stein

Orff

Trionfo di Afrodite (role of Lo Sposo)	February 1953	La Scala, Milan	Herbert von Karajan
Trionfo di Afrodite (concert)	March 1953	Herkulessaal, Munich	Eugen Jochum
Trionfo di Afrodite	March 1953	Zurich Festival	Eugen Jochum

Pfitzner

Palestrina (role of Abdisu)	January 1997	Covent Garden, London	Christian Thielemann

R. Strauss

Der Rosenkavalier	October 1952	Stockholm Opera	Leif Segerstam
Der Rosenkavalier	January 1958	Metropolitan Opera, New York	Karl Böhm, Max Rudolf
Der Rosenkavalier	May 1958	Metropolitan tour	Max Rudolf
Der Rosenkavalier	July 1961	Salzburg Festival	Karl Böhm
Der Rosenkavalier	June 1962	Staatsoper, Vienna	Herbert von Karajan
Der Rosenkavalier	August 1962	Staatsoper, Munich	Karl Böhm

Wagner

Lohengrin	January 1966	Stockholm Opera	Silvio Varviso

Weber

Oberon	February 1954	Paris Opéra	André Cluytens
Oberon (concert)	February 1978	Carnegie Hall, New York	Eve Queler

Russian

Mussorgsky

Boris Godunov	December 1960	Metropolitan Opera, New York	Erich Leinsdorf
Boris Godunov (role of Innocent) (concert)	July 1987	Kennedy Center, Washington, D.C.	Mstislav Rostropovich

Prokofiev

War and Peace (concert)	December 1986	Salle Pleyel, Paris	Mstislav Rostropovich

Tchaikovsky

Evgeny Onegin	December 1958	Metropolitan Opera, New York	Dimitri Mitropoulos
Evgeny Onegin	May 1963	Stockholm Opera	Leif Segerstam
Evgeny Onegin (concert)	October 1976	Carnegie Hall, New York	Seiji Ozawa
Evgeny Onegin (concert)	January 1980	Toronto Concert Hall	Andrew Davis
Evgeny Onegin	February 1980	Budapest Opera	
Evgeny Onegin	March 1980	Bolshoi Theater, Moscow	Fuat Mansurov
Evgeny Onegin	April–May 1980	Metropolitan tour	Emil Tchakarov
Evgeny Onegin	August 1980	Teatro Comunale, Florence	Mstislav Rostropovich

Tchaikovsky

Iolanta (concert)	April 1982	Kennedy Center, Washington, D.C.	Mstislav Rostropovich
Iolanta (concert)	April 1982	Carnegie Hall, New York	Mstislav Rostropovich
Iolanta (concert)	December 1984	Salle Pleyel, Paris	Mstislav Rostropovich

Tchaikovsky

Mazepa (concert)	October 1992	Stockholm Opera	Gennadi Rozhdestvensky

Tchaikovsky

Pique Dame	December 1972	Metropolitan Opera, New York	Kazimierz Kord

Czech

Smetana

Dalibor	January 1977	Carnegie Hall, New York	Eve Queler

Smetana

The Bartered Bride	October 1978	Metropolitan Opera, New York	James Levine
The Bartered Bride	April–May 1979	Metropolitan tour	James Levine

Swedish

Naumann

Gustaf Wasa	December 1991	Stockholm Opera	Philip Brunelle

ORATORIO

Bach

B Minor Mass	June 1958	Musikverein, Vienna	Herbert von Karajan
B Minor Mass	April 1959	Montreal Concert Hall	Igor Markevich

Bach

St. John Passion	March 1961	Düsseldorf Concert Hall	Jean Martinon
St. John Passion	May 1961	Théâtre des Champs-Elysées, Paris	Jean Martinon

Bach

St. Matthew Passion	March 1953	Copenhagen (radio)	Mogens Wøldike
St. Matthew Passion	April 1955	St. Eustache Church, Paris	R. P. Martin
St. Matthew Passion	March 1958	Carnegie Hall, New York	Erich Leinsdorf
St. Matthew Passion	February 1961	Royal Festival Hall, London	Otto Klemperer

Beethoven

Missa Solemnis	September 1958	La Scala, Milan	George Szell
Missa Solemnis	August 1959	Salzburg Festival	Herbert von Karajan

Beethoven

Symphony No. 9	February 1956	Turin (RAI radio)	Artur Rodzinski
Symphony No. 9	September 1957	Berlin Concert Hall	André Cluytens
Symphony No. 9	September 1959	Beethoven Hall, Bonn	George Szell

Berlioz

L'Enfance du Christ	May 1957	Rome (RAI radio)	André Cluytens
L'Enfance du Christ	June 1970	Teatro Comunale, Florence	Georges Prêtre
L'Enfance du Christ	September 1985	Lyon Opera	André Krivine

Berlioz

Requiem	August 1956	Cologne (Radio Köln)	Dimitri Mitropoulos
Requiem	June 1969	La Scala, Milan	Georges Prêtre
Requiem	November 1974	Les Invalides, Paris	Sir Colin Davis
Requiem	September 1985	Lyon Concert Hall	Serge Baudo

Berlioz

Te Deum	September 1985	Lyon Concert Hall	Serge Baudo

Brahms

Rinaldo	February 1983	Milan (RAI radio)	Wolfgang Scheidt

Britten

Serenade	January 1957	Stockholm Concert House	Walter Goehr
Serenade	September 1966	Helsinki Concert Hall	Antal Dorati

Bruckner

Te Deum	May 1962	Musikverein, Vienna	Herbert von Karajan

Handel

Acis and Galatea	March 1970	Alice Tully Hall, New York	Frederic Waldman

Handel

Messiah	December 1956	Storkyrkan, Stockholm	Arne Sunnergårdh

Messiah	September 1959	Lucerne Festival Hall	Sir Thomas Beecham
Handel			
Samson	April 1980	Kennedy Center, Washington, D.C.	Stephen Simon
Haydn			
Die Jahreszeiten	June 1962	Herkulessaal, Munich	Rafael Kubelík
Haydn			
Die Schöpfung	March 1954	Théâtre des Champs-Elysées, Paris	André Cluytens
Die Schöpfung	April 1958	Montreal Concert Hall	Igor Markevich
Die Schöpfung	August 1958	Edinburgh Concert Hall	Mogens Wøldike
Die Schöpfung	June 1968	Musikverein, Vienna	Josef Krips
Janáček			
Slavonic Mass	January 1963	Philharmonic Hall, New York	Leonard Bernstein
Kodály			
Psalmus Hungaricus	March 1970	Alice Tully Hall, New York	Frederic Waldman
Psalmus Hungaricus	October 1988	Odense Concert Hall	James Vető
Liszt			
Psalm 13	1987	Zagreb Concert Hall	Vladimir Kranjcevic

Psalm 13	1987	Stockholm Concert House	

Lully

Te Deum	April 1957	San Francisco Concert Hall	Enrique Jordá

Martin

In terra pax	June 1969	Vatican, Rome (concert for Pope Pius VI)	Georges Prêtre

Martin

Le vin herbé	1951	Stockholm Concert House	Eric Ericson

Mendelssohn

Elijah	June 1968	Royal Festival Hall, London	Rafael Frühbeck de Burgos

Mozart

Requiem	June 1962	St. Stephen's Dome, Vienna	Carl Schuricht

Rossini

Stabat Mater	November 1953	Théâtre des Champs-Elysées, Paris	André Cluytens
Stabat Mater	April 1967	Leeds Concert Hall	Carlo Maria Giulini
Stabat Mater	September 1969	Edinburgh Concert Hall	Carlo Maria Giulini

Stravinsky

Oedipus Rex	November 1952	Rome (RAI radio)	Herbert von Karajan

Oedipus Rex	August 1953	Lucerne Festival Hall	Herbert von Karajan
Stravinsky			
Persephone	January 1955	Théâtre des Champs-Elysées, Paris	André Cluytens
Tippett			
A Child of Our Time	February 1953	Turin (RAI radio)	Herbert von Karajan
Verdi			
Requiem	June 1954	Théâtre des Champs-Elysées, Paris	Jean Martinon
Requiem	November 1954	Musikverein, Vienna	Herbert von Karajan
Requiem	April 1961	Musikhalle, Hamburg	Hans Schmidt-Isserstedt
Requiem	January 1962	Royal Festival Hall, London	Carlo Maria Giulini
Requiem	June 1963	Konzerthaus, Vienna	Lorin Maazel
Requiem	July 1971	Festival Orange	Carlo Maria Giulini
Requiem	June 1972	Venice Concert Hall	Thomas Schippers
Requiem	November 1972	Carnegie Hall, New York	Lorin Maazel
Requiem	November 1973	Radio auditorium, Milan	Claudio Abbado

Requiem	July 1979	Dubrovnik Festival	Lovrò von Matačić
Requiem	July 1981	Hollywood Bowl, Los Angeles	Carlo Maria Giulini
Requiem	September 1982	Helsinki Concert Hall	Leif Segerstam
Requiem	May 1984	Tivoli Gardens, Copenhagen	F. Eckert-Hansen

OPERETTA

Lehár

Das Land des Lächelns	April 1965	Volksoper, Vienna	Anton Paulik
Das Land des Lächelns	December 1984	Kongresspalast, Berlin	
Das Land des Lächelns	February– March 1985	German tour	

Lehár

The Merry Widow (concert)	March 1962	Carnegie Hall, New York	Franz Allers

J. Strauss

The Gypsy Baron	November 1959	Metropolitan Opera, New York	Erich Leinsdorf
The Gypsy Baron	April–May 1960	Metropolitan tour	Erich Leinsdorf

Discography

Title	Composer	Date	City	Conductor	Other Performers	Label*
1. *Boris Godunov*	Mussorgsky	July 1952	Paris	Issay Dobrowen	Boris Christoff	EMI
2. *Die lustige Witwe*	Lehár	November 1952	London	Otto Ackerman	Elisabeth Schwarzkopf	EMI
3. *Das Land des Lächelns*	Lehár	November 1952	London	Otto Ackerman	Elisabeth Schwarzkopf	EMI
4. B Minor Mass	Bach	November 1952	London	Herbert von Karajan	Elisabeth Schwarzkopf	EMI
5. Swedish Songs	misc.	1952	Stockholm	Kurt Bendix		Swedish Odeon
6. *Faust*	Gounod	May 1953	Paris	André Cluytens	Victoria de los Angeles, Boris Christoff	EMI
7. Opera Arias (I)	misc.	April 1954	London	Alceo Galliera		EMI
8. *Der Zigeunerbaron*	J. Strauss	May 1954	London	Otto Ackerman	Elisabeth Schwarzkopf	EMI
9. *Eine Nacht in Venedig*	J. Strauss	May 1954	London	Otto Ackerman	Elisabeth Schwarzkopf	EMI
10. *Wiener Blut*	J. Strauss	May 1954	London	Otto Ackerman	Elisabeth Schwarzkopf	EMI
11. *Mireille*	Gounod	July 1954	Paris	André Cluytens	Jeanette Vivalda	EMI
12. *Il Turco in Italia*	Rossini	September 1954	Milan	Gianandrea Gavazzeni	Maria Callas	EMI
13. *Arabella* (excerpts)	R. Strauss	September 1954	London	Lovrò von Matačić	Elisabeth Schwarzkopf	EMI
14. *Persephone*	Stravinsky	January 1955	Paris	André Cluytens		EMI

*In this list, the label EMI includes recordings made for HMV (England and Italy), Pathé Marconi (France), Angel Records (United States), and Electrola (Germany), as all labels are currently part of EMI.

Title	Composer	Date	City	Conductor	Other Performers	Label
15. *Die Fledermaus*	J. Strauss	April 1955	London	Herbert von Karajan	Elisabeth Schwarzkopf	EMI
16. *Madama Butterfly*	Puccini	August 1955	Milan	Herbert von Karajan	Maria Callas	EMI
17. *Le Devin du Village*	Rousseau	April 1956	Paris	Louis de Froment	Janine Micheau	EMI
18. *The Barber of Baghdad*	Cornelius	May 1956	London	Erich Leinsdorf	Elisabeth Schwarzkopf	EMI
19. *Platée*	Rameau	July 1956	Aix-en-Provence	Hans Rosbaud		EMI
20. *Don Giovanni*	Mozart	September 1956	Paris	Hans Rosbaud	Elisabeth Schwarzkopf	EMI
21. *Der Rosenkavalier*	R. Strauss	December 1956	London	Herbert von Karajan	Elisabeth Schwarzkopf	EMI
22. *Ruslan and Ludmilla* (excerpts; Vol. IX of "History of Music in Sound")	Glinka	1957	Paris	Louis Fourestier	Janine Micheau	EMI
23. *Orfeo ed Euridice*	Gluck	March 1957	Paris	Louis de Froment	Janine Micheau	EMI
24. *Aria Recital*	Mozart	June 1957	Paris	André Cluytens		EMI
25. *Capriccio*	R. Strauss	September 1957	London	Wolfgang Sawallisch	Elisabeth Schwarzkopf, Dietrich Fischer-Dieskau, Hans Hotter	EMI
26. *A Life for the Czar*	Glinka	December 1957	Paris	Igor Markevich	Boris Christoff	EMI
27. *Symphony No. 9*	Beethoven	December 1957	Berlin	André Cluytens		EMI
28. *Vanessa*	Barber	February 1958	New York	Dimitri Mitropoulos	Eleanor Steber	RCA
29. *Missa Solemnis*	Beethoven	September 1958	Vienna	Herbert von Karajan	Elisabeth Schwarzkopf	EMI
30. *Faust*	Gounod	October 1958	Paris	André Cluytens	Victoria de los Angeles, Boris Christoff	EMI (stereo)

	Composer	Date	Place	Conductor	Singer	Label
31. *Carmen*	Bizet	September 1959	Paris	Sir Thomas Beecham	Victoria de los Angeles	EMI
32. *Les Pêcheurs de Perles*	Bizet	October 1960	Paris	Pierre Dervaux	Janine Micheau	EMI
33. *Lakmé* (excerpts)	Delibes	March 1961	Paris	Georges Prêtre	Gianna d'Angelo	EMI
34. *Iphigénie en Tauride* (excerpts)	Gluck	April 1961	Paris	Georges Prêtre		EMI
35. *Alceste* (excerpts)	Gluck	May 1961	Paris	Georges Prêtre		EMI
36. *St. Matthew Passion*	Bach	May 1961	London	Otto Klemperer	Elisabeth Schwarzkopf	EMI
37. *Gedda à Paris* (French arias)	misc.	September 1961	Paris	Georges Prêtre		EMI
38. *La Damnation de Faust* (excerpts)	Berlioz	October 1961	Paris	André Cluytens		EMI
39. *L'Enfance du Christ*	Berlioz	October 1961	Paris	André Cluytens		EMI
40. *Die lustige Witwe*	Lehár	July 1962	London	Lovrò von Matačić	Elisabeth Schwarzkopf	EMI (stereo)
41. *Slavonic Mass*	Janáček	January 1963	New York	Leonard Bernstein		CBS
42. *La Bohème*	Puccini	July 1963	Rome	Thomas Schippers	Mirella Freni	EMI
43. *Requiem*	Verdi	September 1963	London	Carlo Maria Giulini	Elisabeth Schwarzkopf, Christa Ludwig, Nicolai Ghiaurov	EMI
44. *Evening Bells* (Russian songs)	misc.	October 1963	New York	Nicolas Afonsky	Choir of the Russian Orthodox Cathedral of New York	EMI
45. *Die Zauberflöte*	Mozart	March–April 1964	London	Otto Klemperer		EMI
46. *Carmen*	Bizet	July 1964	Paris	Georges Prêtre	Maria Callas	EMI
47. *Les Comtes d'Hoffmann*	Offenbach	September 1964	Paris	André Cluytens		EMI

Title	Composer	Date	City	Conductor	Other Performers	Label
48. Roméo et Juliette (excerpts)	Gounod	September 1964	Paris	Alain Lombard		EMI
49. Messiah	Handel	September 1964	London	Otto Klemperer		EMI
50. Favorite Encores	misc.	October 1964	Munich	Willy Mattes		EMI
51. Die Jahreszeiten	Haydn	October 1964	Munich	Wolfgang Gönnenwein		EMI
52. Le Postillon de Longjumeau (excerpts)	Adam	June 1965	Munich	Fritz Lehan		EMI
53. Bella Venezia (operetta arias)	misc.	June 1965	Munich	Willy Mattes	Anneliese Rothenberger	EMI
54. Lieder der Welt (song album)	Munich	July 1965	Munich		acc. Gerald Moore (piano)	EMI
55. Wiener Blut and Giuditta (excerpts)	J. Strauss and Lehár	July 1965	Munich	Willy Mattes		EMI
56. La Forza del Destino (excerpts in German)	Verdi	August 1965	Dresden	Giuseppe Patanè		EMI
57. Zar und Zimmermann	Lortzing	August 1965	Dresden	Robert Heger		EMI
58. Evangelimann (excerpts)	Kienzl	August 1965	Munich	Robert Heger		EMI
59. Land du Välsignade (Swedish songs)	misc.	1966	Stockholm	Nils Grevillius		RCA
60. Die Entführung aus dem Serail	Mozart	February 1966	Vienna	Josef Krips		EMI
61. Christmas Songs	misc.	June 1966	London		acc. Geoffrey Parsons (piano)	EMI

	Composer	Date	City	Conductor	Soloist	Label
62. Italian Duets	Bellini and Donizetti	June 1966	London	Edward Downes	Mirella Freni	EMI
63. *Don Giovanni*	Mozart	June 1966	London	Otto Klemperer	Nicolai Ghiaurov	EMI
64. *Madama Butterfly* (excerpts in German)	Puccini	August 1966	Berlin	Giuseppe Patanè	Anneliese Rothenberger	EMI
65. *L'Elisir d'Amore*	Donizetti	August 1966	Rome	Francesco Molinari-Pradelli	Mirella Freni	EMI
66. *Undine*	Lortzing	September 1966	Berlin	Robert Heger	Anneliese Rothenberger	EMI
67. *Das Land des Lächelns*	Lehár	January 1967	Munich	Willy Mattes	Anneliese Rothenberger	EMI
68. *Die lustige Witwe* (excerpts)	Lehár	June 1967	Munich	Willy Mattes	Anneliese Rothenberger	EMI
69. German Arias	misc.	June 1967	Munich	Heinrich Bender		EMI
70. *Rigoletto*	Verdi	July 1967	Rome	Francesco Molinari-Pradelli		EMI
71. *Eine Nacht in Venedig*	J. Strauss	September 1967	Munich	Franz Allers	Rita Streich	EMI
72. French Songs	misc.	September 1967	Paris		acc. Aldo Ciccolini (piano)	EMI
73. *Guillaume Tell* (excerpts)	Rossini	September 1967	Paris	Alain Lombard		EMI
74. *Firestone Christmas Album*	misc.	October 1967	New York	Irwin Kostal	Leontyne Price	Firestone
75. *Die Entführung aus dem Serail*	Mozart	October 1967	London	Yehudi Menuhin	Mattiwilda Dobbs	EMI
76. *Recondita Armonia* (aria album)	misc.	November 1967	London	Giuseppe Patanè		EMI
77. B Minor Mass	Bach	November 1967	London	Otto Klemperer		EMI

Title	Composer	Date	City	Conductor	Other Performers	Label
78. Swedish Songs	misc.	1968	Stockholm	Einar Ralf	Student Chorus	EMI
79. *Martha*	von Flotow	March 1968	Munich	Robert Heger	Anneliese Rothenberger	EMI
80. *St. Matthew Passion*	Bach	June 1968	Stuttgart	Wolfgang Gönnenwein		EMI
81. *Elijah*	Mendelssohn	July 1968	Munich	Rafael Frühbeck de Burgos	Dietrich Fischer-Dieskau	EMI
82. *Zarewitch*	Lehár	August 1968	Munich	Willy Mattes		EMI
83. *Der Graf von Luxemburg*	Lehár	August 1968	Munich	Willy Mattes	Lucia Popp	EMI
84. Song Recital	Beethoven	August 1968	Stockholm		acc. Jan Eyron (piano)	EMI
85. *Werther*	Massenet	September 1968	Paris	Georges Prêtre	Victoria de los Angeles	EMI
86. Swedish and Russian Songs	misc.	September 1968	Stockholm		acc. Jan Eyron (piano)	EMI
87. Song Recital	Stolz	October 1968	Munich	Willy Mattes		EMI
88. *Tribute to Gerald Moore*	misc.	1969	London		acc. Gerald Moore (piano)	EMI
89. Russian Arias	misc.	April 1969	Munich	Gika Zdravkovich		EMI
90. *Der Freischütz*	Weber	June 1969	Munich	Robert Heger	Birgit Nilsson	EMI
91. *Der Zigeunerbaron*	J. Strauss	July 1969	Munich	Franz Allers	Grace Bumbry	EMI
92. *The Happy Beethoven* (various songs)	Beethoven	August 1969	Stockholm		acc. Jan Eyron (piano)	EMI
93. *La Damnation de Faust*	Berlioz	October 1969	Paris	Georges Prêtre	Janet Baker	EMI
94. Song Recital	Satie	October 1969	Paris		acc. Aldo Ciccolini (piano)	EMI

	Composer	Date	Place	Conductor	Soloist / accompanist	Label
95. Song Recital	Rachmaninoff	1969	Paris		acc. Alexis Weissenberg (piano)	EMI
96. *Christ on Mount Olives*	Beethoven	March 1970	Bonn	Volker Wangenheim		EMI
97. Operetta Recital	Lehár	April 1970	Munich	Willy Mattes		EMI
98. *Walzer-Traum*	O. Strauss	April 1970	Munich	Willy Mattes	Anneliese Rothenberger	EMI
99. *Manon*	Massenet	July 1970	London	Julius Rudel	Beverly Sills	EMI
100. Tenor Cantatas	Bach	January 1971	Basel	Hans Martin Linde	Ensemble Schola Cantorum Basiliensis	EMI
101. *Idomeneo*	Mozart	May 1971	Dresden	Hans Schmidt-Isserstedt		EMI
102. *La Traviata*	Verdi	July 1971	London	Aldo Ceccato	Beverly Sills	EMI
103. *Requiem*	Mozart	July 1971	London	Daniel Barenboim		EMI
104. *Die schöne Müllerin*	Schubert	August 1971	Berlin		acc. Jan Eyron (piano)	EMI
105. *Die Fledermaus*	J. Strauss	November 1971	Vienna	Willi Boskovsky	Anneliese Rothenberger	EMI
106. *Benvenuto Cellini*	Berlioz	July 1972	London	Sir Colin Davis		Philips
107. *Guillaume Tell*	Rossini	July 1972	London	Lamberto Gardelli	Gabriel Bacquier	EMI
108. *Der Bettelstudent*	Millöcker	February 1973	Munich	Franz Allers		EMI
109. *Palestrina*	Pfitzner	February 1973	Munich	Rafael Kubelík		DGG
110. Symphony No. 9	Beethoven	June 1973	Munich	Rudolf Kempe		EMI
111. *The Happy Schubert* (various songs)	Schubert	June 1973	Munich		acc. Erik Werba (piano)	EMI
112. *La Damnation de Faust*	Berlioz	July 1973	London	Sir Colin Davis		Philips
113. *I Puritani*	Bellini	August 1973	London	Julius Rudel	Beverly Sills	ABC
114. *Paradies und Peri*	Schumann	August 1973	Düsseldorf	Henryk Czyz		EMI
115. *Die Czardas Fürstin*	Kálmán	September 1973	Munich	Willy Mattes	Anneliese Rothenberger	EMI
116. *Gräfin Mariza*	Kálmán	September 1973	Munich	Willy Mattes	Anneliese Rothenberger	EMI

Title	Composer	Date	City	Conductor	Other Performers	Label
117. *Faust* (excerpts in German)	Gounod	September 1973	Berlin	Giuseppe Patanè	Edda Moser, Kurt Moll	EMI
118. *Don Carlos* (excerpts in German)	Verdi	September 1973	Berlin	Giuseppe Patanè	Dietrich Fischer-Dieskau	EMI
119. *Abu Hassan*	Weber	December 1973	Munich	Wolfgang Sawallisch		EMI
120. Song Recital	N. and A. Tcherepnin	December 1973	Paris		acc. Alexander Tcherepnin (piano)	EMI
121. *Lélio*	Berlioz	December 1973	Paris	Jean Martinon		EMI
122. *Così fan tutte*	Mozart	May 1974	London	Sir Colin Davis	Montserrat Caballé	Philips
123. *Euryanthe*	Weber	June 1974	Dresden	Marek Janowski	Jessye Norman, Rita Hunter	EMI
124. *Il Barbiere di Siviglia*	Rossini	August 1974	London	James Levine	Beverly Sills	EMI
125. Duets from French Operas	misc.	September 1974	Paris	Pierre Dervaux	Mady Mesplé	EMI
126. *Baccalauréat—1975* (various songs)	Roussel	December 1974	Paris		Henriette Puig-Roget	EMI
127. *Die Opernprobe*	Lortzing	January 1975	Munich	Otmar Suitner	Walter Berry	EMI
128. *Der betrogene Kadi*	Gluck	January 1975	Munich	Otmar Suitner		EMI
129. *Die Zwillingbrüder*	Schubert	January 1975	Munich	Wolfgang Sawallisch	Dietrich Fischer-Dieskau	EMI
130. *Heitere Klassiker* (various arias)	Mozart and Haydn	January 1975	Munich			EMI
131. Russian Orthodox Hymns	misc.	February 1975	Paris	E. Evetz		Philips

Title	Composer	Date	Location	Conductor	Performers	Label
132. *I Capuleti ed i Montecchi*	Bellini	June 1975	London	Giuseppe Patanè	Beverly Sills, Janet Baker	EMI
133. *The Dream of Gerontius*	Elgar	July 1975	London	Sir Adrian Boult		EMI
134. *Der Schauspieldirektor*	Mozart	November 1975	Paris	Eberhard Schoener	Peter Ustinov, Mady Mesplé, Edda Moser	EMI
135. *Wiener Blut*	J. Strauss	February 1976	Düsseldorf	Willi Boskovsky		EMI
136. *Thaïs*	Massenet	June 1976	London	Lorin Maazel	Beverly Sills	EMI
137. Song Recital	Poulenc	July 1976	Paris		acc. James Dalton (piano)	EMI
138. *Coronation Mass* and *Vespre solennes*	Mozart	July 1976	Munich	Eugen Jochum		EMI
139. *Boris Godunov*	Mussorgsky	August 1976	Katowice	Jerszy Semkow	Martti Talvela	EMI
140. Russian Orthodox Hymns (I)	misc.	February 1977	London	Rev. Michail Fortunatto		Ikon
141. *Paganini*	Lehár	April 1977	Munich	Willi Boskovsky		EMI
142. *Louise*	Charpentier	June 1977	Paris	Julius Rudel	Beverly Sills	EMI
143. Song Cycles	Schumann	July 1977	Berlin		acc. Erik Werba (piano)	EMI
144. Two Songs	Aquilon	early 1978	Stockholm		acc. Barbro Aquilon (piano)	Artemis
145. *Katerina Ismailova*	Shostakovich	April 1978	London	Mstislav Rostropovich	Galina Vishnevskaya	EMI
146. *Cendrillon*	Massenet	June 1978	London	Julius Rudel	Frederica von Stade	CBS
147. Russian Orthodox Hymns (II)	misc.	February 1979	London	Rev. Michail Fortunatto		Ikon
148. *La Belle Hélène* (in German)	Offenbach	July 1979	Munich	Willy Mattes		EMI

Title	Composer	Date	City	Conductor	Other Performers	Label
149. Russian Songs	misc.	March 1980	Moscow		acc. Lija Mogilevskaia	Melodia
150. Baroque Arias	Mozart	September 1980	Stockholm	Claude Génetay		Polar
151. Arias	Handel, Gluck, Mozart	September 1980	Stockholm	Claude Génetay	Chamber Orchestra of the National Museum of Stockholm	Polar
152. Russian Folk Songs	misc.	October 1980	Moscow	K. Ptitsa	Chorus of Moscow Radio	Melodia
153/154. Songs	Peterson-Berger	September 1980	Stockholm		acc. Jan Eyron (piano)	Blue Bell (2 LPs)
155. Russian Folk Songs	misc.	October 1980	Moscow	Nekrassov	Orchestra of Folk Instruments	Melodia
156. Songs	De Frumerie	February 1981	Stockholm		acc. Jan Eyron (piano)	Blue Bell
157. Songs	misc.	February 1981	Stockholm		acc. Lars Blom, Student Chorus	Blue Bell
158. *Scenes from Faust*	Schumann	April 1981	Düsseldorf	Bernhard Klee	Dietrich Fischer-Dieskau	EMI
159. *Opera Composers in Song*	misc.	June 1981	Stockholm		acc. Jan Eyron (piano)	Blue Bell
160. *Ciboulette*	Hahn	December 1981	Monte Carlo	Cyril Diederich	Mady Mesplé	EMI
161/162. Songs	Sjögren	January 1982	Stockholm		acc. Jan Eyron (piano)	Blue Bell (2 LPs)
163. Songs with Orchestra	Fauré	spring 1982	Toulouse	Michel Plasson	Frederica von Stade	EMI

Title	Composer	Date	Location	Conductor	Performer	Label
164. *Padmavati*	Roussel	June 1982	Toulouse	Michel Plasson	Marilyn Horne	EMI
165. *Alceste*	Gluck	June 1982	Munich	Serge Baudo	Jessye Norman	Orféo
166. Songs	Stenhammar	September 1982	Stockholm		acc. Jan Eyron (piano)	Blue Bell
167–169. Anthology of Swedish Songs	misc.	September 1982	Stockholm		acc. Jan Eyron (piano)	Blue Bell (3 LPs)
170. Swedish Duets	misc.	October 1982	Stockholm		acc. Jan Eyron (piano), Rolf Leanderson	Blue Bell
171. Russian Orthodox Hymns	misc.	December 1982	Warsaw	Zurbak	Leonard Mroz	Polish
172. *Romeo and Juliet*	Berlioz	February 1983	Vienna	Lamberto Gardelli		Orféo
173. *Requiem*	Schumann	July 1983	Düsseldorf	Bernhard Klee		EMI
174. *Fra Diavolo*	Auber	September 1983	Monte Carlo	Mare Soustrot		EMI
175/176. Songs	Rangström	December 1983	Stockholm		acc. Jan Eyron (piano)	Blue Bell (2 LPs)
177. *Petite Messe Solenelle*	Rossini	July 1984	Cambridge, England	Stephen Cleobusy	Lucia Popp, Brigitte Fassbender; acc. Peter Katin (piano), Marielle Lebèque	EMI
178. *Giuditta*	Lehár	July 1984	Munich	Willi Boskovsky	Edda Moser	EMI
179. *Diary of the Vanished*	Janáček	August 1984	Prague		acc. Josef Páleníček (piano)	Suprafon
180. *Iolanta*	Tchaikovsky	December 1984	Paris	Mstislav Rostropovich	Galina Vishnevskaya	Erato
181. Swedish Church Music	misc.	April 1985	Stockholm		acc. Lars Blom (organ)	Blue Bell

Title	Composer	Date	City	Conductor	Other Performers	Label
182. Songs by the Bernadotter	misc.	April 1986	Stockholm		acc. Arnold Östman	Blue Bell
183. Twelve Serenades	misc.	April 1986	Stockholm	Erik Westling		Fermat
184. *Kalanus*	Gade	May 1986	Copenhagen	Frans Rasmussen		Danish CD
185. *War and Peace*	Prokofiev	December 1986	Paris	Mstislav Rostropovich	Galina Vishnevskaya	Erato
186. *Evocations*	Roussel	December 1986	Paris	Michel Plasson		EMI
187/188. Songs	Liszt	December 1986	Stockholm		acc. Lars Roos	Blue Bell (2 CDs)
189. *Boris Godunov*	Mussorgsky	July 1987	Washington, D.C.	Mstislav Rostropovich		Erato
190. Songs on Poems by Pushkin	misc.	November 1987	Stockholm		acc. Eva Pataki	Blue Bell (not issued)
191. *Evgeny Onegin*	Tchaikovsky	January 1988	Sofia	Emil Tchakarov	Ingvar Wixell	Sony
192. *Tosca*	Puccini	June 1988	Sofia	Emil Tchakarov	Ingvar Wixell	Sony (not issued)
193. *Holy Night*	Adam	October 1988	Oslo	P. Kran	Oslo Cathedral Chorus	Norwegia
194. *Oedipe*	Enesco	June 1989	Monte Carlo	G. Lawrence		EMI
195. *Candide*	Bernstein	December 1989	London	Leonard Bernstein		DGG

196. *Oedipus Rex*	Stravinsky	May 1991	Stockholm	Esa-Pekka Salonen		Sony
197. *Gustaf Wasa*	Naumann	January 1992	Stockholm	Philip Brunelle		Virgin
198. *The Wonder of Heliane*	Korngold	February 1992	Berlin	G. Mauceri		Decca
199. *Evgeny Onegin* (in English)	Tchaikovsky	July 1992	Swansea, Wales	Charles Mackeras		EMI
200. Russian Folk Songs	misc.	August 1993	Munich	Vladimir Cielkovich	Vocal Ensemble	Philips
201. Russian Orthodox Hymns	misc.	August 1993	Munich	Vladimir Cielkovich	Vocal Ensemble	Philips
202. *Daniel Hjort*	Palmgren	October 1994	Åbo–Turku, Finland	Ulf Söderblom		Finlandia

Index of Names